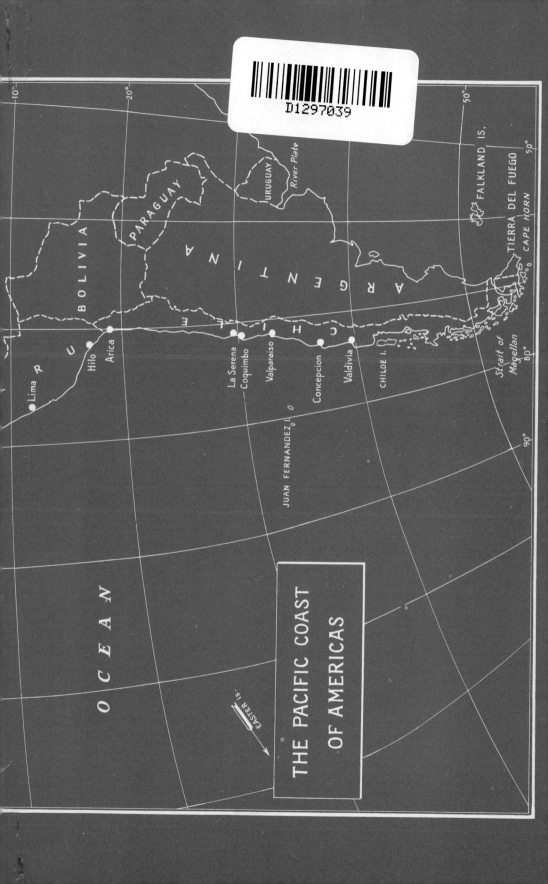

THE PACIFIC COAST

OF AMERICAS

Brethren of the Coast

BRETHREN OF THE COAST

Buccaneers of the South Seas

By

P. K. KEMP

and

CHRISTOPHER LLOYD

❁

New York

ST MARTIN'S PRESS

Contents

List of Illustrations

*Arranged in the following sequence
between pages 120 and 121*

MAPS

Foreword

IN THIS ACCOUNT of the buccaneers and privateers of the West Indies and their incursion into the Pacific in the seventeenth and early eighteenth centuries we have, wherever possible, gone back to the original documents and letters. The earliest printed versions of these journals almost all differ, in a greater or less degree, from the original manuscript accounts kept on board during the voyages, and subsequently printed editions, more often than not, repeat the errors of the first. Though from a literary point of view the published accounts are sometimes superior to the original manuscripts, we have, where possible, checked the one against the other because, where the Brethren of the Coast are concerned, the facts are often stranger than the fictions which they inspired, both in their own day and subsequently from the time of Defoe to that of Stevenson.

We would wish to record our grateful thanks to My Lords Commissioners of the Admiralty, the Trustees of the British Museum and the National Maritime Museum, and the Keeper of the Public Records for the use of original records in their departments. Our thanks are also due to the British Museum for permission to reproduce facsimile pages of the Bartholomew Sharp manuscript; to the National Maritime Museum for permission to reproduce the portrait of Woodes Rogers and his family and the cartouche showing buccaneers; to the National Portrait Gallery for permission to reproduce the portrait of William Dampier; and to the Scheepvart Museum, Amsterdam, for permission to reproduce an illustration of a model of a Dutch East Indiaman.

CHAPTER ONE

The Rise of the Buccaneers

IT IS SAID THAT ONCE UPON A TIME a band of buccaneers forced the gates of Heaven. St Peter was anxious to get rid of these uninvited guests, who had clearly arrived at the wrong place. He hit on a stratagem worthy of the Brethren of the Coast. 'A sail!' he cried, pointing out of the doors of Paradise. 'Where?' demanded the buccaneers. 'To leeward on the port quarter.' *'Chasse dessus!'* they cried as they incontinently rushed out of the gates, which were then slammed securely behind them.

Who were these men we see boarding every Spanish vessel they could come up with in the Caribbean, marching across the isthmus of Panama in their tricorn hats, musket on shoulder and cutlass by side, harrying the Pacific coast and even sailing across the vast expanse of the South Sea in search of loot on the farther shore? Buccaneers were of so many types that a strict definition is impossible. From about 1630, French adventurers, many of them escaped servants from the plantations, began to settle at Tortuga, the turtle-shaped island off the north-west coast of Hispaniola, the modern Haiti. From this centre they spread to the uninhabited south-western part of the larger island, the Spaniards having only settled the area around San Domingo. In the great cul-de-sac formed by the coast north of Cape Tiburon there were many secret anchorages which became their favourite rendezvous – Petit Goave, Isle de Vache (to the south of the cape), or the district of Leogane, named after an illegitimate

1

daughter of Philip II who was supposed to have died in a ruined castle there.

The earliest settlers were hunters rather than sailors, desperate, landless men attracted by the abundance of wild boars and cattle which roamed these parts. They cooked the meat of these animals in little dome-shaped huts called *boucanes,* which were divided into shelves on which strips of meat were laid to be smoked dry by a slow fire on the floor of the grill or barbecue. The strips of what the French called *viande boucanée,* and the English called 'jerked meat' (a corruption of the American Spanish *charqui*) were of excellent colour and flavour, though hard and dry as a board. They were sold by the *boucaniers* in bundles of a hundred for six pieces of eight. In the days before canned meat such victuals were essential for the crews of ships at sea, hence there was a ready market among the corsairs of Tortuga, where, says one of them, 'all the tavern keepers wait for the coming of these lewd buccaneers even after the same manner that they do at Amsterdam for the arrival of the East India fleet.'

By degrees the name spread to cover the corsairs and privateers who roamed the Caribbean in the seventeenth century as the descendants of the seamen of the age of Drake. The Spaniards used to call them *corsarios,* something between a pirate preying on the shipping of all nations *(hostis human generis),* and the legalised privateer who carried a commission or letter of marque in time of war. As there was 'no peace beyond the line' – that is to say a line drawn west of the Azores and north of the tropic of Capricorn, and not, as is commonly supposed, the equator – a state of endemic warfare existed between the corsairs of France, England and Holland, and the Spanish colonists. Hence 'privateer' came to have a very flexible meaning. It is significant that the English documents never use the word 'buccaneer' until the end of the seventeenth century. The seamen who are the subject of this book were called 'privateers', whether they were officially licensed or not, until their depredations became so serious that they were termed pirates and prosecuted as felons. Another English term in frequent use was 'freebooter'. Since the French could not pronounce the word, it became in their language *flibustier*, until it returned into English (or rather American) in the nineteenth century as *filibuster*. Alternatively such men were called *bucaniers* (hence 'buccaneer'); by the Dutch, *zee-rovers*; by the Germans, *Seeräuber*; while the Spanish naturally preferred *piratas*, since they regarded all interlopers in their American empire and the seas surrounding it as such. One cannot blame them for this failure to discriminate, because it is often impossible to determine whether a man was a genuine privateer or not. Commissions issued by the French government of Tortuga or the English governor of Jamaica might well be forged, out of date, or worded with deliberate ambiguity. Nevertheless, such documents were highly prized, because they alone enabled a man to escape the charge of piracy.

The privateer-bands were composed of the outcasts of all nations with the exception of the Spanish, their inveterate enemies. As English colonies began to be established at St Kitts, Barbados and Nevis, with the French at Martinique, Guadaloupe and Tortuga, and the Dutch at Tobago and Curaçoa, their populations were increased by the export of convicts, prostitutes, indentured servants, political or religious undesirables, who formed a fertile source of recruitment for the Brotherhood of the Coast. Such marauding adventurers preferred to live under assumed names such as Pass-Partout, Vent-en-Panne, Brise-Goulets, l'Hallebarde or (strangest of all) Borgne-Fesse, or Half-Buttock. Having neither kith nor kin, they organised their society on a basis of *matelotage*, an older man sharing with a younger all things in common, including wives; since cruises often lasted a year or more, homosexuality was common. Such was the custom of the coast.

3

A curiously democratic discipline was evolved by crews at sea. All captains were elected. If the ship's company grew tired of him, they either marooned him (or any other member of the crew, such as Alexander Selkirk), or they were free to join another ship, provided they paid for their food and arms. When they went cruising 'on the account', as the phrase was, detailed charter-parties were drawn up on the basis of 'no purchase, no pay', using the word 'purchase' in its old sense of prey or loot. The captain's share, and those of the mates, carpenters, surgeons (to the cost of whose chests all contributed) were naturally larger than those of individual members of the crew. But the latter benefited by a detailed insurance scale: in compensation for the loss of the right arm, 600 pieces of eight or six slaves; for the left arm, 500 pieces; for an eye or a finger, 100 pieces.

A curious example has survived in the form of an agreement by the mutinous crew of the *Camelion* slaver on 30 June 1683, whereby they compelled their captain to go off 'on the account'. 'Articles of Agreement between us aboard the *Camelion*, Nic Clough commander, that we are to dispose of all the goods that are aboard amongst us, every man to have his full share, only the Commander is to have two shares and a half for the ship, and whom the Captain pleases to take for the Master under him is to have a share and a half. Now, Gentlemen, these are to satisfy you; as for the Doctor, a share and a half; and these are our Articles that we do all stand to as well as one and all. . . . As you are all here present, you have taken your corporal oath upon the holy Evangelists to stand by the other as long as life shall last.' The signatures, or marks, of twenty members of the crew follow. Unfortunately for them, the vessel was captured three months later. Eight of the signatories were sentenced at New York to twenty lashes and a year's imprisonment each.

'They observe among themselves very good order,' says an old buccaneer, 'for in the prizes they take, it is severely pro-

4

hibited to everyone to usurp anything in particular to themselves. Hence all they take is equally divided, according to what has been said before. Among themselves they are very civil and charitable to each other.' But to the Spaniards they were devils incarnate. 'They have no more religion than the Hottentots,' complains one of the Jesuit fathers, whose description of their habits is the basis of our knowledge of these strange creatures. However, there were exceptions. Père Labat tells the story of a certain Captain Daniel who, having captured a village, asked the priest to celebrate Mass. To announce this unusual occasion a salute of eight guns was fired, followed by a second salvo at the Sanctus, a third at the Elevation, a fourth at the Benediction, and a fifth at the Exaudiat. During the service one of the crew, unaccustomed to such a ceremony, made an offensive remark. Whereupon Captain Daniel shot him dead, consoling the priest with the remark: 'Don't trouble yourself, Father. It's only a rascal who has been punished for disrespect and will not now forget his duty.'

The clothes, arms and ships of these motley bands, composed of the adventurers of all nations, depended on the loot they acquired. The one common feature was the peculiarly long musket which was imported from Nantes or Bordeaux, together with the leaden bullets carried in a leather bag or bandolier. Three or four long knives were stuck in the belt. Priding themselves on their marksmanship, many claimed to be able to hit a coin spinning in the air. Indeed, the Governor of Panama attributed his defeat to the superior musketry of Morgan's men. Their clothes were originally made from the skins of the beasts which they hunted – leather jackets stained red with blood, seamless moccasins shrunk on to the foot when the skin was fresh, curious peaked caps. Many carried mosquito-nets wound round their waists for nights spent in the open. By Morgan's day the caps had changed to tricorns, the bloodstained jackets to faded red coats originally belonging to soldiers of the New Model Army, with boots and bandoliers stripped off Spanish prisoners.

The vessels in which they lay in wait for shipping in the Yucatan or Windward Passage between Cuba and Tortuga, or the Mona Passage between Hispaniola and Puerto Rico, or in which they cruised along the Mosquito Coast of Honduras, the Isthmus of Darien or the South American coasts of the Spanish Main, were equally varied. Some were single-masted, lateen-rigged barques, others two-masted brigantines. They were of all sizes and rigs. A list of thirty-six ships, in Morgan's squadron of 1670, ranges from the flagship of 120 tons and 22 guns to the unarmed *Betty* sloop of 12 tons. An earlier list in the Bodleian Library varies from the *Griffon* frigate of 14 guns and 100 men to Captain Mansfield's brigantine of 4 guns and 60 men. A third, from Paris, dated 1684, includes other famous names such as those of Gramont and Laurent de Graff in large ships of over 50 guns and 300 men, down to two- or four-gun vessels with crews of twenty.

Even if the depredations of the buccaneers prevented the development of peaceful trade with Spain, the loot they acquired immeasurably enriched the infant colonies of Tortuga and Jamaica, so that Port Royal came to be called the richest place in the world. Under the prevailing mercantilist doctrine that riches must be reckoned in precious metals, their chests of pieces of eight, *reales*, dollars and ducats were welcomed by the settlers, even when they were frowned on by the representatives of the home government. It is impossible to give accurate estimates of the value of a piece of eight on account of the inflationary tendencies of the modern world; what used to be reckoned at five shillings should today be multiplied by at least ten. Some of the more successful – Morgan, for example – settled down to enjoy this wealth. One such, to the amusement of Père Labat who first knew him as an indentured servant to a carpenter, was to be seen in his later years doing his shopping with a slave, not only to carry his purchases but to name the required tools because his master affected to be ignorant of such vulgar articles. Most of them, however, spent the results of a successful cruise in a fit of wild debauchery, accompanied by the continual firing of muskets.

Though historically the descendants of the Elizabethan and Huguenot privateers of the previous century, buccaneering may be said to have begun at Tortuga in the sixteen-thirties. Successive governors, such as Levasseur and d'Ogéron, encouraged privateering by the liberal issue of commissions in order that they should bring their loot thither. Three figures of that early barbaric period may be distinguished – Pierre le Grand, who sailed his Spanish prize back to Dieppe to enjoy the fruits of his brief career; Montbars, nicknamed the 'Exterminator' on account of his implacable hatred of the Spaniards, who commanded an early expedition against Mara-caibo, which was to be regularly sacked later on; and his companion, the infamous L'Ollonois named after his birthplace Les Sables d'Olonne, in Brittany. Accounts of his career entitle us to regard him as the worst of the buccaneers, with no re-deeming feature beyond a relentless energy. Sailing with a commission from d'Ogéron, he took a ship off the Main loaded with a cargo of 120,000 cwt. of cocoa, 40,000 pieces of eight and jewels to the value of 10,000 more. 'He never used to make any great account of murdering ten or twelve Spaniards. He drew his cutlass and hacked one to pieces in the presence of the rest saying, "If you do not confess and declare where you have hidden the rest of your goods, I will do the like to all your companions." ' In a raid on Nicaragua he 'grew out-rageously passionate, insomuch that he drew his cutlass, and with it cut open the heart of a poor Spaniard, and pulling out his heart with sacrilegious hands, began to bite and gnaw it with his teeth, saying to the rest, "I will serve you all alike, if you show me not another way." ' It is satisfactory to know that soon afterwards he was abandoned by his com-

7

panions to the Darien Indians, who 'took him prisoner and tore him to pieces alive, throwing his body limb by limb into the fire, and his ashes into the air, to the intent no trace nor memory might remain of such an infamous, inhuman creature'.

To such men (if we are to believe a recently printed account) should be added the name of Louis Le Golif, nick-named Borgne-Fesse on account of an embarrassing wound which necessitated the removal of one of his buttocks. His manuscript autobiography was discovered after the bombing of St Malo towards the end of the last war. Selections which show signs of heavy editing have appeared in print, but we are assured that nothing has been added to the original. If that is so, Captain Le Golif was a remarkable stylist for his age and kind. His scabrous anecdotes, true *contes drôlatiques*, are told with zest of a born story-teller. His account of his 'marriage' with one of the thousand prostitutes sent over to populate the new colonies reads like a film script at its worst: not content with killing a rival named Bâbord-Amure (or 'port tack', on account of his nose being askew) in a duel on the night of his wedding, his *matelot* must needs murder the lady and her lover in bed a few days later. This self-styled buccaneer-leader is reputed to have lived in the West Indies between 1660 and 1675, when he retired to Brittany to compose his memoirs in his old age. His name, however, does not figure in any of the other records of the time, which contain the names of those he claims to have met.

After its capture by the British in 1655, Jamaica began to rival Tortuga as a centre for privateering. The garrison left behind by General Venables, when he returned to be imprisoned in the Tower by Cromwell for failing to capture Hispaniola, was composed of just the sort of men who preferred buccaneering to settlement, 'unruly, raw soldiers, the major part ignorant, lazy, dull; officers that have a large portion of pride, but not of wit, valour or activity', as their commander complained. To these Bobadils were added a thousand Irish emigrants sent out by Cromwell, together with a number of Jews, Quakers, convicts, vagabonds, and other undesirables, for the transportation of whom the Governor's brother was given a five year license in 1664. By that date the population of 'His Majesty's frontier dominion' numbered some 5,000 whites and 2,000 negro slaves. No wonder that early planters lived in continual fear of absconding servants, a negro uprising, or a Spanish invasion.

The first Governor, d'Oyley, encouraged privateering for much the same reason as did d'Ogéron in Tortuga. The policy was continued by his successors, Lord Windsor and Sir Thomas Modyford, until Morgan's successes began to overtop the bounds of what had been hitherto regarded as legitimate self-defence. In early days there was every reason to encourage 'the sweet trade of privateering' because of the lack of adequate naval forces in those seas. Even when a few frigates were stationed there, they were used in a way indistinguishable from that of privateers. Thus in 1659 d'Oyley sent Captain Christopher Myngs with 300 soldiers to harry the coast of the Main, whence he returned with twenty-two chests; each containing 400 pounds of silver, the total value amounting to £300,000. Myngs, however, was sent home in disgrace for plundering one of the ships for his own use. In 1662 he was there again, to be sent by another governor on a similar cruise, this time against Cuba with the young Henry Morgan among his men. As a tarpaulin captain and 'a very stout man', he made a name for himself in the Dutch wars, when Pepys gives a vivid account of his funeral at which his men evinced a touching devotion to his memory.

Privateering was essential to the well-being of the infant colony, as every Governor tried to point out to the Lords of Trade and Plantations at home. In the absence of a regular naval force, it maintained a pool of seamen who could be enlisted in a crisis and who kept the authorities informed of

Spanish plans for the recapture of the island. Such men alone could acquaint themselves with the difficult navigation of those seas before the days of adequate charts, and the loot they brought in certainly enriched the place. Moreover, if the Governor of Jamaica did not encourage them by the liberal issue of commissions, his rival at Tortuga would certainly do so, and if Charles II could not even maintain a fleet in the Channel during the Dutch Wars, how could he spare ships for such distant seas? During the whole reign only one squadron was ever sent to the Caribbean, and that never reached Jamaica. However, under Lord Windsor, efforts were made to regularise the activities of the privateers by the establishment of a Vice-Admiralty Court at Port Royal, of which Morgan himself became a judge.

One of our chief sources of information about the latter's career and those of his predecessors is the book entitled *The Bucaniers of America*, of which two translations appeared in English in the year 1684. The author's name is variously given as Alexander Oliver Oexmelin and John Esquemeling. Both his identity and the bibliography of his book are problems of formidable complexity. The book first appeared under the imprint of Jan Ten Hoorn at Amsterdam in 1678 with the title of *De Amerikaensche Zee-Rovers*, the author's name being given as A. O. Exquemelin. It was soon translated into almost every European language. In 1679 appeared a German edition, *Amerikanische Seeräuber*. In 1681 there came a Spanish translation by a certain Dr Alonso de Bueno Maison entitled *Piratas de la América*, from which the English versions were translated in 1684. In 1686 a further expanded version appeared in French, *Histoire des Aventuriers qui se sont signalés dans les Indes*. In every country fresh editions continued to pour from the press, some including new stories, others omitting old ones for fear of libel actions, some bound up one way, some another, some containing genuine narratives, others inventing what they could not find. It was a book which appealed strongly to the contemporary taste for picaresque or rogue literature which Daniel Defoe was to exploit so successfully. One would indeed like to think he had a hand in the muscular style of the English translation, but he had hardly begun his career as a publisher's hack by that date. It was certainly a book which appealed to the author of *Robinson Crusoe*: after all, Alexander Selkirk, the original model, was himself a marooned buccaneer. A stronger case has been made out on stylistic ground for Defoe's authorship of the best seller which displaced Esquemeling a generation later: Captain Charles Johnson's *General History of the Robberies and Murders of the Most Notorious Pyrates* (1724), for Johnson's identity is even more mysterious than Esquemeling's. Who, indeed, was more likely to write such a Newgate Calendar type of work than the man who faked such admirable narratives as *The Journal of the Plague Year, Captain Singleton, Colonel Jacques*, or the biography of the imaginary Colonel Roberts, not to mention *The Life and Strange Surprising Adventures of Robinson Crusoe of York, Mariner*?

All that Esquemeling says about himself is that he sailed from Le Havre on 2 May 1666 as the indentured servant of a planter, and that he escaped from a cruel master to join the buccaneers at Tortuga in the days of Governor d'Ogéron. He claims to have sailed with many of the famous figures whom he describes, and to have accompanied Morgan on some of his expeditions before he left him because he did not receive his just share after the sack of Panama. After wandering about the place for some years he returned with Admiral d'Estrées to France in 1674. His book was published in Dutch in 1678, but he appears in the capacity of a surgeon in the attack on Cartagena in 1697. After that he disappears from history.

Many such buccaneering surgeons kept journals, but the English translator evidently knew nothing more about this one, because he raises some pertinent queries. 'I take him to be a Dutchman, at least born in Flanders, notwithstanding that the Spanish translator represents him to be a native of the Kingdom of France; his printing this history originally in Dutch, which doubtless must be his native tongue, who otherwise was but an illiterate man, together with the very sound of his name, convincing me thereto. True it is, he set sail from France and was some years at Tortuga, but neither of these two arguments drawn from history, are prevalent. For were he a Frenchman born, how came he to learn the Dutch language so perfectly as to prefer it to his own?' It has been suggested that the name was a pseudonym for a Dutch surgeon called Hendrick Barentzoon Smeeks, who later published with Ten Hoorn a pseudo-autobiography entitled *The Description of the Powerful Realm of Krinke Kesmes*, a romance based on his experience in a Dutch East Indiaman wrecked on the coast of Australia. Since *Robinson Crusoe* appeared in 1719, the 1715 edition of Smeeks's book may have inspired it. It is known that Smeeks entered the service of the French West Indies Company as a surgeon in 1666, returned to Holland in 1672 and fought against the English in the Third Dutch War, which helps to explain the anglophobia of the book. He died in 1721, after further voyages, though not to the West Indies. He may have adopted a pseudonym so that his previous companionship with the buccaneers would not harm his respectable practice in Holland. Moreover, it is known that the Spanish translator was a doctor resident at Amsterdam at that time.

Everything would therefore seem to point to Smeeks's authorship. But in 1934 a Dutch historian, M. Vriejman, discovered that the names of both Esquemeling and Smeeken [*sic*] were on the books of the Dutch Surgeons' Guild as passing their examinations in 1679 and 1666 respectively. He concludes that the Franch translator's preface asserting that Oexmelin (as he calls him) was a native of Honfleur is correct. There would therefore appear to be two persons in the case, both serving with the buccaneers at roughly the same date, and that the Frenchman's rough journal came into the hands of a Dutch publisher who virtually re-wrote it, with or without the assistance of Smeeks, as did all the translators according to their various national prejudices.

The facts relating to the early buccaneers can thus be established by collating Esquemeling's lively memoirs with the more sober accounts of the Jesuit fathers, Père Labat or Père Charlevoix, together with references to them in the official records when they got into trouble, or with the reliable account of Jamaica which Charles Leslie wrote within a generation of their time. Like Esquemeling, Leslie describes these 'people of desperate fortunes and those who could not endure the unactive state in which England then was'. Such an adventurer was Bartholomew the Portuguese, who with thirty men and a leaky ship took a twenty-gun Spanish brig off Cuba with 70,000 pieces of eight on board. He was later caught, but managed to escape by using two wine-jars as floats because he could not swim.

A more bloodthirsty rogue, as his portrait suggests, was Rock Braziliano, a Dutchman so called from long residence in Brazil before he came to Jamaica. He seems to have been chiefly remarkable for the amount of hair on his chest, which gave him the appearance of a bear, and for the prodigal way in which he spent his ill-gotten gains. 'They have been known to spend two or three thousand pieces of eight in one night, and one of them gave a strumpet five hundred to see her naked. They used to buy a pipe of wine, place it in the street and oblige everyone that passed to drink; at other times they would scatter it about in large quantities thinking it excellent diversion to wet the ladies' clothes as they went along, and force them to run from the showers of wine.'

Rather than cruise in search of Spanish vessels at sea, Lewis Scott and John Davis began the raids on the Campeachy or Mosquito coasts which became so familiar in the Spanish com-

13

plaints that have been preserved among the English State Papers of the seventies and eighties. Davis plundered the town of Nicaragua so successfully that his band of eighty men escaped before the Spanish troops arrived on the scene. Encouraged by this success, he got together a fleet of seven vessels to attack St Augustine on the Florida coast as Drake had done seventy years previously.

Edward Mansfield (whom Esquemeling calls a 'Scot' of the name of Mansvelt) is another genuine historical character who captured the island of Santa Catalina off the coast of Honduras as a base from which to attack the isthmus. Because of its excellent strategic position on the route of the treasure fleet from Porto Bello, it changed hands regularly for the next thirty years. By capturing it, Mansfield must be regarded as something more than an adventurer. He was the progenitor of later successes, because his grandiose plans came to be implemented during the decade after his death. Besides, with him sailed Henry Morgan, the greatest of them all.

CHAPTER TWO

Sir Henry Morgan

IN THE YEAR 1684 Governor-General Admiral Sir Henry Morgan, Justice of the Peace, Judge of the Vice-Admiralty Court, Custos Rotulorum, and one of the richest planters in Jamaica, heard that two obscure London publishers, William Crooke and Thomas Malthus, had simultaneously produced translations from the Spanish edition of Esquemeling's book. That edition was entitled *Piratas de la America*. Throughout the text Sir Henry was referred to as a pirate, reflections were cast upon his character and (what was far worse) his birth, and even his Christian name was wrongly given as John. Though the author, as he claimed, may well have accompanied Morgan on the famous expedition to Panama, his account of the leader's early career and character abounds in inaccuracies which the Spanish translator took pains to embroider when dealing with his nation's greatest enemy.

At this stage of his life Morgan did not relish reminders of his early adventures, nor did he care to be classed with blood-thirsty villains such as L'Ollonois. He therefore sued the book-sellers in the Court of the King's Bench for £10,000 damages for 'cunningly contriving to injure his good name and fame by printing, spreading and publishing a certain false, malicious and famous libel entitled *A History of the Bucaniers*'. He got £200 from each bookseller, £9 costs, together with abject apologies in subsequent editions (though the libellous remarks remain unchanged in the text of the second edition, at least). Cooke assured his readers that nothing was intended to mis-

15

represent 'the unparralleled exploits of that valiant and heroick gentleman, Sir Henry Morgan', nor were any of the remarks about his low birth or his cruelty towards prisoners intended to reflect upon his honour. Malthus was even more fulsome, claiming that 'the filth and ordure' of the Spanish version had now been cleared away entirely. Moreover, when another bookseller printed the journal of Bartholomew Sharp (in a sense Morgan's disciple) later that year, he included a 'true relation' of the Panama expedition 'that I might in some measure rescue the honour of that incomparable soldier and seaman from the hands of such as would load him with the blackest infamy'. Philip Ayres, the editor of this volume, was the first to point out that Morgan sailed with an official commission and that 'those dismal stories of murdering in cold blood, torturing, ravishing, starving and other such barbarities, are foisted in by the author to lard his history with delightful variety, and to fix an odium on the English nation in general, that they may be hated by others'. In spite of all this, the damage was done. Esquemeling's book was indeed a 'famous libel' with an international circulation. The picture of Morgan as a rum-swilling, nun-raping pirate has remained fixed in the popular imagination ever since. Esquemeling's pen was indeed mightier than Morgan's sword.

It must be admitted that any statement about Morgan's early life can be easily challenged. It is now generally accepted that he was born in 1635, the eldest son of Robert Morgan of Llanrhymney in the county of Glamorgan. He named his Jamaican estate after his birthplace and he had every reason to be proud of his family. Uncle Thomas, Monck's second-in-command, was knighted when he became Governor of the island of Jersey. Another uncle, Colonel Edward, was a Royalist exile who became a noted Jamaican soldier after the Restoration. But how Henry himself ever reached the island, or what happened to him when he got there, remains a mystery. He himself was the first to admit the deficiencies of his education: writing as a middle-aged respectable citizen, he said that 'the office of Judge Admiral was not given to me for my understanding of the business better than others, nor for the profitableness thereof, for I left the schools too young to be a great proficient in that or other laws, and have been more used to the pike than the book'. But he was at pains to deny the story that he had been sold as a servant to a planter. More probably he sailed with Penn and Venables in 1654 and as a boy belonged to that ill-assorted army from which so many of the early buccaneers were recruited. Certainly some of that riff-raff served under him later, marching in the faded red coats of the New Model Army across the Isthmus of Panama sixteen years later.

Morgan always claimed that he sailed as a genuine commissioned privateer. Probably his first expedition was under Captain Myngs in 1662 against Cuba. After that he may well have sailed off 'on the account', but from the start he differed from his fellow buccaneers in his attitude towards money. Leslie, the earliest historian of Jamaica writing within a few years of his death, says that 'because he saw the Excess and Debauchery of his fellows, and that they became reduced to the lowest shifts by their lavish Expenses on their Arrival, he, having Vast Designs in View, lived moderate and got together as much money as purchased a Vessel for himself; and having a fine Crew, put to Sea'. A responsible character, noted for his courage, was bound to become the natural leader of such adventurers, hence he soon became second-in-command to Mansfield in his operations against the Dutch possessions during the Second Dutch War. He may also have accompanied his uncle Edward in 1665, when (as the Governor reported) 'the good old colonel, leaping out of a boat and being a corpulent man, got a strain, and his spirit being great, he pursued over earnestly the enemy on a hot day, so that he was surfeited and suddenly died'. He certainly married Edward's daughter the next year. When Mansfield himself was killed,

Morgan succeeded to the leadership of the privateers and also of the regular forces stationed on the island. In 1668, at the age of thirty-three, he was made their colonel and from that point onward his story is well authenticated either by official letters of successive governors, or by his own business-like despatches. Esquemeling may provide the colour and the scandal, but the broad achievements of Henry Morgan are a matter of history.

The reason he was appointed colonel was the outbreak of fresh hostilities with Spain. He was told to collect a force of twelve ships and 750 men for an attack on Santa Maria de Puerto Principe, the second largest town in Cuba, now known as Camagüey. Years of cruising in those seas had taught him all there was to know of the value of surprise tactics, secret anchorages, ambuscades and forced marches over broken ground. Leaving his ships in the maze of 'keys' which the Spaniards called by the romantic name of Los Jardinios de la Reina, he landed his men in a secluded bay to march thirty miles inland through forest country as far as a hill overlooking the town. A scratch garrison was dispersed with two volleys, and though there was some violent fighting in the streets, the place was easily taken. A ransom saved it from the usual fate of any place which fell into the hands of the buccaneers, but the sum was hardly sufficient to pay for the costs of fitting out the expedition, so that the French contingent left Morgan's colours in disgust.

For his part Morgan was determined to reimburse himself before returning to Jamaica. A peace with Spain was being negotiated and the governor sent him a copy of the articles. Curiously enough, the vessel carrying the letter failed to find him before he had turned his attention to the much larger city of Porto Bello on the eastern coast of the isthmus of Panama. Puerto Velo (as older writers call it) was the best defended harbour in the Caribbean because, in spite of its unhealthy situation, it was the main entrepôt of the American trade and the scene of a famous annual fair of merchants. Morgan's great exemplar, Sir Francis Drake, had died of fever off the town, and seventy years after his day, Admiral Vernon, with a fully equipped fleet bombarded the castles defending the harbour with well-advertised success, though he never had to storm the town. Though Morgan's force amounted to 1,800 men, nearly all of them buccaneers, it was a scratch body to assault such a well-garrisoned place. But to the faint-hearted he replied in true Roman style, 'If our number is small, our hearts are great. And the fewer persons we are, the more union and better shares we shall have in the spoil.'

A frontal attack on the castles was out of question because he lacked guns of any sort, so a landing was made two leagues up the coast to disembark canoes in which they could get well inland across the swamps. Even the landward fortifications were strong. Using broad scaling ladders, and carrying 'fire-balls' in their hands, Morgan's men stormed a town held by 3,000 men with the loss of only eighteen killed and thirty-two wounded. 'And for the better vindication of our-selves against the usual scandals of that enemy,' writes Morgan in his despatch, 'we aver that having several ladies of great quality and other prisoners, they were proffered their liberty to go to the President's camp, but they refused, saying they were now prisoners to a person of quality, who was more tender to their honours than they doubted to find in the Presi-dent's camp among his rude Panama soldiers, and so voluntarily continued with us till the surrender of the town.' Esquemeling's account is very different. As usual, Morgan's men commit all manner of debauchery and excess, the miserable citizens only escaping from their 'cruel captivity' after payment of 100,000 pieces of eight. He adds the story that the President of Panama asked Morgan to send him a specimen of the arms with which he had captured so great a city. Morgan obliged with the gift of a pistol and a few small bullets, desiring him 'accept that slender pattern of the arms wherewith he had taken Porto Bello and keep them for a twelvemonth, after which time he promised to come to Panama to fetch them away'. Though Don Guzman begged him not to take the trouble, he was as good as his word.

Loaded with loot, they returned to Jamaica, where the inhabitants relieved them of their silver as easily as they had taken it from the Spaniards. Reduced to a starving condition, the privateers welcomed the news that a fresh expedition was fitting out under the now famous leader, so that in a short time he found himself with a thousand rude fellows at his command. Though peace negotiations still continued in Europe, Governor Modyford promptly sent the *Oxford* frigate to join Morgan as soon as she arrived from England. The rendezvous was at the Isle de Vache, where she caught up with Morgan's ten vessels in January, 1669. A council of war was held on board to decide whether Caracas or Cartagena on the coast of South America should be their objective. But the decision was cut short by an extraordinary accident which Esquemeling (or rather his Spanish translator) regarded as an example of 'divine punishment, as we may very rationally conceive'. Even more rationally we may explain it as the consequence of that habitual carelessness with firearms which ruined so many buccaneering expeditions. The drinking of healths around the council table being accompanied as usual by an inordinate firing of muskets, a spark ignited a barrel of powder in the waist. Three hundred and fifty men were killed in the explosion which followed. The newly-joined surgeon, Browne (to whose letters we owe valuable sidelights on Morgan's career), saved himself by clinging to part of the mizzen mast after it had been blown overboard. 'Admiral Morgan and those captains that sat at that side of the table he did,' wrote Colonel Beeston in his unpublished journal, 'were saved, but those captains on the other side were all killed, and this accident stopped the attempt on Cartagena.'

A fresh force had to be collected before they could proceed

to attack Maracaibo instead. This was done on the advice of a pilot who had taken L'Ollonois thither three years previously. The town lay near the entrance of the great indentation of the Venezuelan coast which goes under the name of Lake Maracaibo, at the head of which there stood the smaller town of Gibraltar. The fortifications at the entrance of the lake had been strengthened since the buccaneers were there last, but Morgan's men found the town deserted by the inhabitants, who had fled at the news of this fresh incursion. Bands of angry and disappointed men were despatched to round-up what prisoners they could, and no doubt many such miserable wretches were tortured to reveal where their treasures lay. 'Amongst other tortures then used, one was to stretch their limbs with cords and at the same time beat them with sticks and other instruments. Others had burning matches placed between their fingers, which were then burnt alive. Others had slender cords or matches twisted about their heads, till their eyes burst out of the skull. Thus all sorts of inhuman cruelties were executed upon those innocent people. These tortures and racks continued for the space of three whole weeks.' To what extent must we hold Morgan personally responsible for such barbarities? The commander of a buccaneering expedition had small control over the behaviour of the irresponsible adventurers who formed the majority of its members once a town was put to the sack. The historian Leslie claims to have seen a document which 'vindicates Morgan from these black aspersions', but he cannot have been ignorant of what was going on.

After proceeding up the lake to Gibraltar, Morgan heard that three large Spanish ships had arrived to station themselves at the entrance in order to dispute his return. First, he tried bluffing the enemy with threats of further depredations unless he was allowed free passage to the open sea, but the Spaniards replied that nothing would deter them from doing their duty unless all the loot already taken was restored.

Morgan read this reply to his followers assembled in the market place. All agreed that that they would fight their way out before they would accept such terms. So a fire-ship was secretly prepared, on the decks of which a number of logs were stood upright with hats nailed to the ends in order to give the illusion that the vessel was fully manned. Tar and other combustibles were ignited as she got under way. In spite of all efforts to push her off, she drifted alongside the Spanish flagship and her flames soon spread on board. A second ship withdrew under the guns of the fort which had repelled Morgan's attack before he went up the lake. The third vessel was captured. But the ships of the buccaneers had still not passed the entrance, so that another ingenious diversion had to be devised before a favourable wind enabled Morgan to get clear with booty valued at £30,000. His ingenuity and determination on this occasion earned him the affectionate respect of the Brethren of the Coast. 'That is Harry Morgan's way', became a common phrase on their lips.

His return coincided with the arrival of letters expressing strong disapproval of the Porto Bello operations. Modyford therefore preserved a discreet silence about the success of the Maracaibo raid and prevailed on Morgan to remain quietly on the estate (still known as Morgan's Valley) which he bought with the proceeds. But shrill complaints soon emanated from Spain about this new desecration of her territory, and on the Campeachy coast the local authorities began to prepare for reprisals in the form of a landing on Jamacian soil. A certain Captain Pardal (contemptuously dismissed by Morgan as 'the vapouring admiral of Santiago') even landed at Jamaica to nail a challenge to a tree on 5 July 1670. 'I, Captain Manuel Rivera Pardal to the chief of privateers in Jamaica. I am he who has done that which follows. I went on shore at Caimanos and burnt twenty houses and fought with Captain Ary and took from him a catch [ketch] laden with provisions and a canoe. And I am he who took Captain Baines and did carry

the prize to Cartagena, and now am arrived to this coast and
have burnt it. And I am come to seek Admiral Morgan with
two ships of war of twenty guns, and having seen this, I crave
he would come out upon the coast and seek me, that he might
see the valour of the Spaniards. And because I had no time, I
did not come to the mouth of Port Royal to speak by word of
mouth in the name of my King, whom God preserve.'

Morgan himself took no notice of this quixotic behaviour,
but a month later an old comrade of his, named Captain
Morris, accidentally encountered Pardal off the coast of Cuba,
boarded his ship and killed the captain. Morris brought
back the original of the challenge written on canvas to the
Governor, who forwarded it with delight (since it provided
him with a justification of his attitude to Morgan) to the
Lords of Trade and Plantations.

The truce was obviously wearing thin, so the Council of
Jamaica commissioned Morgan as 'Admiral and Commander-
in-Chief of all the ships belonging to this harbour'. By beat
of drum it was announced in the market place that he would
raise a force to attack Santiago, 'or any other place belonging
to the enemy'. Ships and men were soon ready, the force sailing on 14 August 1670, for the old rendezvous at Isle de
Vache, where three hundred French buccaneers joined it.
Morgan had in fact been given full powers to go where he
wished and do what he would with the largest force ever seen
in those seas – twenty-eight English ships (though the flagship
herself, suitably named the *Satisfaction*, was only of 120 tons
and 22 guns), eight French ships and 1,846 men all told. Since
a list of the squadron has been preserved, it is interesting to
compare it with Esquemeling's figure of thirty-seven ships
and 2,000 men, thereby confirming the fact that this part of
his book, at any rate, is accurate as far as the facts go, and
that he himself did accompany the expedition, though it is
still possible to detect malicious overtones added by the
Spanish translator.

What was to be their objective? Cuba? Cartagena? Or Panama? A council of war held on 21 December decided on the latter place, the capital of the Spanish American empire which even Drake had not attained. Yet it was probably Drake's example which inspired Morgan, as did his tactics. The narrative of the famous attack on Nombre de Dios, one of the most stirring adventure stories in the language, had been printed by Drake's nephew under the title of *Sir Francis Drake Revived, Calling upon this Dull and Effeminate Age to Follow his Noble Footsteps for Gold and Silver* only a few years before Morgan's birth, so that the reading of it may well have fired his imagination as a boy. Even if he recalled that some of Drake's men under John Oxenham had indeed crossed the Isthmus to attack Panama, only to be caught and hanged on the other side, Morgan's record at this date determined him to attempt something which would win him undying fame. His band of desperadoes were of superb fighting quality, confident in their power to defeat any Spanish soldiery, avid for loot, seasoned by years of such warfare by sea and land, in fact, fit for anything.

Loot being the consideration uppermost in all minds, Morgan drew up a detailed plan for the division of the booty before he sailed. It was agreed that one-fifteenth was due to the King, a tenth to the Duke of York as Lord High Admiral, this being nominally an official expedition in which the laws governing prize money should prevail, though indeed such laws were not yet officially laid down. Morgan himself was to receive one-hundredth part of the whole, each captain being allowed the share of eight men. Carpenters were to receive 100 pieces of eight in addition to their shares, and surgeons 200. The customary insurance payments were listed – 1,500 pieces of eight or fifteen slaves for the loss of two legs, 600 for the loss of one, 100 for the loss of an eye, etc. All this seemed fair enough; but there was a different story to tell when the booty came to be divided in fact.

In order to secure a base, the island of Providence (or Santa Catalina) was recaptured once more, as it had been before by Mansfield. The small garrison which the Spaniards had left there made little resistance and a useful store of powder and ammunition fell into Morgan's hands. The castle of Chagres at the mouth of the river of that name was the next point of attack, because canoes could be taken up-river to a point half-way across the Isthmus, which was at its narrowest here. Chagres is only a mile or two east of Colon, the new town built at the entrance of the modern Panama Canal which for much of its way runs through the lakes created by damming the Chagres river. Since this was the key point on the Caribbean side of the Isthmus, it was a strongly-fortified place, sited on a hill or cliff and surrounded by palisades. Once more Morgan preferred to attack from the landward side, his men advancing as before with a cutlass in one hand and a 'fireball' in the other. The vanguard, or 'forlorn', was heavily repulsed, but a lucky accident gained them entry at last. An Englishman having been hit with an arrow, he pulled it out of the wound, wrapped some smouldering tow around its head and fired it back. The flaming arrow stuck in a thatched roof, which caught fire and exploded a powder barrel beneath. While some of the defenders strove to extinguish the blaze, others 'cast down many flaming pots full of combustible matter and odious smells'. Resistance was indeed desperate, only thirty of the 300 defenders surviving the attack, and it cost Morgan 100 of his best men; but at last it was in his hands, with his ships riding securely at anchor below.

With his striking force he could now begin to cross the Isthmus. A flotilla of canoes was used to go up the river towards the watershed, until the rapids forced their crews to continue along the jungle track used by the mule trains from Panama. This was the hardest part of the journey. For a week they were tormented by mosquitoes and leeches, ambushed by parties of Indians, suffering terribly from thirst and hunger. Only the chance finding of a barn stored with maize saved them from starvation, and even then they were reduced to chewing the leather of their ammunition pouches and drinking the stagnant water of forest pools. But on the ninth day they came at last, says Esquemeling, to a high mountain (probably Gold Hill, the watershed), whence, like Drake, they descried the broad expanse of the South Seas ten miles away. 'This happy sight, as if it were the end of their labours, caused infinite joy among the pirates.' Below them lay open pastures, in which browsing cattle were rounded up and roasted with all speed, 'for such was their hunger that they more resembled cannibals than Europeans, the blood running down from their beards to the middle of their bodies'.

They were now on the paved highway leading to the city where, on 18 January 1671, they found the Governor's force drawn up in battle array to receive them – two squadrons of cavalry, four regiments of foot and over a thousand wild bulls driven by Indians: according to Morgan's estimate, 2,100 foot and 600 horse; according to the Spanish commander's report, 1,200 men. Don Guzman had chosen a bad battlefield. The swampy ground on either side of the causeway prevented him from deploying his cavalry. Though according to the English translation of his dispatch he led his men to the attack with the cry of 'Come along, boys, there is now no other remedy but to conquer or to die,' the first volley fired by the buccaneers scattered the bulls which were intended to break their lines. Their effect on the Spanish lines was far more devastating on account of the closer formation of the enemy. In two hours the battle for Panama had been won. Four hundred Spanish dead lay on the ground, while the rest escaped into the hills beyond the city. The action itself only cost Morgan half a dozen men, but casualties were higher in the street fighting which followed. When the defence collapsed, warehouses stacked with silks and linen lay open to the eager hands of the buccaneers. Most of the inhabitants had fled, but enough booty remained to stock an empire. It was Morgan's critical moment as a leader. Wisely, he spread the rumour that the wine was poisoned, but any restraint on that score could not last long.

Esquemeling's story that he deliberately fired the town is obvious nonsense, because there was nothing he could desire less at the moment. Nevertheless the city, built of cedar houses, was soon a flaming mass. As Morgan later reported: 'Thus was consumed the famous and ancient city of Panama, which is the greatest resort for silver and gold in the whole world, for it receives all the goods that come from Spain in the King's great fleet, and delivers all the gold and silver that comes from the mines of Peru and Potosi.' Nothing remains today of Old Panama except the ruined tower of what was once the largest cathedral in America. A new city had to be built a few miles away at the foot of Ancon Hill, where the canal enters the Pacific Ocean. The scene of Morgan's victory is commemorated by a small overgrown plaque. A British naval officer recently visited the site in company with some American tourists, one of whom was overheard to remark, as he read the tablet, 'Christ, these limeys get everywhere.'

The consequences of lack of discipline among the buccaneers was particularly evident when it came to dealing with the shipping in the harbour. Had a few sober men been available to give chase, the *Santissima Trinidad* galleon from Lima might have been taken with all her treasure. But seeing the smoking ruins of the town as he approached from the southward, her captain turned back in time – only to fall victim some years later to men who were probably with Morgan at that time: Sawkins, Coxon and Sharp. Another later figure in our story, Charles Swan, now captain of the *Endeavour*, was so impressed by the chance of buccaneering in the Pacific that he tried to desert in one of the captured vessels. Morgan heard of the attempt just in time to order all shipping in the harbour to be sunk. He did not realise that what he had done was to open the door to the Pacific to the resolute men who would follow in his footsteps.

To read of the fate of the prisoners in Esquemeling's account is to be satiated with horrors: 'They spared, in their cruelties, no sex nor condition whatsoever,' says the man who, after all, was one of the invaders. He concludes with a pathetic story of the Admiral's attempt to seduce a rich and chaste lady, of which he claims to have been an eye-witness. On the other hand, Surgeon Browne says that such stories 'are a great deal worse than it was. As to their women, I know not, nor even heard of anything offered beyond their wills; something I know was cruelly executed by Captain Collier (the second in command) in killing a friar after quarter given, but for the Admiral, he was noble enough to the vanquished enemy'. It would be absurd to hold Morgan personally responsible for the excesses of his men, nor can Browne's evidence be lightly set aside, for he was no friend of the Admiral. On their return three weeks later (a miserable procession of prisoners, slaves and pack-mules shepherded by a vanguard and rearguard of exultant buccaneers) Morgan called a halt and much to Browne's anger had every man searched from head to foot. The French contingent, unused to this sort of behaviour on such expeditions, departed as soon as they reached Chagres on 26 February. Out of a booty estimated by the Spaniards at six million crowns, each man received a pittance of £10, for which, complains Browne, 'we must be content or else clapped in irons'. Deserting his starving and disgruntled troops, Morgan himself with a few favoured captains departed silently in the night for Jamaica with three or four ships. 'We were left,' complains Esquemeling, 'in such miserable condition as might serve for a lively representation of what reward attends wickedness at the latter end of life.'

Writing about a century later, the historian Edward Long

gave the following estimate of Morgan's loot between the
years 1669 and 1671:

Puerto del Principe	50,000	pieces of eight.
Porto Bello	250,000	,, ,,
Maracaibo	250,000	,, ,,
Panama	400,000	,, ,,
Total	950,000	[£237,500]

'Beside an immense quantity of silks, linen, gold and silver
lace, plate, jewels and other valuable commodities, which
probably amounted to near as much more. By this means
money grew to be in vast plenty, and returns easy to England,
into which many hundred thousand of those pieces of eight
were imported.'

Morgan's triumph meant Modyford's fall. In the eyes of
the English Government, Porto Bello was bad enough, but
Panama was insupportable. The treaty signed at Madrid in
1670 for 'composing the differences, restraining depredations
and establishing peace' in return for the Spanish recognition
of British sovereignty in Jamaica had just been ratified. 'It
is impossible for me to paint to your Lordships,' wrote our
harassed ambassador in Spain, 'the face of Madrid upon the
news of this action, nor to what degree of indignation the
Queen and minister of state have taken it to heart.' Colonel
Thomas Lynch was immediately sent out to arrest the
Governor for having, 'contrary to the King's express commands, made many depredations against the subjects of His
Majesty's good brother, the Catholic King'. The inhabitants
of Jamaica were well aware of the hypocrisy of such language;
but it was clear that reasons of state necessitated the arrest
of Governor Modyford and his incarceration (for a suitably
short time) in the Tower of London.

Towards Morgan, Lynch's attitude was more circumspect.
He reported how unpopular he was for the desertion of his

followers, but in view of Spanish threats of revenge he was bound to rely on his advice for the defence of the island. Even when orders arrived to send him home under arrest, he delayed at first to enforce them. 'However, I shall send him home so as he shall not be very much disgusted, yet the order obeyed and the Spaniards satisfied. I cannot do it now, for he is sick and there is no opportunity. To speak the truth of him, he's an honest brave fellow. However, it must be confessed that the privateers did barbarous acts, which they lay to the Vice-Admiral's [Collier's] charge.'

Thus it was that on 2 April 1672, Morgan sailed for England under arrest in His Majesty's unsuitably-named frigate *Welcome*. He prepared his defence in advance by writing a statesmanlike memorandum on the necessity of encouraging privateers as long as there was no adequate naval force in those seas, and he wisely armed himself with testimonials as to his character and ability. The Commander of the Forces, for instance, informed Lord Arlington (a member of the Cabal government) that he was 'a well-deserving person, and one of great courage and conduct, who may, with His Majesty's pleasure, perform good public service at home and be very advantageous to this island if war should again break forth'. There is therefore some doubt if Morgan was ever sent to the Tower on his arrival, and though the government censor tried to suppress narratives of his exploits, the story of Panama was soon known all over England. As Evelyn noted in his diary, 'such an action has not been done since the famous Drake', and like the lion-hunter he was, both Modyford and Morgan were soon invited to a dinner, at which Morgan told him that a thousand men could conquer the whole of the Spanish Indies. By that date the services of such a man could not be dispensed with, because the Third Dutch War had broken out and every regular naval ship was required in the Channel. Hence, on 22 January 1674, Morgan was appointed Deputy-Governor of Jamaica. 'His

Majesty reposing particular confidence in his loyalty, prudence, and courage and long experience in that colony,' the words being written by the philosopher John Locke, at that time Secretary to the Council of Trade and Plantations. At the same time he was knighted and given a snuff-box with a portrait of the King set in diamonds on the lid. He was also (we happen to know) suffering from boredom and the cold weather.

The new Governor, Lord Vaughan, later Earl of Carberry, was not at all Morgan's type of man. The pupil of Jeremy Taylor, the friend of Dryden, he was fitted to become President of the Royal Society. Except for the fact that, according to Pepys, he was 'one of the lewdest fellows of the age', he was totally unfitted for the rough ways of Jamaica. The two men were to have left England together on 8 January 1675, but Morgan's ship parted company as soon as they were out of sight of land. Strangely enough, she ran on a reef near the old rendezvous at Isle de Vache and became a total wreck. One of Morgan's buccaneering friends gave him a passage to Port Royal, where he arrived a fortnight before Vaughan's frigate in spite of his mishap. With such news to welcome him, it was not long before Vaughan was complaining of his assistant's behaviour. 'Sir Henry has made himself and his authority so cheap at the Port, drinking and gaming in the taverns, that I intend to remove there speedily myself for the reputation of the island.' 'What I most resent,' he wrote a few months later, 'is that I find Sir Henry, contrary to his duty and trust, endeavours to set up privateering and has obstructed all my designs for the reducing of those that do use that curse of life.' But the authorities turned a deaf ear to such complaints, telling him to remain on civil terms with his subordinate. When at last it became obvious that the two men could not get on together, it was Vaughan who was recalled.

Before the new Governor, the Earl of Carlisle, arrived, the

31

situation in the Caribbean had become ominous. Hostilities
between England and France might break out at any minute,
and Admiral d'Estrées had already made an appearance off
Hispaniola. On the very day that Vaughan left, Morgan set
about restoring the defences of the island: troops were drilled,
and with Morgan's example before them, says Colonel
Beeston, 'everyone applied themselves heartily to the business'. But d'Estrées's flagship was wrecked and he returned
to France, probably taking Esquemeling with him.

The latter part of Morgan's career belongs to the history of
Jamaica rather than to that of the buccaneers, nevertheless his
attitude towards his old companions is of great importance
in the gradual suppression of the Brethren of the Coast in
those seas. He was now a different man, living the life of an
affluent planter, busy with public responsibilities and the
administration of the colony. He did not choose to be re-
minded of the long way that he had come. His vices – exces-
sive love of money and drink, a tendency to disown his old
comrades in arms – were not uncommon. As a self-made man
who had won honour and riches by dubious means, his attitude to the privateers was hardening. He vehemently denied
that he encouraged them because, as he wrote in 1680, he
now regarded them as 'ravenous vermin' who were ruining the
prospects of peaceful trade with Spain. But it was no good,
he pointed out, sending out an occasional frigate to put them
down because they knew the secret anchorages better than
any naval officer could ever hope to. 'Nimble frigates' or
'yatches' (the yacht, of which the first example was presented
to Charles II by the Dutch, being still regarded as a warship)
should be stationed there permanently. When the redoubtable Peter Harris took a Dutch vessel and H.M.S. *Success* was
sent to arrest him, it was the naval vessel which ran on a reef.
The arrival of H.M.S. *Norwich* satisfied Morgan better. In
February she brought in the privateer James Evertsen to
await trial for his life. 'Such is the encouragement privateers

receive from my favours,' he wrote as Acting-Governor; but he could not resist reminding their Lordships that such desperate men 'can be no more easily extirpated than robbers on the King's Highway in England.'

It was wise not to be too complacent. That summer the news arrived of the second raid on Panama. It had been inspired by his example, though Sawkins, Sharp and company now sailed without a vestige of legality. The survivors took good care not to revisit Jamaica on their return. Those few on whom Morgan managed to lay his hands were arrested, and 'one of the condemned is proved a bloody and notorious villain, and fit to make an example of. . . . I abhor bloodshed and I am greatly dissatisfied that in my short government I have been so often compelled to punish criminals with death'. Strange words for the hero of Panama! However, he is generous enough to add that 'the passage of this people is extraordinarily remarkable, for in little more than four months they came from Peru to Barbados'. Such was the message he sent home by his friend Captain Swan, in March, 1682.

Though he had by now identified himself with the official anti-privateering attitude, the reappearance of his old enemy Sir Thomas Lynch a few months later meant the decline of his influence in the island. He was forced to hand over his offices without any reason being given for his dismissal. Lynch, like Vaughan, complained of his dissolute behaviour and of his disloyalty to the established order; robbed of responsibility, he naturally reverted to his old ways. But the only witness which could be called against him was a female tavern-keeper who swore that as Morgan passed her door she heard him say: 'God damn the Assembly.' He now spent most of his time with his Tory cronies in a place called the Loyal Club. 'In his debauches which go on every night, he is much magnified and I criticised by the five or six little sycophants that share them. . . . In his drink Sir Henry reflects on the government, swears, damns and curses most extravagantly.' He sent his cousin Charles to England to protest at his treat-ment by Lynch, but before the matter could be thrashed out Lynch himself was dead and the year 1685 saw the death of the King and the accession of James II. Changes highly favourable to Morgan's party ensued. Friends – 'gentlemen of great convivial talents' – were re-elected to the Assembly, and the new Governor, the Duke of Albemarle, made it his busi-ness to reinstate Morgan as soon as possible. This was done on 12 July 1688, but, says the duke, 'I am afraid he will not live long, being extraordinarily ill.'

The duke had brought out as his personal physician, young Dr Hans Sloane, who spent his time collecting the flora and fauna of the island, together with any buccaneer's journals he could get hold of. This collection of manuscripts and books formed the core of the British Museum library when it was founded some years later. He gives us clinical details of Morgan's last days. 'Sir Henry Morgan, aged about 45 (he was actually 53), lean, sallow coloured, his eyes a little yellowish and belly jutting out or prominent, complained to me of want of appetite to victuals; he had a kicking or reaching to vomit every morning and generally a small looseness attending him, and withal was much given to drinking and sitting up late, which I supposed had been the cause of his present indisposi-tion.' Scarifying details of the treatment of this old Falstaff follow. After a temporary recovery, 'falling into his old course of life, and not taking any advice to the contrary, his belly swelled so as not to be contained in his coat, on which I warned him of his very great danger because he being so very weak and subject to looseness, there was no room for purging, medicines, which seemed to be the greatest remedy for his dropsy, threatening his life'. Thoroughly alarmed, the old man called in a number of quacks, including a negro witch-doctor, who 'plastered him all over with clay and water, and by it augmented his cough. So he left his Black Doctor and sent for another, who promised him cure, but he languished and his cough augmenting, died soon after', on 25 August 1688.

The doctors and the drink had succeeded where the climate of Panama and the bullets of the Spaniards had failed. It was right that one of the two ships which fired a salute of twenty-two guns at his funeral should be called the *Drake*. As the log of the *Assistance* records, 'and after we and the *Drake* had fired, all the merchantmen fired also'.

'He showed the world that he was qualified to govern as well as to fight, and that in all stations of life he was a great man', is Leslie's epitaph. It was his success, based on the example of the Elizabethan privateers, which unveiled the weakness of Spanish power in those seas and inspired his followers to repeat his incursion into the South Seas. Had opportunity been provided for him to play his part on a national rather than on a colonial stage, his name might still be linked with that of his predecessor in those parts, Sir Francis Drake.

CHAPTER THREE

The First Invasion of the
South Seas

IN MARCH, 1 6 8 0, when Morgan as Deputy Governor of Jamaica was beginning to speak of his old companions as 'ravenous vermin' who ought to be destroyed in the interests of trade with Spain, there assembled at Golden Island off the eastern seaboard of the Isthmus of Panama a band of 336 buccaneers under the command of John Coxon. They included many redoubtable leaders, such as Bartholomew Sharp (occasionally spelled 'Sharpe'), Edmund Cook, Richard Sawkins, Peter Harris the elder, and many others whom Morgan knew and disapproved of. Who they were, and what – as far as can be ascertained – became of them afterwards, we must postpone until a later chapter. At this date, however, they were a formidable body with a force of eight ships ranging in tonnage from 150 tons to a mere fourteen-ton pinnace. Two of these vessels were manned by Frenchmen; but they, having no stomach for the coming adventure, parted company shortly afterwards.

The English party was in high spirits. They had recently sacked Porto Bello after a march of indescribable hardship through the tropical jungle. Their reward having been small at that place, they now all decided to follow the precedent set twelve years earlier by the present Deputy Governor of Jamaica, the sack of Panama. 'That which often spurs men on to the undertaking of the most difficult adventure is the sacred hunger of gold,' runs the opening sentence of one of the printed accounts of the adventure. 'And 'twas gold was the bait that tempted a pack of merry boys of us, near three hundred in number, being all soldiers of fortune, under the command (by our election) of Captain John Coxon, to list ourselves in the service of one of the richest West Indian monarchs, the Emperor of Darien.' The said emperor was in fact an escaped Spanish slave named Don Andreas, a Cuna Indian who had vowed eternal enmity against the oppressors of his race. The buccaneers thought he was a hundred and ten years old: he was certainly old enough to be a grand-father, and his son Don Augustine (called 'Golden Cap', be-cause of a brass helmet he had somehow got hold of) proved a faithful guide to this motley band of adventurers.

The plan proposed by the Indians was an attack on Santa Maria, described as a large gold-collecting centre situated midway across the Isthmus, to be followed by a repetition of Morgan's raid on Panama. The risk was tremendous, because this band possessed no leader of the calibre of Morgan and only half the size of his force; nor had they much more in the way of provisions, though they were never driven to the extremes of hunger experienced by Morgan's men. The lure of gold was sufficient: 'Though the undertaking seemed imprudent, we having no shipping of our own over there, and there being no other way home for us but through the Straits of Magellan when we should have made ourselves masters of some of their vessels, yet the encouragement we had in the expedition of freighting home our coffers with Spanish gold and pieces of eight overcame all difficulties.' Therefore, continues the manuscript of the New Englander, John Cox, 'we fitted ourselves for the march, taking with us every man a French fusil and about 2 1lbs. of powder and shot in proportion; as for provisions for the march we had none fitting save for flour, which we made into cakes and boiled them'. 'Johnny cakes' they called them, or 'journey cakes';

'doughboys' or doughnuts, according to Basil Ringrose, the young apprentice to a West Indian planter who had rashly joined this band of hardy pirates. He was compelled by circumstances to accompany them, but he never showed much relish for the prospect of adventure. He it is who has left us by far the most detailed and colourful account of the ensuing voyage.

On 5 April they left their ships behind them under the care of Captains Allison (or Alleston) and Magott (or Mackett), who were too ill to march, and struck boldly forward into the jungle with fifty Indian guides to lead them. They divided themselves into companies, Captain Sharp leading the way with a red flag to which was attached a bunch of white and green ribbons. Although 'very faint and weak' because he was recovering from a bout of fever, nothing could prevent Sharp from an enterprise in which he was soon to prove the most skilful, if not the most popular leader. The red and yellow striped flag of Sawkins's company came next, followed by Harris's green and Coxon's red colours; Edmund Cook's division, which brought up the rear, displayed a striped flag on which was the suitable device of a hand holding a sword.

Among this heterogeneous company were at least two very remarkable men – Lionel Wafer and William Dampier. The former was a young surgeon who, after a voyage to the East, had tried unsuccessfully to set up as a general practitioner at Jamaica. Meeting on the waterfront a sea captain who called himself Edmund Cook, he had easily been persuaded to go off 'on the account'. Dampier, even more of a rolling stone and sharing with Wafer an insatiable curiosity for adventure combined with the gifts of a natural scientist, had drifted (as we shall see) into the company of the logwood cutters in the Bay of Campeachy, on the coast of Honduras, a fertile nursery of British buccaneers. He was to go round the world three times in the course of the next fifteen years, but at the moment he, Ringrose and Wafer were among the youngest and the least influential of the band.

Though the march across the Isthmus was made tedious and difficult by necessity of hacking their way through the undergrowth, wading across marshes and frequently carrying their canoes from one river to another, at least the Indians were friendly. Don Andreas was an imposing figure in his 'mantle of pure gold, extraordinarily splendid rich', with his 'belt of tiger's teeth, and a hat of pure gold, with a ring and a plate of gold like a cockle-shell hanging in his nose'. All the Indians wore this crescent of gold in their noses, holding it up with one hand when they lifted a cup with the other. Some were albinos, seeing better in the dark, 'fairer than the fairest of Europe, with hair like finest fleece'. The women were 'generally very fine, airy and brisk, yet withal very modest and cautious in their husbands' presence, of whose jealousy they stand in fear'. Wafer was to get to know them better when he spent four months among them two years later recovering from a wound. Indeed, the Cunas must have afforded a splendid contrast to the tattered buckskin coats of the buccaneers and their mouldering tricorn hats with the brims cut off in front, as they marched forward, festooned with bandoliers. musket on shoulder and cutlass in hand.

The attack on Santa Maria was a disappointment. The place turned out to be a mere palisaded huddle of huts, nothing in comparison with a city like Porto Bello. At the first onset the 'forlorn hope' broke into the place, whereupon the Spanish garrison, four hundred strong, surrendered. They had received intelligence of the approach of the buccaneers and had sent off what little gold dust they had in store to a safer place. In their anger the Indians began killing the prisoners in cold blood until even the buccaneers had to stop such naked savagery.

Unwilling to have come so far for so little, they decided

to press on to Panama, 'that city being the receptacle of all
the plate, jewels and gold that is dug out of the mines of all
Potosi and Peru'. On reaching the Pacific coast a barque was
seized and put under the command of that 'sea artist and
valiant commander, Captain Bartholomew Sharp'– a tribute
to Sharp's character inserted (as were others of like nature) by
his friend William Hack, the copyist of Wapping, into the
original and more objective narrative of Basil Ringrose.
Accompanied by a flotilla of canoes, and having rid themselves of their prisoners by leaving them on shore to fend
for themselves among the savage and revengeful Indians, the
buccaneers sailed for Panama, arriving within sight of the
city on St George's Day. The date may have been thought
propitious, but the sight of a squadron of eight ships of war
under the island of Perico near the harbour of the city somewhat daunted their spirits.

This *armadilla* was commanded by the same 'old and stout
Spaniard' who defied Morgan's ravenous horde – Don
Francisco de Peralta. He was not the man to stand on the
defensive. With orders that no quarter should be given to
the invaders, he sailed to attack the approaching fleet of
canoes. The buccaneers were tired and dispirited after
paddling about for a whole week in a tropical downpour.
Sharp was away in chase of another ship, and their numbers
were sadly depleted. But Coxon's men were desperate. Battle
was joined and the Spanish flagship was boarded. Peralta and
Sawkins fought it out ship against ship, 'giving and receiving
death unto each other as fast as they could charge', writes
Ringrose about tactics which seem reminiscent of the Middle
Ages. Harris was shot through both legs as he led a boarding party against another vessel, but Coxon succeeded in
capturing the 400-ton ship named the *Trinidad*. This
was the same ship in which Peralta had escaped from
Morgan twelve years before, the buccaneers having then been
too drunk to pursue her – a grave mistake because (as Peralta

now informed Dampier) on that occasion they had on board 'friars and nuns, with all the old gentlemen and matrons of the town, to the number of fifteen hundred souls, besides an immense treasure in silver and gold'. Dampier attributes her capture to Sharp, but other accounts make it clear that Coxon was the victor, though indeed the ship became Sharp's flag-ship under the name of the *Trinity*. Peralta tried to prevent her falling into the hanas of the buccaneers by setting her on fire, but she was saved and converted for the time being into a hospital ship, on which Harris died shortly afterwards. It was his nephew who succeeded four years later in taking Santa Maria with 120 pounds of gold and a nugget the size of a hen's egg.

By the end of this desperate engagement five Spanish ships had been captured. But the buccaneers had lost forty men and it was obvious even to the boldest that an attack on the city was out of the question. As soon as the loot was divided, the usual arguments among such an undisciplined body became fierce and noisy. Murmurings were made against Coxon's leadership. He was accused of 'backwardness', a fatal failing in such company. So he and fifty others decided to return home across the Isthmus, together with the Indian chiefs and the surgeon, who, unknown to the rest, took with him the priceless medicine chest. He tried to persuade Sharp to go too but, says that virtuous character, 'I would by no means condescend to so base and dirty an action.'

Prospects would be brighter, thought Sharp, if they turned south to lie across the track of shipping coming up to Panama from Lima; but it was Sawkins who was elected to replace Coxon as their leader, since (according to Ringrose) he was 'a valiant and generous-spirited man, and beloved above all others we ever had among us'. Under him they 'eased' a vessel that very evening of 50,000 pieces of eight, 2,000 jars of wine and fifty kegs of gunpowder, which, says Sharp, 'did produce great content to our dissatisfied minds'. At the same time every little coaster gave them news of richer vessels carrying treasure to the northern capital.

Since an attack on the city now seemed unlikely, the President of Panama, alarmed by the presence of the first marauders in those seas since the days of Drake and Cavendish, demanded to know by what right they appeared in what he regarded as a Spanish monopoly area. Sawkins's reply was 'that we came to assist the King of Darien, who was the true Lord of Panama and all the country thereabouts. And that since we were come so far, there was no reason but that we should have some satisfaction. So that if he pleased to send us 500 pieces of eight for each man and 1,000 for each commander, and not any further to annoy the Indians, that then we would desist from all further hostilities, and go away peaceably; otherwise that we should stay there, and get what we could, causing to them what damage was possible'.

A second, and, as it would seem, unnecessary, enquiry was made about what commissions they carried, seeing that Englishmen and Spaniards were nominally at peace. To this Sawkins replied more shortly 'that as yet all his company was not assembled, but that when they were come up we would come and visit him at Panama, and bring our commissions on the muzzle of our guns, at which time he should read them as plain as the flame of gunpowder could make them'.

Sawkins was as bold in action as he was on paper. When a landing was made at Pueblo Nuevo on the mainland opposite Quibo Island, he led the attack in person, but he was killed at the first onset, together with a few other of the bolder spirits. This catastrophe, says Ringrose, caused another party of men to mutiny and return overland, as Coxon had already done. In Sharp's manuscript there is no mention of mutiny, the suggestion being that they were allowed to depart of their own free will. For the second time he had been out of the way at the critical moment. Fortunately for his claim to the leadership now that Sawkins was dead, he had captured a valuable cargo of indigo, butter and pitch in a small vessel which he renamed the *Mayflower* and put under the command of Edmund Cook. At a full council of the buccaneers his proposal to sail south with the two ships and return through the Straits of Magellan did not satisfy the mutineers, who thereupon returned across the Isthmus, leaving 146 men behind under Sharp's command. Ringrose would have liked to have gone too, but he was afraid of falling into the hands of the wild Indians, and so felt compelled to continue on this 'hazardous adventure'. For some undisclosed reason no one on board the *Mayflower* would accept Cook as a commander, so he was brought over to the *Trinity* and Sharp appointed his old acquaintance John Cox, the New Englander, to the command of the smaller ship. As the event proved, it was not a wise appointment because loyalty was not one of Cox's virtues.

With high promise of loot to the value of £1,000 to each man who would accompany him to the southward, Sharp took his two ships to the Isle of Gorgona to careen them before pursuing his voyage off South America. On this island (which Cowley, his successor in these seas, renamed Sharp's Island) and in the Galapagos group farther out to sea, giant turtles abounded. They were highly prized by buccaneers and Sharp's popularity must have been considerably enhanced when he 'showed himself very ingenious in striking them'. It was a pleasant place to refresh themselves after the hardships of the isthmian crossing, but Ringrose was right when he considered it mistaken strategy to stay there. The alarm had spread quickly down the Peruvian coast, so that when Sharp once more went a-roving he met with small success.

Cruising off the north coast of Peru in the summer of 1680, they parted company with the *Mayflower* in thick weather. The two ships did not see each other again until they met, apparently by chance, at the Isle of Plate a month later. The

43

island was so called by the Spaniards because it was the spot
where Drake was supposed to have divided his spoil after his
successful cruise northward in 1579, each man (so the story
went) receiving twelve tons of plate and sixteen bowls of
coined money. We know now that Drake, with his obligations
to the Queen as the principal investor in his famous voyage,
was far too careful to make any final distribution at that stage
of his circumnavigation, but it is easy to see how such a story
must have invigorated the minds of Sharp's buccaneers when
they found themselves in those seas, the first Englishmen to
view the fabulous coast of Peru for a hundred years.

Arica was the port at which they aimed, a silver town once
attacked by the legendary El Draque himself. But before they
made their landfall Sharp decided to scuttle the *Mayflower*
after taking her in tow for several days. In her rotten state she
was more of a hindrance than a help, so all his followers were
now crowded on board *Trinity*. Soon afterwards they spied a
sail with which they closed after a long chase. They boarded
her after a half-hearted action and found among her passengers the late Governor of Guayaquil, from whom they
learned that the coast was in a state of alarm and that men-of-
war were fitting out at Lima to chase these intruders out of
the South Sea. The captured vessel was therefore pillaged
without delay, 3,276 pieces of eight being divided at the capstan head among the members of the crew. For some undisclosed reason the chaplain of the Spanish ship was shot on
deck and his body heaved overboard without more ado before
he was dead. 'Such cruelties,' wrote Ringrose, 'though I
abhorred very much in my heart, yet here I was forced
to hold my tongue and contradict them not.' As Sharp
now had 140 men and fifty-five prisoners on board the
Trinity his immediate aim was to get rid of the useless
mouths. One of them, a noted Spanish pilot, might be useful
later on, but the rest were put on board their next prize after
the crew had taken the precaution to cut down the main

and mizen masts so that they could not reach land before their captors. The ex-Governor, together with three other gentlemen and the pilot Moreno, were detained in the hope of ransom, along with twelve slaves to do the drudgery of the ship.

It was a long voyage made tedious by light airs before they arrived off Arica on 26 October. A reconnoitring party which was landed some way above the town brought news that their arrival was anticipated. This news, together with the high sea that was running, decided them against any attempt on the place, so they bore away to the smaller town of Ilo. The place was taken without difficulty, English colours being hoisted above the town and a garrison established, while a flying column was sent out to see what the country afforded. But Spanish troops soon appeared in the vicinity, with whom a ransom of cattle was arranged. When, as they half expected, the buccaneers were cheated of their payment, they enjoyed themselves by sacking the neighbouring sugar factory until Spanish cavalry appeared on the scene. In a running fight they were forced back to the boats and wisely made their way back to the ship under cover of darkness.

The same trouble occurred when they landed at Coquimbo farther south within the borders of what we call Chile. Moreover many of the company were now suffering from scurvy, which the surgeon rightly ascribed to their diet of bread, water and meat. At that date no one realised that the disease was due to a deficiency of vitamin C, the vitamin found in fruit and vegetables. It was therefore the scourge of all long voyages except those in East Indiamen, in which a lime juice issue had long been the practice. It was in these same seas that Anson's men died by scores some fifty years later in the circumnavigation which became the classic instance of the incidence of this disease. Sharp's men were only saved from a similar fate by their frequent landings and lootings.

Notwithstanding the news that they were expected on this coast, they landed near the town of La Serena, a city 'most excellent and delicate, and far beyond what we could expect in so remote a place'. The inhabitants fled on their approach, carrying with them their jewels and burying their less portable plate in the ground. Under flag of truce a deputation offered a ransom of 95,000 pieces of eight, but once again the buccaneers were cheated of their reward. Whereupon Sharp ordered his men to set fire to the town and make their way back to the ship, leaving the gentlemen prisoners on shore because they did not know what else to do with them. Under Sharp's leadership his men fought their way back to the ship, which they reached only just in time to save her from the effects of an underwater stratagem which the Spaniards had employed to burn the ship while the crew was on shore. A man had been floated out on an inflated horse's hide to fill the space between the rudder and the sternpost with combustibles, to which he had set fire.

After these disappointments it was decided to spend Christmas on the lonely and uninhabited island of Juan Fernandez, an experience which proved of great strategic importance during the next fifty years, when the place became almost a British base in the South Seas. Successive circumnavigators invariably visited the island, following the precedent set by this buccaneering band, and plans were made more than once to annex it for strategic purposes.

'This day being Christmas Day we gave in the morning early three volleys of shot for solemnization of that great festival.' But the jollifications of the season could not obliterate the sense of disappointment which they all felt now that their cruise down the American coast had ended. The memory of Drake had been ever before them, but they had not met with a tenth of his success. Sharp had promised them £1,000 a man. Where was their reward, beyond a few thousand pieces of eight which most of them had already gambled

46

away? Certainly Sharp was not Drake. He had none of the latter's tactical genius, and although evidently a courageous and intelligent man – subsequent events proved him to be a first-class navigator – he lacked the qualities which enabled Drake to impose his personality on his crew. But Drake in founding the tradition of naval leadership had the help of semi-official backing in his cause which allowed him to strengthen his discipline with sanctions. Sharp found himself in command of a refractory crew, each man of which re-garded himself, in the tradition of the Brethren of the Coast, as the equal of the captain 'by election'. No wonder, then, that when all the wine had been drunk and all the muskets fired off at random into the darkness of this uninhabited isle, murmurs of discontent began to gather in volume. Accord-ing to Sharp, John Cox was the moving spirit in the mutiny – 'the promoter of which design as I was creditably informed was a true-hearted dissembling New England man, whom I for old acquaintance sake had taken from before the mast and made him my vice-admiral; it was not at all for his manhood or art, for he had none; and as they consulted, so they acted, and took my ship by force out of my possession, and kept me a prisoner there.' Cox, of course, never mentions his part in the affair. He merely says that the argument whether they should return with the 3,000 pieces of eight which still remained in their pockets became so fierce that blows were exchanged. Sharp's party insisted on an immediate return through the Straits of Magellan (for it was high summer in those lati-tudes), while 'the cabal' wanted another cruise to the north-ward to make more money.

On Thursday, 6 January 1681, 'our differences being now grown to a great height', says Ringrose, Sharp was deposed and a certain John Watling elected in his stead, articles being signed to this effect as was the buccaneer custom. Nothing is known about Watling beyond the fact that he gave his name to the West Indian island which Columbus first sighted. It

seems that he was a religious type, for the first thing that
Ringrose records of his rule was that he clapped one of the
servants in irons for suspected treachery; actually the man
was Edmund Cook, and according to Sharp's unprinted
account, it was for his addiction to the unnatural vice
common in buccaneering communities. Furthermore, the
next Sunday was kept as a holy day for the first time since the
death of Sawkins.

In this aura of respectability, they set sail northward to try
their luck once more. When the ship had to leave Juan Fernandez in a hurry a Mosquito Indian named William could
not be found. This man – historically the first Robinson
Crusoe – was left behind by mistake; he was taken off again
by Eaton and Dampier four years later, having nearly lost
the gift of speech. [See page 90.]

The new captain was not a success. Ringrose was soon complaining that he was 'fainthearted as a leader', and of course
Sharp took every opportunity to undermine his authority. On
one occasion a friar, taken out of a captured prize, gave such
unsatisfactory answers to the questions put to him that he was
shot out of hand, Sharp thereupon assumed the role of
Pontius Pilate and rebuked Watling for such unnecessary
cruelty. 'Gentlemen,' he cried, ostentatiously washing his
hands in a bowl of water, 'I am clear of the blood of this old
man; and I will warrant you a hot day for this piece of cruelty
whenever we come to fight at Arica.'

For Arica was once more the point of their attack. On 30
January, they landed four miles south of the city. The men
were carefully divided up into landing parties, boat guards,
assault parties and grenadiers to storm the forts. The greater
part of the town was occupied after a desperate fight, but
the forts held out and they soon heard that enemy reinforce-
ments were expected. Watling himself was killed at the head
of his men and the number of casualties suffered was so great
that the remainder were forced to beg Sharp to resume the

command. 'Now they came about me begging me to take command of them anew upon me, the which I absolutely refused.'
But the situation was so serious and the instigation of his
friends so pressing that he agreed at last on condition that a
new oath of obedience should be sworn. This done, they re-
treated to the boats in as good order as Sharp could muster
them, the only loot which they managed to carry away
amounting to thirty-seven pieces of eight per man.

Ringrose agrees that this was how things fell out, but the
following testimonial to Sharp's character in the printed
version of the latter's narrative finds no place in the original,
since it is another of Hack's interpolations: 'Sharp is a man of
an undaunted courage, and of excellent conduct, not fearing
in the least to look an insulting enemy in the face, and a
person who knows both the theory and practice of navigation
as well as most do.' Such at least is the way the testimonial
appears in the printed version; but what actually appears in
the manuscript sent to the booksellers (or publishers, as we
should call them) runs thus: 'A man of excellent conduct, not
fearing to look the insulting enemy in the face and one that
hath the theorique and pratique of navigation as well as most
men have it.' Hack's worst sin was not the insertion of this un-
solicited testimonial (for Sharp was out of the country when
he wrote it) but the omission on the beautifully decorated
title page of his copy of the manuscript of all mention of the
name of Basil Ringrose, the real author.

After this date Ringrose kept no regular journal, 'my
disease and sickness being the occasion of intermitting what
I had never failed to do in all the course of this voyage till
now.' Occasionally he felt strong enough to describe a remarkable place or action, but for the long voyage home his journal
amounts to little more than a list of navigational observations
such as one finds in a ship's log. Sharp's journal throughout is
much briefer and this too deteriorates into a mere log for the
latter part of the voyage. Cox is little better, and since

Dampier and Wafer broke with Sharp in order to return overland, the evidence of what occurred during the last year the
buccaneers were at sea becomes very meagre.

The occasion of the breach between Sharp and the party of
which Dampier was a member was a second mutiny on board
the *Trinity* which occurred when they returned to the Isle of
Plate, which they had visited a year previously. A number of
the crew had never been reconciled to Sharp's resumption of
the command. The second attack on Arica had failed as miserably as the first, though this was not Sharp's fault. With forty-
seven men, including Dampier, Wafer therefore decided on
17 April 1681, to return across the Isthmus as their predecessors had done. Dampier complains that it was 'the
meaner sort' who supported Sharp, the rest of the company
(meaning his own party) 'being not satisfied either with his
courage or behaviour'. Wafer justifies his conduct in the same
way, adding that in Sharp 'we experienced neither courage
nor conduct'. Because the accounts of these two men have
been more accessible, later writers have too easily repeated
such charges, which are indeed belied by Sharp's conduct
both before and after the mutiny. The facts never seem to
warrant calling him a coward on any occasion, and his conduct as a leader and as a seaman certainly excelled that of any
other member of the crew. All that the much-maligned commander has to say in his own journal about the event is that
'forty-five of our men left us with a free consent'. No doubt
he was glad to see them go and willingly gave them the
long boat and two canoes for the 600-mile voyage to the
Bay of Panama. He had far too many men on board the
Trinity, and he must have hoped that he would never see or
hear of this discontented minority again. But these remarkable men not only completed their voyage safely, but after
many adventures (which will be recounted in a later
chapter), crossed the Isthmus to rejoin their friends on the
other side. Most of them, including Dampier, re-entered

the Pacific again by the Straits of Magellan three years later, inspired by the prospects of this, the first, invasion of the South Seas.

Those remaining under Sharp's command must now have amounted to about 73 men, though it is impossible to be precise as to the number. It was as well that they 'fully resolved and faithfully promised to each other that they would stick close together', because they were about to embark on one of the longest and most difficult voyages ever recorded in the history of sail. At first they continued their northerly course to a point well above Panama; then they turned south 'under the equinoctial', where another example of the luck which always accompanied Sharp's leadership occurred. They made prize of one of the same ships returning from Panama which they had looted on her way thither the previous year. This time they were more fortunate, since she was carrying no less than 21,000 pieces of eight in chests and another 16,000 in bags. It is difficult to imagine what became of all this money, because the final dividend proved somewhat meagre.

A much more valuable prize was the *Santi Rosario*, taken on 19 July 1681 off Cape Francisco on the coast of modern Ecuador. All that Ringrose has to say about this episode is that, besides taking much plate and coin, they found on board 620 jars of brandy (with which they made 'very merry') and 'the most beautiful woman I ever saw in all the South Sea'. But a much fuller account appears under the signature of W.D., William Dick, who rushed into print before Ringrose's narrative was published and by so doing committed such a serious breach of security that the authorities took care to censor his account in all succeeding editions, and to replace it with that by Ringrose. In the first place, Dick relates the incredible story (supported by another printed narrative) of how they all mistook for tin what were really ingots of silver direct from the mines of Peru. Part of one such ingot was retained by an economical fellow who wished to make bullets of it, the rest was abandoned. Back in Bristol, this same fellow sold a single pig of what remained for £75, when it was found to be pure silver.

That probably annoyed Sharp's followers when they heard of it; but what outraged the authorities was the way Dick went on to speak of a great book of sea charts and maps which they found on board. 'This book serveth them (the Spaniards) for an entire and compleat Wagenaer[1] in those parts, and for its novelty and curiosity was presented to His Majesty after our return into England. It hath since been translated into English, as I hear, by His Majesty's order and the copy of the translation, made by a Jew, I have seen at Wapping; but withal the printing thereof is severely prohibited, lest other nations should get into those seas.'

Since at that date charts were regarded as state secrets, it is understandable why Sharp's own account of this episode has never appeared in print. 'In this prize I took a Spanish manuscript of a prodigious vallue – it describes all the ports, roads, harbours, bayes, sands, rocks and riseing of the land and instructions how to work the ship into any port or harbour between the latt. of 17d. 15′N to 57d. S latt. – they were goeing to throw it overboard but by good luck I saved it – the Spaniards cryed out when I gott the book (farewell South Seas now) – allso I took in this prize another jewell viz, a young lady about 18 years of age – her name was Dona Juana Constanta – a very comely creature – her husband's name was Don Juan, etc. . . . The ship was called the *Rosario*.'

He was intelligent enough to realise that this 'waggoner'

1. A version of the name of Waghenaer, the Dutch publisher of *The Mariner's Mirrour* in 1586. A century later his name, corrupted into the form of 'waggoner' was applied to any sea atlas, rutter [*routier*] or pilot. The Spanish collection of charts has been identified by Mr R. A. Skelton of the British Museum as either that now in the Houghton Library or that in the Huntington Library, U.S.A., probably the latter (See page 59).

was far more valuable than all the pieces of eight they had so arduously collected. It was, indeed, a case of 'farewell South Seas now'; if he could get in touch with the King, all his crimes as a pirate (or at least as a privateer sailing without a commission) would be forgiven him. Whether he took any of the crew into his confidence we shall never know, but it is significant that within a few weeks it was unanimously agreed to return into the Atlantic through the Straits of Magellan. A final failure to take Paita by surprise settled the matter. On 29 August, says Ringrose, 'all our hopes of doing any further good upon the coasts of the South Sea being now frustrated, seeing we were descried before our arrival wherever we came, we resolved unanimously to quit all other attempts and bear away for the Straits of Magellan.'

They drove south through terrible weather, though it was the summer season in those parts. Equinoctial gales, 'prodigious cold weather', and high seas battered the *Trinity* as she approached the southern extremity of the continent. Poor Ringrose was in bad shape, being 'still much tormented with the gripes as before', nor did the rocky shores and innumerable inlets of this fiord coast, inhabited by Indians kept alive by a diet of shellfish, afford them any refuge. On 6 November they lost sight of land in a fog and from that date until they made their landfall in the West Indies three months later they never sighted land on a voyage of some ten thousand miles. The weather being 'very dark, foggy and windy, with a huge sea which oftentimes rolled over us', they missed the entrance to the straits altogether and were driven down to the latitude of Cape Horn (55° 59′) in order to make their easting. They were thus the first Englishmen to make, albeit involuntarily, that famous passage, and it is a tribute to Sharp's skill and resolution that they ever reached the Atlantic Ocean. A comparison of their observations does not permit us to say exactly on what date they doubled the Horn, but it was probably on 17 November.

SHARP	*RINGROSE*
15 November: 58° 13′	58° 25′
16 November: nil	'the weather was dark'
17 November: 58° 15′	58° 23′

Not even Drake had ventured as far south as this, so that when they were able to haul away to the northward their hearts filled with joy. Sharp kept on promising them that Christmas Day would be celebrated in due style in a safer latitude, but some of the ungrateful wretches whom he commanded took the opportunity to plot his assassination at the height of the anticipated festivities. Rumours of the plot fortunately reached his ears, so he directed that the wine should be shared out before the promised day, 'being persuaded they would scarce attempt any such thing in their sobriety'. When Christmas Day dawned off the coast of Brazil they were allowed to regale themselves by roasting an enormous sow which had been a mere sucking pig when she was first taken on board. It was the first meat they had tasted for four months. There was still enough wine to gladden their hearts, but not enough to allow matters to get out of hand. With great satisfaction their commander was able to note in his journal, 'we eat our hogg and dranck severall jarrs of wine and was extraordinary merry, whome god preserve and send us in safety to our desired port; no observation.'

The most amazing thing about the whole voyage was the accuracy with which they made their intended landfall. On Saturday, 28 January 1682, 'in the morning about 6 of the clock I made the island of Barbadoes – it bore SW distant about 4 leagues – and I stood in to Spike's and the first boat that we spake with was the *Richmond*'s barge, which made us bare up for the island of Nevis, not staying for any refreshment'.

54

CHAPTER FOUR

What Happened to Sharp

IT WAS NOT A HAPPY RETURN. The encounter with the *Richmond*'s barge at Barbados seems to have given Sharp and his crew a more acute apprehension of danger than of the vicissitudes of the voyage. For three years they had been preying on Spanish shipping without any sort of commission beyond that which they once boasted lay in the muzzles of their guns. How would the authorities regard them – as pirates, corsairs, marauders, or as legitimate privateers, possibly even as explorers? It is this anxiety which causes the discrepancies between the various accounts of the voyage to become most marked in the concluding pages of the journals which have survived.

Ringrose gives the fullest account, and the most ingenuous: the *Richmond*'s men, he says, refused to come on board, but he refrains from adding that this was probably because they feared to have their throats cut by the set of unkempt desperadoes whom they saw leaning over the taffrail. For similar reasons the crew of the *Trinity* wished to have as little as possible to do with a man-of-war: every member had a bad conscience and the news shouted up by the *Richmond*'s men exacerbated it – there was peace at home. That meant that marauders of Spanish shipping were not at the moment encouraged. Sharp had the misfortune to return when the policy of suppressing the privateers was beginning to be taken seriously, even by the Governors of the West Indies. In the face of Spanish diplomatic pressure in

London, the Board of Plantations and the Admiralty had long since ceased to condone such characters.

There is a wealth of meaning in Sharp's short phrase that they therefore bore up for Nevis 'not staying for any refreshment'. After their long voyage in an unseaworthy ship the victualling situation was desperate. Two days before they made their landfall at Barbados they had decided to eat 'a little Spanish shock dog' if they did not see land very soon. Refused entry at the port where they thought they would have found refuge, they were hunted men once more. They had already divided the spoil, promising themselves 'drinking bouts' and 'public merriment' as soon as they landed. Even the dog had fetched forty pieces of eight at the masthead. The gamblers had counted up the money they had won during the past months. A dividend from sharing 'some small parcels of money that had not as yet been touched of our former prizes' amounted to only twenty-four pieces of eight for each man. 'We also gave to our good commander a mulatto boy, in token of the respect we all were owing to him for the safety of our conduct through so many dangerous adventures.'

But now they were so short of food that they even decided to risk breaking their voyage to Nevis at Antigua in the hope that some refreshment would be offered them there. 'The gentry of the place and common people were very willing and desirous to receive us,' complains Ringrose, 'but the Governor flatly denied us entry' – and this in spite of a proffered bribe of jewellery for his lady, adds William Dick. Matters were so desperate that a final division of the spoil was made and it was decided that every man should shift for himself. The ship itself was handed over to seven men who had been unlucky enough to lose their all in the countless games of chance with which they had whiled away the long hours at sea. Sharp jealously conserved for himself the book of charts which he had taken out of the *Rosario*, determined to buy his pardon with them. On reaching Nevis (where at last they were allowed to come to anchor) he, Ringrose, Dick, and Cox and most of the officers prevailed upon the owners of two vessels about to sail for England to give them a passage, in order, says Cox, 'to give the King an account of our discoveries' – in reality, to buy their pardons. Some of the crew made their way to New England, but the majority determined to try their luck at Jamaica, trusting that Morgan, the Deputy-Governor, would show his old leniency towards old buccaneers. In this they were disappointed. In a letter dated 8 March 1682 Morgan informed the Secretary of State that he had arrested all who landed on the island and (as we have seen) that he had hanged one of them 'who is proved a bloody and notorious villain and fit to make an example'.

Sharp's narrative concludes with these words, 'We came as passengers in two ships, one of which was commanded by Capt. Charles Howard, and the other by Mr. Porteen [her name was the *Lisbon Merchant*], and in safety we all landed at Dartmouth. *Laus Deo.*' The date was 26 March 1682. Less than two months later he and three of his officers were up for trial on a charge of piracy before the Court of Admiralty sitting at the Marshalsea.

The proceedings at this trial breathe the very spirit of *Treasure Island*, and from the depositions we can piece together some of the most curious episodes in Sharp's career. On reaching London from Dartmouth he took lodgings with one Captain Peadly, living near the Tower. Meanwhile a sixteen-year-old Spanish boy, named Calderon, whom he had been unwise enough to bring home with him, had got into contact with the Spanish ambassador, who immediately demanded that proceedings should be taken against Sharp on account of what happened to the *Rosario*.

It was for this reason that on 19 May, Bartholomew Sharp, described as 'formerly living in Jamaica, born in the parish of Stepney in the County of Middlesex, mariner, aged about 32 years', together with William Dick, John Cox and two others stood their trial before the Court of Admiralty. Calderon deposed that Sharp had first fired on the Spanish vessel. Her captain had been killed, a number of her crew tortured to reveal the whereabouts of the silver which she was supposed to be carrying, and the ship's store of wine and brandy thoroughly plundered. His evidence was supported by that of two negroes who, says Dick, 'turned Cat in the Pan and had a spleen against Capt. Sharp'. One of them added that Sharp had been heard to say on landing in England that he would try to get another ship to go to America 'upon the same account'.

Another hostile witness was Thomas Camp of Stepney. He had a friend who was landlord of the Anchor tavern, where Sharp lodged for a few weeks. Sharp had apparently informed the landlord that he had been a pirate for sixteen years, robbing all nations 'but espccially the King of Spain,' and that he 'had often expressed himself to the following effect, viz., that he had lived a wicked course of life abroad and thought he would never die a natural death; that he had come home to sue out his pardon, which he had no great hopes to obtain, and if he did not, that he would return again to the West Indies, or words to that effect'. Camp had of course asked his friend the landlord what money this self-confessed pirate possessed, upon which he received dark hints of 'some thousands of pounds, several portmanteaux of gold and silver coined and uncoined'.

Naturally Sharp and his companions dismissed all this as mere hearsay, since they could rely on a stronger line of defence. While Calderon was persuading the Spanish ambassador to press for a trial, Sharp had not wasted his time. He had made contact with a certain William Hack of Wapping and other 'gentlemen' who may themselves have been buccaneers at one time but had now settled down to

the more respectable task of copying charts. Another probable contact was the Admiralty, since his journal and the
first copy of his *Wagoner of the Great South Sea* was deposited there. Information about certain valuable charts of
the Pacific taken out of a Spanish ship must have reached the
ears of the court, possibly those of the King himself. It looks
as if Hack was commissioned to make a copy of the charts,
getting a Jewish friend named Phillip Dassigny, later a ship-
mate with Cowley, to translate the sailing instructions at the
very time the formal trial was taking place at the Court of
Admiralty.

Be this as it may, Sharp and his friends were acquitted
on the charge of piracy on a plea of self-defence, and in
October a wonderfully ornate copy of the *Rosario* charts was
presented to the King under the title of *A Wagoner of the
Great South Sea*. The frontispiece of this book reproduces
the title-page of the first copy of 1682, which was deposited
at the Admiralty, and recently presented by the Lords
Commissioners to the British Museum. The full title
runs *To the high and mighty monarch, Charles the Second,
King of great Britaigne, France, Ireland etc. This Wagoner of
the Great South Sea is humbly dedicated and presented by
your majesty's ever loyal subject Barth. Sharpe, 1682.*
Another copy, dedicated to James II in much the same
terms in 1685, is signed William Hack, no mention being
made of Sharp. Sharp's title-page, in spite of the crudity of its
drawing, has the additional interest of illustrating the navigational instruments then in use – the cross staff, octant and
quadrant for taking sights, and the dividers to lay off a
course on a globe. The latter part of the seventeenth century
saw the publication of the most beautiful sea atlases that
have ever been printed, but though the delicacy of engraving and the elegance of the cartouches of such great atlases
as those of Blaeu and Van Keulen are superior, none of the
manuscript collections of charts can equal Hack's Wagoner

for full-bodied richness of colouring. It is true that the draughtsmanship is crude in comparison with the work of the Dutch, but the generosity with which Hack lad on his red, gold and green colouring, the magnificence of his heraldic emblems and dedicatory title-pages, quite apart from the intrinsic value of the first accurate navigational charts of the Pacific to be seen in England, certainly impressed the authorities favourably enough to win a pardon for the buccaneers.

The consequence was that, instead of being hanged as a pirate at Execution Dock, Sharp was given a captain's commission in the Navy on 25 November and appointed to the command of the *Bonetta* sloop of war, fifty-seven tons and fifteen men, then lying at Deptford. But if we turn the page of the same List of Ships in Commission which gives us this information, we note that the next month Captain Edward St Lo of the Royal Navy was appointed to the command of the *Dartmouth* frigate, likewise destined for the West Indies. The paths of the buccaneer and the naval officer were soon to cross, with serious consequences for Sharp. But for the moment, having attained a respectable status, the latter decided that he had had enough of law and order. When the *Bonetta* sailed on 13 April 1683 she sailed under Captain Edward Stanley with orders to search for a Spanish treasure-ship reputed to have been wrecked off the shores of Hispaniola.

How Stanley, with the assistance of William Phips, later Governor of Massachusetts, succeeded in locating this treasure ship is another story. But if Sharp never sailed in the *Bonetta*, what happened to him? According to his friend Dick, 'he wasted his money on good fellowship' – exactly what one might have expected him to do. When funds sank low 'he got together a little money, and with this he bought an old boat, which, as I am told, used to lie above London Bridge, for the sum of £20 sterling. Into this boat he put a small quantity of butter and cheese, and a dozen or two pieces of beef'. With a crew of sixteen men as adventurous as himself he sailed this old hulk as far as the Downs, where he 'clapt aboard' a French vessel, seized her in true buccaneering fashion, victualled her by rounding up some cattle which he 'espied' grazing on Romney Marsh, and disappeared over the western horizon.

Shortly afterwards rumours reached the ears of the Secretary of State that he had returned to the South Seas and that the Viceroy of Peru was arming 'divers considerable ships, so that if he comes he will not escape without a new miracle'. These rumours, however, did not in fact relate to the redoubtable Sharp but to a band of his former shipmates who were now following in his footsteps – Davis, Cook, Dampier, Wafer and Ambrose Cowley, whose adventures in the *Batchelor's Delight* form the subject of a later chapter.

By the time this company reached the Pacific, Sharp had in fact turned respectable once more. What occurred during the early months of his cruise in the Caribbean we have no means of knowing, but we do know that on 29 January 1684 the Governor of the Leeward Islands, Sir William Stapleton, gave him a commission to apprehend Indians and pirates, presumably on the principle of setting a thief to catch a thief. About the same time his old companion Coxon received a similar commission, the authorities now reverting to their previous practice of employing buccaneers to police the Caribbean in the absence of a suitable naval force. There were, however, one or two small warships, either sloops or frigates, in those seas, so that a complicated situation arose, no one knowing who was a pirate, a legitimate privateer or a naval officer. Needless to say, Sharp's career was as ambiguous as it could possibly be. On 31 October he took a ship off Jamaica which he renamed *Josiah* and used for his own purposes. Previously she had been owned by a Spaniard and called *Valdivia*; then she had been captured by a New Eng-

61

lander called Thomas Henley, who renamed her *Resolution*. According to Sharp, Henley was a notorious pirate; according to others, Sharp himself was just as bad.

A year after this event he had to face a charge in the Vice-Admiralty Court at Nevis that he 'did feloniously and piratically make a violent incursion upon, rob, plunder, kill and destroy' the Spanish settlement at Campeachy at a date when Britain and Spain were supposed to be at peace with each other. Furthermore he was accused of carrying into captivity twenty Spaniards and Indians, which he sold as slaves at Bermuda. Finally he was accused of seizing a Spanish sloop 'sailing about her lawful occasions' and converting her to his own use. To all of which Sharp replied that he had been carried to Campeachy against his will, having fallen into company with some French marauders, and it was these villains who compelled him to participate in the raid on Campeachy, that ancient haunt of logwood cutters and buccaneers.

No ordinary court of law would have paid much attention to such slender grounds of defence had it not been for the fact that the political situation complicated the case. The previous autumn those of the Monmouth rebels who had been sentenced to the plantations by Judge Jeffreys had begun to arrive. Some of the more spirited allied themselves with the 'maroon' Indians, who were, as always, disaffected against the government, and in their company created a number of disturbances in Jamaica and elsewhere. Sharp was at Bermuda in the *Josiah* at the time when a similar situation began to develop there. In addition to the trouble caused by the arrival of the Monmouth rebels, this island had recently passed from the hands of the Company to the Crown. A large section of the population resented this transfer of power and attacked Governor Cony as the representative of a despotic government at home, a view strongly supported by the newly-arrived rebels. At the moment when his authority and even his personal safety was jeopardised, Cony found in Sharp a redoubtable ally against people who, he complained, were 'mutinous, turbulent, hypocritical and wholly averse to kingly government'.

Thus on 21 January he describes Sharp as 'very zealous for the King's service, though the people have offered him large sums to desert me'. Nothing averse to gilding his own testimonial, Sharp himself tells the Secretary of State that he is busy protecting the life of the Governor with the assistance of a certain Captain Conway, against people 'who will not believe that any king but Monmouth is living'. At the same time we find the inhabitants of the island petitioning the government against the oppressive rule and 'enormous crimes' of Governor Cony and his friend 'Sharp the pirate'. More specifically a certain Captain Peniston calls Sharp a proclaimed pirate, an absconding debtor, a cattle thief and a traitor who had sold his services to the French, in whose company he had massacred the Spaniards at Campeachy and sold others into slavery. When writs had been served on the said Captain Sharp, he had lit his pipe or wiped his breech with them. Another petition from the master of the *Bachelor's Adventure* complained that Sharp had seized his ship and that he, the rightful master, was now languishing in jail.

So the quarrel continued until in July the Deputy Governor of Nevis, Sir John Russel (Stapleton being absent on sick leave) decided that it was time to find out what was really going on in that turbulent island. He therefore ordered Captain St Lo to take H.M.S. *Dartmouth* to Bermuda, where he was 'to seize Capt. Sharp the Pirate . . . and to find out how he came into possession of his present ship'. If the answer were unsatisfactory, Sharp was to be brought back for trial at Nevis.

Edward St Lo was a typical product of the Pepsyian revolution in naval administration, as a result of which the modern professional naval officer began to emerge at the end of the

seventeenth century. He was a man of good birth, honest,
zealous, inclined to domineer and therefore somewhat difficult to get on with. His natural truculence of temperament
which made him jealous of the rights and privileges of His
Majesty's Navy was not an asset in the confused situation
which prevailed at that moment in the Caribbean. Even a
century later an equally zealous young naval officer named
Horatio Nelson failed to understand the rights and wrongs
of the inhabitants of the West Indies and did himself no good
in his attempts to suppress what he called smuggling and
what the West Indian community regarded as legitimate
trade. One can hardly blame St Lo for being unable to make
up his mind who was on whose side, who was a pirate and who
a protector of law and order. Like most officers in a similar
predicament he fell back on the letter of his orders, determined to carry them into effect come what may.

So, when he arrived at Bermuda he arrested Sharp as a
pirate, though Governor Cony protested to his colleague at
Nevis that he himself had been 'forced to retain Sharp for
the King's service to suppress the rebellion here, which he
did. What may be proved against him, I know not, but he
has shown himself a loyal and good subject, and a extraordinary instrument in preserving the Kings' peace'. In a
second letter on Sharp's behalf he begs Russel to let Sharp
off lightly if anything should be proved against him.

Such testimonials undoubtedly stood Sharp in good stead
when St Lo carried him back to Nevis to stand his trial at
the Vice-Admiralty Court there on 30 December 1686. Indeed, it was a fortunate moment for him, because the new
Governor of Jamaica, the Duke of Albemarle, had reverted to
the precedent of offering a free pardon to all pirates and
privateers who submitted themselves to the royal clemency
within a specified number of months. The tide was running
strongly in Sharp's favour. Indian and mulatto witnesses
against him at the trial were brushed aside by the Grand Jury,

who took remarkably little time to bring in a verdict of *ignoramus* to clear the prisoner by proclamation.

St Lo, however, was not so easily satisfied. He felt that he had done his duty in seizing Sharp. He was convinced that the man was a pirate, and he was determined that he should not get off so lightly. He therefore compelled him to stand another trial on 12 February 1687, by himself testifying against Sharp's commission which he declared was 'out of date and for another ship'. In his view the *Josiah* had been piratically seized from her New England owner, since the accused had been heard to swear that he 'would be plague to the New England men and the Bermudians'. He had refused to lower his topsail in salute to one of His Majesty's frigates on her arrival at Bermuda and had even had the effrontery to steal part of her mainsail while she lay in harbour. To support these charges St Lo brought forward a number of witnesses, one of whom avowed that he had seen Sharp 'put the broad arrow upon the mainmast' of the *Resolution* when he named her *Josiah*. Another averred that he had seen Sharp selling slaves at Bermuda at prices ranging from £14 to £3 a head. Not that he seems to have regarded this as in any way morally reprehensible, since the trade was strictly legal, but that Sharp was acting like an interloper by selling goods obtained from an unlawful source.

Sharp's defence was, of course, that the master of the *Resolution* was himself a pirate whom he was justified in apprehending by the commission issued by Governor Stapleton. The Petty Jury of this island of 200 souls were clearly satisfied, knowing their Governor's point of view in the matter. For the second time Sharp was acquitted. He even had the satisfaction of seeing his accuser ordered back to England for exceeding his orders and for insolent behaviour towards the Governor, who complained that he had been sailing about the islands 'for recreation'. One entirely sympathises with St Lo when he justified himself by pointing out that he had only carried out his orders, and that far from sailing 'for recreation' he had been busy rounding up witnesses against a notorious miscreant. When he adds that the trial was a farce because the Governor 'God-damned' all the hostile witnesses which St Lo had been at pains to collect, swearing that the evidence of 'a crew of dogs should not take away the life of an Englishman', it is obvious that the verdict on both occasions had been rigged by Governor Russel in agreement with Governor Cony. Sharp's case was by no means the only one at that period in which the process of law as practised in the West Indies seemed incomprehensible to an Englishman. At least it is satisfactory to know that the honest St Lo got his reward in the end by becoming Commissioner of Plymouth dockyard and later Commander-in-Chief at the Nore.

As for Sharp, he passes out of history at the conclusion of his second (or, if we take into account his trial in England, his third) acquittal on a charge of piracy. Only one further fact can be gleaned about him, a fact which suggests that to the last he continued to follow in Morgan's footsteps, as he had done for the previous ten years. In 1688 he is mentioned as commander – not quite governor – of the tiny island of Anguilla, otherwise known as Snake Island, the northernmost of the Leeward Islands. Its population is described as being 'without government or religion', and it later became the haunt of notorious pirates.

CHAPTER FIVE

The Suppression of the Buccaneers
in the Caribbean

THE STORY OF SHARP'S LATER CAREER shows how the authorities were at last attempting to suppress those whom they had previously referred to as 'privateers' and now (flatly) called 'pirates'. They had undertaken to do so by the terms of the Treaty of Madrid as far back as 1670, and Morgan's enemy, Governor Lynch, had taken steps to issue free pardons to those who came in. Morgan himself, as we have seen, loyally accepted this policy during his years of office, but 'privateering' still continued in the Caribbean because it was both popular and necessary. Some, like Sharp, turned honest for a spell, until the outbreak of the general war in Europe in 1689 gave them a chance to become privateers in the proper sense of the word. Others attempted to make a living as logwood cutters in Honduras. If that failed, they degenerated into pirates. By the last decade of the seventeenth century the old buccaneers in that area had been replaced by genuine privateers or by felonious pirates, and the attractions of the South Seas displaced those of the Caribbean.

The career of John Coxon (or Coxen) was similar in outline to that of his friend Sharp. Unfortunately we can only piece together what happened to men like him from stray references in the official correspondence of the period. It is clear that the reason why he was elected to the command of the band which crossed the Isthmus in 1680 was his success

67

three years previously at Santa Marta, a few miles east of Cartagena, where his prisoners included the Governor and the Bishop. On that occasion plunder amounted to only £20 a man, but ransom offered greater possibilities. However, as the Governor complained when he reached Jamaica, Coxon's men had been too drunk to discuss the question when they were on the Main.

With Coxon was Edmund Cook, whose name appears in many of the later raids and who is easily confused with his contemporary, John Cook. He is one of the few whose reasons for joining the Brethren of the Coast can be ascertained. On 5 December, 1673, his 'pink', the *Virgin* of 130 tons, was captured by a certain Don Philip Hellen, alias Fitzgerald, captain of a Spanish man-of-war. Cook was returning to England with a cargo of sugar, logwood and indigo when he was taken off Havana and subjected to 'barbarous treatment'. John Cannon, master of the *Rebecca*, makes a similar complaint. Asked by his Spanish guards if he did not realise that it was a crime to trade in those seas, he replied that he thought he was free to sail from one English port to another. 'At which they said it was contrary to their articles for any English dog to go into their ports', and condemned him to three years' slavery in the quicksilver mines. Cook escaped this fate, to bring a complaint before the courts at Jamaica, claiming £12,863 8s. 1d. compensation; failing that, the grant of a letter of reprisal under the terms of the Treaty of Madrid. As soon as he got this, he joined Coxon, Sharp and the others in 1679.

Highly successful raids followed. On the Honduras coast they took 500 chests of indigo and a great quantity of cocoa, cochineal, tortoise-shell, money and plate. Early in 1680 they sacked Porto Bello, but as their loot only amounted to £24 per man they proceeded on the grand design against Panama which we have already described. Their experiences on the march to Porto Bello must have toughened them for the hard-

68

ships which were to follow. It was at that time, says Dampier, that they opened some merchant's letters which contained warnings that the privateers 'would open a door into the South Seas, which they supposed was fastest shut; and the letters were accordingly full of cautions to their friends to be very watchful and careful of their coasts. This door they spoke of we all concluded must be the passage over the land through the country of the Indians of Darien, who were a little before this become our friends. . . . From henceforward we began to entertain such thoughts in earnest, so that the taking these letters gave the first life to those bold undertakings; and we took the advantage of the fears of the Spaniards, for we sealed up most of the letters again and sent them ashore to Portobel'.

We have seen how, after the attack on Panama, Coxon returned across the Isthmus. While his companions were sailing illegally around South America, he was cruising in the Caribbean with a commission from the Governor of the Bahamas. His new crew, however, did not appreciate this change of status. When the ship was off Honduras, they mutinied. Coxon was not the man to stand for this. He defended himself so stoutly that he drove eleven of the mutineers overboard and brought the rest back to Jamaica, where Governor Lynch hanged two of them in chains as an example to others, although one of them [Peter Johnson] had actually been drinking with one of the judges who had acquitted him at his first trial. The virtuous Coxon was then employed to convoy a Spaniard to Havana; but he appears to have tired of such employment fairly soon, because in 1683 he was said to be 'again in rebellion' and soon after was arrested for piracy. He escaped to Campeachy, was declared an outlaw, and in 1688 voluntarily surrendered under another act of oblivion. He died among his old friends, the Mosquito Indians, the next year.

The Bay of Campeachy (or Campeche) on the coast of

Yucatan, to which reference has already been made, har-
boured a colony of between 200 and 300 logwood-cutters.
In answer to Spanish complaints that this was an infringement of their monopoly, the English Government asserted
that this was not an officially occupied area and that therefore they were not responsible for what went on there. The
same attitude prevailed with regard to the Mosquito Coast
farther south, from which the colony of British Honduras
ultimately grew. Here the Indians were more friendly, claiming that they lived under British protection since the days of
Charles I because their king at that date, named Oldham
[Old 'un?], bequeathed to his son Jeremy an old laced hat
and a piece of parchment as proof of his title. A rare act of
friendship on the part of a buccaneer named Wright sealed
this curious alliance against the Spaniards. His crew took a
fancy to an Indian fisher-boy who fell into their hands. They
trained him as a turtle-striker, taught him English, dressed
him up in European clothes and called him John Gret. The
boy became their interpreter and negotiator with the Indians,
whom he persuaded to ally themselves with the buccaneers to
facilitate their passage to the South Seas through the land
of their friends, the Darien Indians.

The early buccaneers had not appreciated the value of logwood, which was highly prized by the Spaniards as a dye. But
the chance sale in Europe of a cargo brought over by a certain
Captain James opened great possibilities to later privateers
when the policy of suppression began to make things too hot
for them at Jamaica. They were, says Dampier, 'put to their
shifts, for they had prodigally spent whatever they got, and
now wanting in subsistence were either forced to go to Petit
Goave, where the privateering trade still continued, or into
the bay for logwood. The more industrious sort came hither,
yet even these thought it a dry business to toil at cutting
wood. . . . Besides, they had not forgot their old drinking
bouts, and would spend £30 or £40 at a sitting aboard the

ships that came hither from Jamaica, carousing and firing of guns three or four days together. And though afterwards many sober men came into the bay to cut wood, yet by degrees the old standards so debauched them that they could never settle themselves under any civil government, but continued in their wickedness till the Spaniards, encouraged by their careless rioting, fell upon them and took most of them singly at their own huts'.

Such is Dampier's account of his brief sojourn among them, before he joined the buccaneers under Coxon and Sharp. Since he was thereafter involved in so many of the voyages described in this book, it will be best to treat his career in a later chapter. As for his experiences at Campeachy, suffice it to say that he arrived at One Bush Key on the Terminus Lagoon, near the island of Trist, in the year 1675 when he was twenty-four years old. This romantic spot was nothing but a reef of oyster-shells, over which trailed the roots of a few mangrove trees. He arrived in a small cargo vessel from Jamaica which traded rum for logwood, the rum being sold as a formidable punch, 'wherewith they grew frolicksome'. At the huts of the wood-cutters he was so 'kindly entertained with pig and pork and pease, or beef and doughboys [dumplings]' that he grew to like this strange way of life. There seemed great possibilities if one worked hard and kept off the drink, for which he did not have much taste at that time. So he returned to Jamaica to buy himself axes and saws and 'a pavilion to sleep in', and reappeared next year. But a series of misfortunes brought all to nought. First, he was afflicted with a sore on his legs out of which he extracted a Guinea worm some two feet long by rolling it out daily, inch by inch, on a stick, according to the advice of an Indian. His clinical description of the operation is done with all the accuracy he devotes to his descriptions of the flora and fauna of the coast. Next, a hurricane destroyed all hope of making an honest living. In a destitute state he, like so many others, joined

71

the privateers who were always cruising along the coast. Opportunity enabled him to return to England, but in 1679 he was in Jamaica once more, anxious to try his luck a second time. But, as he politely puts it, 'it proved a voyage round the world', because he fell in with Coxon's band. How it took him eight years to get round the world is another story which we may defer for the present.

So far we have been concerned with the activities of the English buccaneers. Their French brethren followed the same course of life, sometimes going off 'on the account' from Petit Goave, sometimes becoming legalised privateers if the liberal-minded Governor of Tortuga was so inclined. On one such occasion in 1678 the French admiral d'Estrées recruited a powerful armament for a proposed attack on the Dutch colony at Curaçoa. He had a fleet of fifteen men-of-war under his command, which was joined by no less than 1,200 buccaneers. Since they knew the coast, some of the latter were sent on ahead to act as look-outs for the fleet, but their vessels drew too little water to serve as guides to the bigger ships. Consequently seven men-of-war were wrecked on a reef and d'Estrées retired to France without achieving anything. The buccaneer Laurent de Graff was left to see what could be done to recover something from the wrecks. According to what he told Dampier later, they enjoyed themselves well enough: indeed, there is a strong suspicion that some of them had acted as wreckers. 'They kept in a gang by themselves, and watched when the ships broke to get the goods that came from them; and though much was staved against the rocks, yet abundance of wine and brandy floated over the reef, where the privateers waited to take it up. They lived here about three weeks, waiting an opportunity to transport themselves back to Hispaniola; in all which time they were never without two or three hogsheads of wine and brandy in their tents, and barrels of pork'.

Laurent de Graff, Grammont and Van Horn were the lead-

ing adventurers at that time. In 1684 they made a grand
attack on Vera Cruz with seventeen ships, which almost vies
in success with Morgan's sack of Panama. It was a real united
nations effort – De Graff, Van Horn and three others being
Dutch by birth (although we have seen that the first of them
was quite prepared to fight with the French against his
countrymen), two others were English and the remainder
French. Just as Porto Bello was the entrepôt for the treasure
of South America from Panama, so Vera Cruz farther up the
coast was the port visited by the *flotas* from Spain to bring
home the wares carried by the famous Manila galleon to
Acapulco and thence transported overland. For such reasons
it was sacked in 1659, again in 1678, and now in 1684. Both
the latter attacks were surprises, the inhabitants waking up
from their sleep to find the raiders in the market place. The
Governor was ransomed for 70,000 pieces of eight and the free-
booters sailed away in the face of a Spanish fleet of fourteen
vessels which made no attempt to interfere with them. Booty
to the value of 150,000 pieces of eight and 1,300 slaves were
taken back to Petit Goave.

The news arrived just in time for an account of the expedition to be included in the volume which contains Sharp's
voyage. For once the Spanish home government acted with
firmness. The Governor was sentenced to death for failing to
defend the city, and even the French and English Governors
began to take stricter measures to suppress such marauders.
Van Horn died of wounds received during the attack.
Grammont was made respectable by being given a commission as Lieutenant du Roi (until he sailed off on his own
account and was never heard of again), De Graff became Lieutenant du Roi, Capitaine de Frégat and Chevalier de Saint
Louis. He lived to play an active part in the wars against the
English and is said to have been the founder of the city of
Mobile in Louisiana before his death in 1704.

Thus by the outbreak of the war of the English Succession

in 1689 the original Brotherhood of the Coast had been broken up. The stricter measures adopted by De Cussy at Hispaniola, and by Lynch and Molesworth at Jamaica, drove some to the Pacific coast, the successes of Morgan and Sharp pointing the way. The despatch by James II of a naval squadron under Sir Robert Holmes was the first practical measure to suppress those who remained behind in the Caribbean, the various Acts of Oblivion having been largely ineffective. When Captain Spragge, another veteran of the Dutch Wars, sailed into Port Royal in January, 1687, with four buccaneers hanging from his yardarms, it was clear that times had changed. It was, says the Governor, a spectacle of great satisfaction to all good people, and of terror to the favourers of pirates'. Among such must be accounted the Duke of Albemarle, who temporarily reversed this policy; but a petition from the planters shows that privateering was no longer as popular as in former days. On the death of the Duke, Molesworth resumed his authority and the outbreak of the Revolution, with the war which followed, gave him an opportunity of transforming the remaining buccaneers into genuine privateers. In later years some, of course, reverted to plain piracy. Others, as the following chapters show, extended their operations to the Pacific. A few turned honest planters; one became an archbishop.

The Rev. Lancelot Blackburn had been sent out in 1681 by the government to preach the Gospel to the benighted inhabitants of Antigua. Scandal said that he also acted as chaplain to the privateers and shared the loot which they brought to the island. When he returned to England ten years later, his rise in the church was rapid, first as Dean, then Bishop of Exeter, and finally Archbishop of York. He appears to have retained the manners he learned in the Caribbean, since he used to demand tobacco and wine in the vestry 'for his refreshment after the fatigues of Confirmation'. Horace Walpole declared that he kept a seraglio of women, for 'the jolly old Archbishop of York gained more hearts than souls'.

What, to conclude, was the importance of the buccaneers in the history of the European colonies in the West Indies? There can be no doubt that for the first thirty years or so their activities were invaluable, not only in defending the islands themselves in the absence of any regular naval force, but in enriching them with loot either in the form of precious metals, or in cargoes of indigo, cocoa and sugar. At the time of the death of Charles II a Spanish governor estimated the total losses of his nation during the past twenty-five years at sixty million crowns. On the other hand, their marauding activities obviously obstructed the establishment of any regular trade with Spanish possessions and bred a lasting suspicion on both sides which was one of the causes of the wars of the eighteenth century, particularly that of Jenkins's Ear. Those wars were fought by regular navies, the Jamaican and Leeward Islands stations having been established to accommodate a vastly increased British naval power. Men-of-war under the command of regular naval officers replaced the vessels of licensed privateers. But the latter continued throughout the century as an important secondary element in naval power, and ex-pirates were found useful by such commanders as Admiral Vernon, on account of their local knowledge. But even in Vernon's day few such pirates remained in the Caribbean, because the rule of law was beginning to be maintained by the exercise of naval power.

CHAPTER SIX

The Second Voyage into
the South Seas

IT WAS FROM THE MUTINY which occurred among Sharp's crew at the Island of Plate on 17 August, 1681, that the second invasion of the South Seas by the buccaneers began. It will be recalled that on that occasion forty-seven of the ship's company decided to return home by way of the Isthmus of Panama. The party was led by Captain John Cook, 'a sensible man who had been for some years a privateer', says Dampier. He was a Creole, born of European parents on the island of St Kitts, and is to be distinguished from another member of the same party, Edmund Cook, who had proved unpopular as one of Sharp's captains and had been put in irons by the saintly Watling on a charge of unnatural vice. He is also to be distinguished from Edward Cooke, the captain on one of Woodes Rogers's ships of a later date.

The most remarkable member of the party was undoubtedly young William Dampier. When he published his first book in 1697 he called it *A New Voyage Round the World*, but it must not be imagined that it was a single or continuous circumnavigation. It took him eight years, with innumerable changes of ships and captains, to reach home, and he arrived with nothing but his journal concealed in a hollow bamboo to show for his pains. That did not really matter to him because, unlike his fellow buccaneers, at that stage of his life at least he was not interested in money. He says that he joined the Brethren of the Coast 'more to indulge my curiosity than to get wealth', just as he kept changing his allegiance from captain to captain because 'the further we went, the more knowledge and experience I should get, which was the main thing I regarded'.

If ever there was a rolling stone, a man avid for experience, no matter of what kind, it was Dampier. He joined the buccaneers because they alone offered him the opportunity of seeing new countries and peoples, though as he continued with them their vices of brutality and greed seem to have affected his character. There is a distinct difference between the young Dampier and the old. With his cast of mind, he at first held himself aloof from crews which he regarded as drunken, ignorant rabble. 'The mildest-mannered man that ever scuttled ship or cut a throat,' Byron called him, and it is the modest, quiet personality of the young man which attracts the readers of his books. But he could not have continued to be so retiring or he would never have got where he did, and there is plenty of evidence in, for example, the voyage of the *St George* some years later that he was by no means an easy man to get on with when he was in command. Though he became the most famous of all the buccaneers, it is by his writings and his early adventures that we know and like him best. At that stage he was such a modest young man that the other buccaneers hardly mention his name; in later life he was well known to French and Spanish alike, and his behaviour to his own men was almost that of a bully, and on occasion that of a coward. He was too rational a person, perhaps, to have a taste for boarding and hand-to-hand fighting, nor did he ever possess the personality of a leader. His only command of a naval ship, H.M.S. *Roebuck*, when he was sent in 1698 on a fruitless search for Terra Australis Incognita, resulted in a court martial for 'many irregularities and undue practices'. He was found guilty, forfeited all his pay, and declared 'not a fit person to be employed as commander of any of Her Majesty's ships'. In fact he entirely lacked what are nowadays called officer-like qualities. Yet had it not been for him we should know little about the second invasion of the Pacific, nor would contemporary novelists such as Swift and Defoe (however much they might despise him as a mere tarpaulin) have had anything to go on. His historical importance is more than this, because the extraordinary popularity of his books turned men's minds to the task of the serious exploration of the Pacific, a task which culminated with Captain Cook, and Cook, we know, was conversant with the work of his predecesssor in those parts.

It is Dampier the writer, not Dampier the meteorologist (on which he most prided himself), who attracts us today. Typically modest about his style, he begs the readers not to expect polite manners in prose from a man such as he, 'but I am persuaded that if what I say be intelligible, it matters not greatly in what words it is expressed.' From the time of James Burney, Cook's lieutenant and the author of the earliest and best history of the Pacific, his claims as a serious observer have been recognised, since his works have, as John Masefield well says, 'the supreme merit of surveying the lesser kingdoms with a calm, equable, untroubled, and delighted vision'.

This thirst for scientific knowledge in a man of no education is remarkable. The work he prized most was his *Discourse of Winds*, which provided the first exploration of the wind system of the Pacific, and it is obvious from a reading of his journals that the story of the movements and bloodthirsty actions of his shipmates is a mere thread on which to hang accurate and picturesque descriptions of the flora and fauna of the countries which he visited. In later and more peaceful days, and with a sounder scientific education, he might have been another Darwin on board another *Beagle*.

The characteristic which most impressed the diarist Evelyn when (with some trepidation) he asked Dampier to dinner in

London to meet Samuel Pepys, was his modesty – 'a more modest man than one would imagine by relations of the crew he had assorted with'. One would hardly guess from his own works that he was a skilful navigator. But remarks which appear in his much more personal manuscript journal show, for example, that it was on his advice that Captain Swan crossed the Pacific. Such details are omitted in the printed form of the journal which, as with others of like character, was evidently seen through the press by a practised hand. The original of the journal is lost, but a copy, with marginal additions in Dampier's hand, has been preserved among the Sloane manuscripts in the British Museum, and it would be silly to imagine that the finished work was not his own, as was suggested by some envious contemporaries.

We have already seen him on the coast of Campeachy and in the company of Bartholomew Sharp. At this point it may be as well to give a short connected account of his early career. He was born at East Coker in Somerset, probably in 1651. Love of the sea led him to sign on for a voyage to Newfoundland (which he disliked because he preferred warm climates) and then to India, having served in the interval in the Third Dutch War. In 1674 he went out to the West Indies on a visit to a relative and was attracted by the possibilities of making a living out of Campeachy logwood. He returned home to get married, but when he revisited Jamaica (apparently with the most serious intentions of making an honest living) he fell in with Coxon and Sharp. Since he had no money and they offered him riches and adventure, he accompanied them across the Isthmus on the first invasion of the South Seas. His journal, under the heading *The Adventures of William Dampier and others who left Captain Sharp in the South Seas and travelled back through the land of Darien*, begins on 17 April, 1681, the date when he parted with Sharp. Another member of the party who was his particular friend was Lionel Wafer. He had a similar career, though he was a trained surgeon and originally shipped on board an East Indiaman as a loblolly-boy, or sick-berth attendant. Later he practised as a doctor at Port Royal. Why he joined Sharp we do not know, but he certainly found in Dampier a congenial temperament and they refused to be parted, even when Basil Ringrose, the third of these journalists, preferred to go south with Sharp rather than face another crossing of the Isthmus.

When their party, led by Cook, reached the mainland they expected the Spaniards to be on the look-out for them, but they encountered no opposition either on landing or on their way across to what they called the North Sea. Their real enemies were hunger and thirst and disease. As before, Mosquito Indians were their guides; so, having dried their clothes, cleaned their guns and 'fixed our snapsacks', they began their march. They had no illusions about the dangers before them, but by the time they reached the other side, twenty-three days later, their worst fears had materialised. 'Not a man of us but wished the journey at an end; our feet blistered, and our thighs stripped with wading through so many rivers, the way being almost continuously through rivers and pathless woods'. In order to preserve his precious journal, Dampier put it in a hollow bamboo case, the ends of which he sealed with wax, and that is how he carried it with him round the world for the next six years.

Some of those who crossed the Isthmus with him were not so fortunate. A certain Gayny was drowned in one of the swollen rivers, weighed down by a bag of 300 silver dollars strapped to his back. So exhausted were his companions that they did not trouble to take the bag off his body when it was washed up a few miles farther on. Only a few days after the march began a careless buccaneer, drying some gunpowder on a silver plate, caused an explosion which scorched Wafer's knee to the bone. He tried to 'jog on' with his companions, but when an Indian ran away with his medicine chest and the wound turned gangrenous, there was nothing for it but to throw himself on the mercy of the Darien Indians. With him stayed John Hincent and Richard Gopson. Hincent we shall hear of again, when he shared a prison cell with Wafer. Gopson was a remarkable character, the apprentice of a London druggist who was a good enough scholar to translate from a Greek Testament which he always carried with him 'to such of the company as were disposed to hear him'.

Some friendly natives cured Wafer in a few weeks by apply herbal poultices. Others, resenting the presence of these useless mouths, 'looked on us very scurvily, throwing green plantains to us as we sat cringing and shivering, as you would bones to a dog'. They would have been burnt as sacrifices had it not been for the intervention of a friendly chief, who arranged for them to be taken down to the coast. Before he reached his destination, Wafer made a name for himself by lancing the arm of the chief's wife instead of letting her be pierced all over with arrows, as was the native method of blooding. The result was that the chief would not let him go for three months, and then only on condition that he would return to marry his daughter and bring some English mastiffs with him for hunting.

Wafer's stay with the Darien, or Cuna, Indians enabled him to describe their way of life in a book which is still of value to the anthropologist. Like Dampier, he was a natural scientist, more interested in the ways of the natives and the topography of the country through which he passed than in descriptions of sacked towns and violated prisoners. The tribe he lived with painted their bodies in a peculiar fashion and compelled Wafer to do the same, as well as to wear one of the nose plates which so intrigued Cox when he met King Golden Cap. So thoroughly was he adopted into the tribe that when he reached the coast to find an English vessel riding there at anchor and went on board with some of his Indian friends, 'I was willing to try if they would know me in this disguise, and 'twas the better part of an hour before one of the crew, looking more narrowly upon me, cry'd out: "Here's our doctor"; and immediately they all congratulated my arrival among them. I did what I could presently to wash off my paint, but 'twas near a month before I could get tolerably rid of it, having had my skin so long stained with it. And when it did come off, 'twas usually with the peeling off of the skin and all. As for Mr Gopson, tho' we brought him alive to the ship, yet he did not recover from his fatigues and his drenching in the water, but having languished aboard about three days, he died there at La Sound's Key.'

After this reconciliation took place, Wafer found that his old companions had been in the Caribbean for some time. When they reached the coast they had discovered one of the French buccaneers, Captain Tristian, lying off-shore. They bought their way into his company in the usual way, and two days later joined a buccaneer fleet which was some twenty-five miles away at Springer's Cay. Four of the eight ships there were English, commanded by Captains Coxon, Payne, Wright, and Williams, some of whom we have met before; of the other four, three were French and one Dutch. The new recruits were distributed among the fleet, Cook going as quartermaster, or second-in-command, to Captain Yankee, the Dutchman, and Dampier as navigator to 'Archembo' [Archambeau], captain of a French vessel of eight guns.

The usual wrangling began almost at once. The lure of the South Seas, the dreams of Spanish treasure, the hopes of easy conquests, were proving as strong as ever and the captains of the buccaneer fleet were anxious to follow Sharp into those golden seas. It took all the persuasiveness of Dampier to dis-illusion them, 'giving them an account of the fatigue of our march and the inconveniences we suffered by the rains; and disheartened them quite from that design'.

Alternative projects proved equally difficult of decision. No sooner was a town on the Main proposed than one or other of the captains raised an objection. For eight days the fleet lay idle before finally agreeing on a suitable objective, though in the end even that agreement meant little. Three only of the eight ships which sailed from Springer's Cay reached their destination; the others stole away one by one on designs of their own.

One of the three was the ship commanded by 'Archembo', another was that of Captain Wright, who on the way had the good fortune to capture a small Spanish vessel armed with a few long guns. Dampier, tired of the company of the French, whom he found 'the saddest creatures that ever I was among; for though we had bad weather that required many hands aloft, yet the biggest part of them never stirred out of their hammocks but to eat or ease themselves', persuaded Wright to man his small Spanish prize with those English who had returned overland from Sharp's expedition. Thus manned, she remained under Wright's direct command.

For some weeks Wright's ship and her small consort cruised among the islands off the Spanish Main, existing somewhat precariously. Dampier has a note in his journal about eating half-grown tortoises, peccary, monkeys, pigeons, and parrots, and occasionally what he calls 'soldiers', 'a little kind of animals that live in shells, and have two great claws like a crab, and are good food'. It appears on the whole to have been an unprofitable cruise, for no ships were taken and a visit to the Pearl Islands with a view to capturing a few Indians and selling them as slaves came to naught. Fortunately for the Indians the two ships were seen approaching and the inhabitants hid themselves so effectively that none was found.

Shortly after this, as they were cruising along the coast of Darien, they met Wafer once more, as recorded above. He went on board Wright's ship and for some weeks the buccaneers continued to cruise between the islands and the main, though still with indifferent success. They captured a ship laden with sugar, tobacco, and ten tons of 'Marmalett', but had difficulty in disposing of the sugar and quarrelled over the ownership of the ship herself. Three more small vessels fell to their guns, variously laden with hides, miscellaneous trade goods, earthenware, and brandy. Again they quarrelled over the distribution, and this time so seriously that they unanimously decided to separate. In the division of the captured goods the brandy presumably fell to the share of Captain Wright, for Dampier remarks that all the crew were drunk and quarrelling for four days.

To Dampier, and to some twenty others of the English companions, buccaneering began to pall. As was their right under the buccaneering code, they chose to leave the party, claiming one of the captured ships and part of her cargo as their share. In her they sailed to Virginia, and there sold the ship and her contents. It can hardly have brought very much, if we can judge from Dampier's share, for during the next thirteen months he lived in great hardship and trouble. His twenty friends appear to have fared no better.

Meantime, John Cook, at the meeting with the privateer fleet under Tristian, had joined Captain Yankee as quartermaster, and as was his right claimed the first captured ship as an independent command, manning her with his English companions. Cook, however, had no commission to act as a privateer, and so was forced to remain with the fleet in order to be covered by the doubtful legality of the commission held by the other captains. They, 'grutching the English such a vessel, all joined together, plundered the English of their ship, goods, and arms, and turned them ashore'.

Tristian, however, found himself under-manned. He took Cook and about ten others on board to make up his complement and sailed away, leaving the remainder marooned. At his next port of call, however, when Tristian and some of his men were ashore, Cook and the English rose, overpowered the Frenchman left on board, bundled them out of the ship, weighed anchor, and sailed off. He first picked up those other marooned English and, now with an adequate crew, captured a French merchant ship laden with wine. A day or two later they took another, armed with eighteen guns – a handy enough vessel in which to 'set off on the account'.

The South Seas, as ever the fabulous fount of gold, silver, and precious gems, was still in their blood in spite of their quarrel with Sharp. They had a ship now in which a voyage around the Horn, though precarious, was not impossible, and a march across the Isthmus was no longer the only doorway to those enchanted waters. They took a resolution to cruise again in the South Seas and take their toll from the coasts of Chile and Peru. To do so, however, they needed new sails and provisions for the long voyage, and where could they more safely acquire these than in an English possession, secure from the anger of the French whom they had tricked? So they sailed to Virginia, there to sell the wine and the ship which carried it and to invest the proceeds in suitable equipment and stores. They arrived there in April, 1683.

Dampier, as we have seen, was already there. Wafer was there. Some twenty others, experienced in the buccaneering trade, were there. There was also (though we do not know how he got into such company) a man who had taken a Master of Arts degree at Cambridge and had some skill as a navigator. Although, for a reason not hard to discover, he concealed for a time his name under the pseudonym of 'an ingenious Englishman', he was in fact William Ambrose Cowley. Oddly enough, Dampier makes no mention of him in his very detailed journal of this voyage, which may indicate that his anonymity was preserved at least until the original buccaneering expedition broke up some eighteen months later, when Dampier and Cowley parted company.

Cook's little company, some seventy souls in all, sailed from Virginia on 23 April, 1683. They had named their small ship the *Revenge*, but Cook hoped to pick up a larger and better found vessel on the way. His only access to the Pacific was round Cape Horn, a terribly long voyage in so small a ship, with its limited capacity for carrying stores. A larger vessel, if one could be acquired, would obviously save much hardship for the crew.

As we have already seen, the only newcomer to buccaneering in Cook's party was Cowley. He must have been considered at first as a weak link in the chain, for the object of the voyage was withheld from him. Signed on as navigator, Cowley was told to shape a course for the island of Hispaniola, and it was only when the ship was at sea that the true destination was revealed to him. He says in his account (the manuscript version of which is very much longer than the printed one) that he was 'forced' to alter his course for the Cape Verde Islands en route for Guinea, 'and then, when they had got a better ship, to the great South Sea in America'. It may be in this that there lies the reason for his anonymity.

They reached the Cape Verde Islands in September, avoiding the more populous of them and anchoring only at one which promised little danger of discovery. Here they replenished their stock of salt and acquired three or four lean goats, which cost them no more than sufficient second-hand clothes to rig out the local 'governor' in a new suit.

That buccaneers were as credulous as other sailors is borne out by an incident which happened at this island. One of the few inhabitants arrived on board with a large lump of what he described as ambergris. He found a buyer in one of the buccaneers named Coppinger, who exchanged his personal wardrobe for it. Dampier, who records the incident in his journal, unfortunately fails to give us the sequel, when Coppinger discovered that his 'ambergris' was no more than a lump of compressed goat's dung.

There was hope that the Cape Verde Islands might provide the larger ship which the buccaneers needed for their long voyage to the Pacific, and for a moment or two these hopes looked like being fulfilled when the masts of a ship were

seen in the port of Santiago. But it was not to be. She was a
Dutch East Indiaman, of fifty guns and 400 men, and soon
showed herself more than ready to receive Cook and his men.
'We thought it more advisable to bear away before the wind;
the Hollander at the same time sending ten shot after us; but
all in vain, for we got presently to sea again,' wrote Cowley.

'Hereupon,' he continues, 'we came to a resolution to sail
to the coast of Guinea, and as soon as we arrived upon the
coast near Cape Sierra Leone we alighted upon a ship of
40 guns, which we boarded and carried her away. We
found she was very fit for so long a voyage, for she was well
stored with good brandy, water, provisions, and other
necessaries.'

She was a Danish ship, and the act of seizing her was one
of pure piracy. The only excuse which the buccaneers had
for their existence was the extremely dubious commission
they carried to act against the ships and territories of Spain,
and by no stretch of the imagination could Denmark be considered an ally, or even a friend, of Spain at that time. That
Dampier does not even mention the incident in his journal
must surely arise from a sense of shame at the act.

What happened to the *Revenge* is not known for certain.
One account suggests that she was burned 'that she might tell
no tales'; another and possibly more likely statement is that
she was exchanged farther down the coast at Sherbro (near
Freetown) for sixty young negro girls who served as a diversion for the buccaneers until they perished miserably one by
one in the icy wastes of the Antarctic. It is certainly true that
Cowley, who did the negotiating with the native chief ashore,
was presented with a black woman for his private use, but
refused the gift 'by reason I misliked her hide'. Certainly it
was at this place that the buccaneers renamed their new ship.
They called her the *Batchelor's Delight*, which may possibly
give some small credence to this typical buccaneering desire
for debauchery. Certainly also they stripped the *Revenge* of

all her water-casks, for water was a more vital necessity for the long voyages ahead than black girls, even for buccaneers. There would have been no lack of a market for the ship, for she would have been useful in the slave trade, and a good ship in exchange for sixty black girls was no bad bargain for a slave trader.

They set out for the South Seas in mid-November, reaching the latitude of Cape Horn in mid-February. On the 14th, 'we choosing of Valentines and discoursing of the intrigues of women, there arose a prodigious storm, which did continue till the last day of the month, driving us into the latitude of 60 degrees and 30 minutes south, which is farther than ever any ship hath sailed before south; so that we concluded the discoursing of women at sea was very unlucky and occasioned the storm'. They made another discovery too, that in these southern latitudes it 'was so extreme cold that we could bear drinking three quarts of brandy in 24 hours each man, and be not at all the worse for it, provided it were burnt'.

Early in March the wind, which for so long had been blowing out of the west, backed to the southward, and a little later blew from the east. This was the wind which was fair for the South Seas, and the *Batchelor's Delight* made the most of it. She stood up to the northward, up the coast of Chile, though out of sight of land, reaching almost to the latitude of Lima. These were the waters that held the promise of rich prizes; broad-beamed, deeply-laden Spanish ships engaged in carrying the produce and the silver of Chile and Peru to the capital at Panama. On 19 March, away to the south, the buccaneers sighted a ship. She was carrying all the sail she could. 'We lay muzzled to let her come up with us,' wrote Dampier, and the guns of the *Batchelor's Delight* were run out.

The newcomer came up apace. She, too, had run out her guns. Each thought the other a Spanish ship from Valdivia bound for Lima; each thirsted after an early prize to christen their South Seas adventure. As they approached each other they discovered their mistake in time to hail each other as compatriots. The newcomer was the ship *Nicholas* under the command of Captain John Eaton, who had fitted her out in London with a piratical cruise in the South Seas in view. He had not been idle on the voyage out, and a trail of destruction and savagery marked his passage down the coast of Brazil and across the estuary of the Plate.

Eaton brought with him news of yet another adventurer to these waters. This was Captain Charles Swan, in the aptly named ship *Cygnet*. His was indeed an absurd, and somewhat pitiful, case. He had been with Morgan at the sacking of Panama and had later joined forces with Basil Ringrose, trading on the latter's knowledge of these waters to persuade a company of London merchants to fit out a ship for lawful trade along the western coast of South America. How either Swan, Ringrose, or the merchants expected to be permitted to trade in these waters is not explained, and Swan at least should have known the realities of the case. Yet, in spite of his record with Morgan, which was none too good even in that dubious company, Swan seems to have been sincere in his desire to keep within the law on this occasion. Later, he was forced by his crew to turn buccaneer, but by then he had long since ruined any chance that he, or any other of the Brethren, might have had of getting rich at the expense of the Spaniards. Right at the start he had made his presence known on the coast in an abortive attempt to open a trade at Valdivia, and everywhere the word had gone forth that the English were back in the Pacific. Spanish ships about to sail were held back in their harbours; gold, silver, jewels, and church plate were removed inland to be concealed in places of safety.

The *Cygnet*, however, was not yet to join the Brethren. She had kept company with the *Nicholas* in the passage of the Straits of Magellan, but the two ships had become separated in the great storm of 14 February. Though Eaton

89

brought news of her arrival in the South Seas, he was unable to give any indication of her position or her possible course of action.

The *Batchelor's Delight* and the *Nicholas*, so opportunely met in the South Pacific, kept company to Juan Fernandez Island. Dampier, of course, knew it well, as also did Cook, Wafer, and many of the crew, for they had been there in 1681, when Sharp had been deposed from the captaincy and Watling had assumed leadership. In their hurried departure from Juan Fernandez on that occasion, driven away by the three Spanish ships, they had been forced to leave behind them the Indian called William, who had been too far away to rejoin the ship before she sailed.

Dampier tells the story. 'This Indian lived here alone above three years, and although he was several times sought after by the Spaniards, who knew he was left on the island, yet they never could find him. He was in the woods, hunting for goats, when Captain Watling drew off his men, and the ship was under sail when he came back to shore. He had with him his gun and a knife, which a small horn of powder and a few shot; which being spent, he contrived a way of notching his knife to saw the barrel of this gun into small pieces, wherewith he made harpoons, lances, hooks, and a long knife, heating the pieces first in the fire, which he struck with his gunflint and a piece of the barrel of his gun, which he hardened, having learnt to do that among the English. The hot pieces of iron he would hammer out and bend as he pleased with stones, and saw them with his jagged knife, or grind them to an edge by long labour, and harden them to a good temper as there was occasion . . .

'With such instruments as he made in that manner he got such provision as the island offered: either goats or fish. He told us that at first he was forced to eat seal, which is a very ordinary meat, before he had made hooks, but afterwards he never liked killing any seals but to make lines, cutting their skins into thongs. He had a little house or hut half a mile from the sea, which was lined with goats' skin; his couch or "barbecue" of sticks, lying along about two foot distant from the ground, was spread with the same and was all his bedding. He had no clothes left, having worn out those he brought from Watling's ship, but only a skin about his waist.

'He saw our ship the day before we came to an anchor, and did believe we were English, and therefore killed three goats in the morning and dressed them with cabbage to treat us when we came ashore. He came then to the seaside to congratulate our safe arrival.

'And when we landed a Mosquito Indian, named Robin, first leaped ashore, and running to his brother Mosquito man, threw himself flat on his face at his feet, who helping him up and embracing him, fell flat with his face on the ground at Robin's feet, and was by him taken up also. We stood with pleasure to behold the surprise and tenderness and solemnity of this interview, which was exceedingly affectionate on both sides, and when their ceremony of civilities were over, we also that stood gazing at them drew near, each of us embracing him we had found here, who was overjoyed to see so many of his old friends come hither, as he thought purposely to fetch him. He was named Will, as the other was Robin. These were names given them by the English, for they had no names among themselves; and they take it as a great favour to be named by any of us; and will complain for want of it if we do not appoint them some name when they are with us.' Such was William, the first Robinson Crusoe.

The two ships landed their sick, mainly scurvy cases, and filled with wood and fresh water. Being well supplied with surgeons – Eaton had no less than four in the *Nicholas* – the patients rapidly recovered on a diet of fresh goat's flesh and green vegetables, but with one exception. This was John Cook, and though he was well enough to be taken back on board, his disease defied diagnosis.

They sailed after sixteen days at Juan Fernandez, standing over towards the mainland and altering course to the northward when in sight of the coast. On 3 May they captured their first prize, a small ship laden with timber, and thus of no value to the buccaneers. Here they held a Council of War, whether to go into Arica Bay in search of booty, or whether to make Cape Blanco, some 750 miles south of Panama, and lie in wait for the Spanish plate fleet as it made up the coast. The vote fell for Cape Blanco, and according to Cowley the choice was an unfortunate one, for in Arica Bay they would have found a ship with 300 tons (barrels) of silver aboard. This may have been, of course, no more than wishful thinking on Cowley's part.

Once more, however, scurvy began to make its appearance among the crews of the two ships. There was nothing for it but to seek a suitable anchorage and, together with their small prize, they made for the small island of Lobos, a few miles to the southward of Cape Blanco and about fifteen miles out to sea. And there, 'much troubled that we were out of action', they held another Council of War to decide future policy. The prisoners out of the prize were 'examined' for information about the state of the Spanish defences, and as a result the Council decided that the town of Truxillo, 'as the most important, was therefore the likeliest to make us a voyage if we could conquer it'. Out of the two ships they were able to muster 108 men fit for service.

Next morning, however, just as they were about to weigh their anchors, three ships were sighted in the offing. They were all quickly captured and plundered, producing a quantity of flour and fruit, eight barrels of quince marmalade, a stately mule which had been destined for the President of Panama, and a large image of the Virgin Mary in wood, carved and painted. The largest of the three had also been carrying 800,000 pieces of eight, but it had all been ordered ashore as the alarm that English buccaneers were in the

Pacific spread up the coast. This of course was due to Captain Swan's attempts to open a legitimate trade farther south.

It must have seemed to the Brethren at that moment that fate was set dead against them. The whole coast was in a state of alarm, and nothing worth the taking was moving on the sea. The blundering Swan had provided the Spaniards ample warning, and they were taking no chances. 'So that now we sought for a place to erect a magazine, to lay up our stores in serenity for a reserve, and to lie still five or six months to make them think that we had sailed out of the South Sea.'

They found the place they sought in the Galapagos Islands, which those who had served under Sharp knew well. In the most westerly of the many islands in the group they found good wood and plenty of fresh water, both of them necessities for sailing ships, and multitudes of guanas and giant tortoises. 'I do believe,' wrote Dampier, 'that there is no place in the world that is so plentifully stored with these animals. The guanas here are fat and large as any that I ever saw; they are so tame that a man may knock down 20 in an hour's time with a club. The land-turtle (tortoise) are here so numerous that 5 or 600 men might subsist on them alone for several months without any other sort of provision. They are extraordinary large and fat; and so sweet that no pullet eats more pleasantly. . . . There are great plenty of turtle-doves, so tame that a man may kill 5 or 6 dozen in a forenoon with a stick. They are somewhat less than a pigeon and are very good meat, and commonly fat.'

Ambrose Cowley amused himself by naming the islands of the group, all after living people. Thus King Charles Island was guarded on either side by islands named after two of the buccaneers, Crossman and Brattle. Sir Anthony Deane, the famous shipwright, kept company with Eure and Bindloss, two more of the buccaneers. The Duke of York, Duke of Norfolk, and Duke of Albemarle had Dassigny, the draughtsman of the *South Sea Wagoner*, as a fellow. There was also a

93

'small one which my fancy led me to call Cowley's Enchanted
Island, for we having had a sight of it upon several points of
the compass, it appeared always in as many different forms,
sometimes like a ruined fortification, upon another point like
a great city, etc.'

The buccaneers laid up their reserve store on the Duke of
York's Island, landing some 5,000 sacks of flour out of the
prizes they had captured and storing them against further use.
But alas! for the good resolution of lying low for six months
to allow the alarm to die down. One of the prisoners offered
to guide the ships to Rio Lexa, in Honduras, where he stated
that the town was poorly defended but exceedingly rich. The
temptation was too great and, taking the largest of the prizes,
they set off upon his new adventure.

But again everything went amiss. They made the mainland
at Cape Blanco (a different cape, though with the same name,
on the coast of Mexico), but as they were standing in towards
it, Captain Cook 'died of a sudden, though he seemed that
morning to be as likely to live, as he had been some weeks
before, but it is usual with sick men coming from the sea to
die off as soon as ever they come within view of the land'.

They took him ashore to bury him, the operation being
watched by three native Indians, who demanded who they
were and where they came from. The three, 'drawing near,
asked many silly questions and our men did not stick to
sooth them up with as many falsehoods purposely to draw
them into their clutches. . . . At length they drilled them
by discourse so near that our men laid hold on all three at
once', but by carelessness one of them was allowed to escape.
He ran to the town and gave the alarm, and by the time the
buccaneers reached it the place was not only in a good state
of defence, but all the valuables had also been removed to a
place of safety.

Cook was succeeded in command of the *Batchelor's Delight*
by Edward Davis, who had been quartermaster and second-

in-command. He was yet another of Sharp's companions on the earlier voyage and was no mean buccaneer on his own account. One of his early French companions says that he was of Flemish birth, but there is nothing to confirm this. All we know is that he remained illiterate to the end of his life, unable even to sign his name. Dampier regarded him with considerable respect, and he certainly seems to have been a moderate, sober, humane man, a much better leader than Sharp and just as good a navigator, to judge by his passage of the Horn. Even he, according to Dampier's manuscript, had some trouble with his crew: 'Some of his men (fellows without sense or reason) conspired to turn him out and choose another commander of a rougher temper, for the greatest fault they could find with him was that he was too mild.'

Davis and Eaton immediately held a Council of War and decided to sail to the Gulf of Amapalla, to the northward of Cape Blanco, in order to find enough Indians to help in careening the ships. Eaton was to remain with the ships, while Davis took a couple of boats ashore in the hope of finding Indians.

As Davis and his men reached the shore, the Indians scattered into the woods. And then the Englishmen had a tremendous stroke of fortune. Visiting the neighbourhood that day was the Spanish friar, the local overlord and the only white man in the district. He was too stout to run, and fell easily into Davis's hands, together with his 'secretary', an Indian who had learned to speak and write Spanish.

With him as their prisoner, they marched up to the Indian town, with the friar kept well to the fore. The sight of him was some reassurance to the Indians, and the 'secretary' had little difficulty in persuading them that Davis, whom he took to be a Spaniard, newly arrived from Spain, was a friend. Davis's plan was to get them all into the church, lock them inside, and then persuade them to help with the work of careening and cleaning the ship. All was going well, with himself, the friar, and the secretary leading the way and the

Indians following, though slowly. 'But before they were all in the church one of Captain Davis's men pushed one of the Indians to hasten him into the church. The Indian immediately ran away, and all the rest taking the alarm, sprang out of the church like deer; it was hard to say which was first; and Captain Davis, who knew nothing of what had happened, was left in the church only with the friar. When they were all fled, Captain Davis's men fired and killed the secretary; and thus our hopes perished by the indiscretion of one foolish fellow.'

Disconsolately they returned to the ships, taking the friar with him, and it was he who solved their difficulties for them. He managed to persuade half a dozen Indians to lend their assistance, and in due course the ships were put ashore, heeled and cleaned, and well stocked with water and beef from a nearby *estancia*. By the beginning of September they were fit for sea again.

Six months had now elapsed since the buccaneers had first arrived in the Pacific, and their cruise had so far yielded them little of value beyond the prizes laden with flour.

It was at this stage of the joint expedition, in September, 1684, that the two ships parted company. The cause of the disagreement was a claim by Davis's crew that, as their ship was the stouter and better found, they should have the larger share of any plunder. Unable to agree, Eaton 'broke off consortship', and Ambrose Cowley left the *Batchelor's Delight* to join Eaton in the *Nicholas* as master. Taking 400 sacks of flour out of the prize, the *Nicholas* sailed away on 2 September 1684, now a lone ship cruising in the Pacific on her solitary account. She was, however, to meet up with the *Batchelor's Delight* once more, three weeks later, and Eaton on that occasion offered to forget the quarrel and continue the original partnership, 'but Captain Davis's men were so unreasonable that they would not allow Captain Eaton's men an equal share with them in what they got'. Once again the *Nicholas* sailed away, this time for good.

CHAPTER SEVEN

Cowley's Voyage round the World

BEFORE CONTINUING with the operations of the main body of buccaneers remaining in these Pacific waters, it will be as well to follow the fortunes of Eaton and Cowley in the *Nicholas*. After parting from Davis in the Gulf of Amapalla, they cruised in the waters around Panama with as little success as before. There was no Spanish shipping to seize, no town ashore that was not on the alert for an attack. Finally they stood into Paita Bay and, keeping out of range of the guns mounted ashore, took two small ships which were lying there at anchor, hoping that the Spaniards would ransom them. They met with a blank refusal, which enraged our Captain to that degree that he commanded our men either to sink or burn them; which was our farewell to that coast'.

And farewell it was. In the face of so barren a prospect of obtaining wealth by piracy in these waters, Eaton and Cowley decided to try their hand in the East Indies. They made for the island of Gorgona, filled up with water and wood, and on 22 December 1684, ventured out on their long voyage westward. Their next port of call was to be Guam, 7,646 nautical miles away according to Cowley's calculations, but in fact some hundreds of miles farther.

The great sea scourge of the period, scurvy, hit them hard. In Cowley's journal of the voyage, whenever he could tear himself away from details of his navigation, references to the

97

disease keeps cropping up. Thus, on 3 February, 'we throwed overboard Rod Cap, one of our company, who died with the scurvy,' on the 19th, this day heaved overboard Long Peter, the negro'; on the 22nd, 'John Holden departed this life'. The following day Cowley recorded, 'we have now a very sickly ship, our men being extraordinary weak, and our fare for the most part being water and flour, chocolate in the morning, pease every other day, and two "dow boyes" [dough-boys] a day. Yet our men full of the scurvy; no man in the ship free but all in a consuming condition.' One hardly wonders at this, for Cowley's 'fare' contains nothing of an anti-scorbutic nature.

So the voyage continued, with a growing tale of men being 'heaved overboard'. Yet they were nearing their destination, and on 14 March Cowley was able to enter in his journal: 'Saturday, we have had the wind at ENE, distance run 76 miles, and about seven of the clock we saw the land bearing from us west . . . the land maketh indifferent high.' It was a remarkable feat of navigation on Cowley's part, for his desired landfall – Guam in the Marianas – was dead ahead of the ship.

On the following day 'we came to an anchor in the bay and sent a boat on shore with a flag of truce, but when we came on shore we found that the natives had burned their houses and run away by the light of them. But we felled some coco-nut trees and brought about 200 of the nuts on board to refresh our men, which were exceeding weak. As we put off with our boat there appeared a party of Indians rushing out of the bushes with their lances, but we called to them and told them we were friends, but they would scarce believe us. At length, we having a flag of truce, the Indians went into the wood and peeled a stick so that it was white. In coming down, one of his mates saw that the messenger who had the stick had never a cap to put off to compliment our men and call'd him back and gave him a cap.

'From Sunday the 15th to Monday the 16th, we lying at an anchor, we went on shore and got some coconuts and had a free trade with the Indians. The next morning, being the 17th day, on which day, our men going on shore, in crossing to the low island which lieth on the west side of Guam, the Indians fell upon our boat with stones and lances, but we made some shot at them and killed and wounded some of them, so that the men in the boat got no harm.'

News of the arrival spread rapidly across the island and the Spanish Governor came to see the ship, sending on board a letter, written in Spanish, Latin, and Dutch, demanding to know who they were, whence they came, and whither bound. Eaton, 'thinking the French would be welcomer than the English, returned answer that we were employed by some gentlemen of France upon the discovery of the unknown part of the world'. This reply appeared to satisfy the Governor, and arrangements were quickly made to exchange gunpowder, of which the Spanish garrison were sadly in need, for fresh-killed pigs, potatoes, oranges, lemons, plantains, paw-paws, and red pepper. And, remarks Cowley, 'we satisfied the Governor that we had killed some of the Indians in our own defence, and he gave us a toleration to kill them all'.

For twelve days trade with the Indians went smoothly enough, though the buccaneers raised some resentment among them when they 'chased some Indians and made them forsake their boats and get on shore. We took their boats with all their furniture with them, which was useful to us to carry a guard for our canoe when she went to fetch water or coco-nuts'. This resentment flared up the following day when about a hundred Indians attacked the boat's crew ashore with stones and lances. They were, however, easily driven off, leaving four of their number as prisoners in the hands of the buccaneers.

Their fate was an unhappy one. 'Saturday, while our ship was watering and the boat was on board [alongside], three of the Indians leapt overboard, with their hands bound behind them. We shot one of them by the ship's side, the boat going away to kill the other two. One of our men was shot through the side; I myself got a terrible fall on shore against a rock, which bruised my side very sore and hurt me inwardly. The boat, coming up with the Indians, killed them, they had received many shot in them before they died. One of them, for all his hands were bound, swam above a mile.'

It is difficult to account for this savagery, for the general run of buccaneers, though ruthless so far as Spaniards, and women of any colour, were concerned, usually treated natives reasonably well. Eaton, however, was no leader of men, and his crew was getting out of hand. It may well have been a lack of all discipline which was the cause of this unnecessary slaughter, of which Cowley records that 'they died in mere wantonness of sport'. On the next day, still more fell victims to this hideous sport, 'our men saluting them by making holes in their hides'.

The *Nicholas,* replenished with water and provisions and with her crew recovered from the scurvy, sailed from Guam on 21 April 1684, heading north for the Ladrones. There were now plenty of islands along this course which could provide fresh water, fresh meat, and fresh fruit, and the buccaneers had few worries on that score. The early breaking of the monsoon, presenting them with a head wind, forced them north-westward, but it made little difference to them. In that direction lay China, which for their purpose held as rich a promise of plunder as did the East Indies.

They reached Canton in May and lay there for a month, refitting their ship and undoubtedly acquiring considerable wealth, though Cowley is silent about the methods they employed. He does, however, lament one lost opportunity which might have made them richer still. 'While we lay there,' he confided to his journal, 'here came thirteen sail of Tartar ships, out of which we might with ease have laden our ship with the best of their cargo, but our men, being under no command, said that they would not be made pedlars to carry packs at their backs, for they came there for gold and silver and not for goods. Insomuch that they would not meddle with them, and the thirteen ships sailed all away about their business, being all richly laden with the best of the plunder of China, which the Tartars had taken two years before from the Chinese and lay all that time near to Canton to be shipped off.'

They slipped out of Canton during June, having received information about a Tartar ship bound for Manila, half laden with silver. They sighted her and gave chase, but she was too fast for the *Nicholas* and got away. There was, however, consolation of a different sort in store. They reached a small island to the north of Borneo where they decided to beach the ship and clean her bottom of the long growth of weed which had held her back in the chase of the silver ship.

'We hauled our ship ashore, planting ten guns on the shore, and built a tent to put our goods in. Which done, we went to seek the natives to trade, but they were afraid of us, they never having seen a white man before. We coming up with one of their boats, which was full of women, being the Governor's lady and her attendants, which when they saw our complexion leapt overboard into the sea, but we soon got them out again and made them more friendly before we parted.'

By November they were in Borneo, 'which island is plentifully stored with food and rich commodities as diamonds, pepper, camphor, and fine woods'. Cowley enlarges upon the 'very large eliphats (*sic*), tygers, panthers, leopards, antilopes and wild hoggs', but in general he lacks the authentic Dampier touch when describing flora and fauna. Navigation was always his chief delight, and no sooner does he let himself get launched into these descriptive rhapsodies than he must break off to recount in detail his calculations of longitude and de-

parture in navigating the ship from place to place. It is apt
to make his journal tedious reading for modern tastes.

Leaving Borneo in December, the buccaneers steered south
through the Celebes, the Molucca Passage, and the Banda Sea,
calling at odd islands en route. They picked up a few prizes
here and there, adding to their booty of gold, silver, and
precious stones, but naturally enough found no cities worth
holding to ransom, so profitable a source of income in the
Spanish domains of South America. They appeared to find,
throughout this passage, the East Indian women generally
receptive to their proposals of pleasure, though of course we
do not know what threats, if any, accompanied the proposals.
If one can take former buccaneer behaviour as a guide, the
threats were not lacking.

After a good passage the *Nicholas* reached Timor, a destination to be made famous a century later as the termination of
Captain Bligh's superb voyage of 1,700 miles in an open boat
after the mutiny in H.M.S. *Bounty*. Now, in 1685, Timor was
the scene of another, though less dramatic mutiny. 'Finding
the ship's company factious', writes Cowley, 'and not under
command of our captain, myself with nineteen men more
joined our forces together and bought a large boat in which
we sailed to the island of Java.'

By this stage in the adventure, Cowley had become a rich
man. If the pickings off the South American coast had been
meagre, those in Chinese waters and around the East Indian
Islands had undoubtedly added substantially to the haul. If
one may judge from his journal, Cowley was a methodical
man who would not suffer from the almost universal buccaneering habit of gambling away his gains, and no doubt he
left the *Nicholas* with his share of the proceeds of the voyage
intact.

Cowley and his nineteen men did not stick together for
long. In January, 1689, 'we having stayed at Cheribon to
refresh ourselves, we thought it fit to divide our twenty men

into three parties, two of which were bound for Bengal and the third were resolved to take their chance with me.

'I with my small party hired a boat at Cheribon to go to the city of Batavia, in which is the Hollanders' magazine for India. We arriving there were courteously received by the governor, the general promising a passage for myself and my two friends for Holland, in Europe. This city is extraordinary well fortified, with a high stone wall about the town with four spacious sundials within the town, and a very strong castle commanding the whole town, the castle being double-walled. To this city come many rich ships from China, which come for trade, the city of Batavia being peopled with above one-half of Chinamen, which maintain the greatest factory. The Island of Java hath one Emperor governing it and many petty kings and princes under him, yet they are all under slavery to the Hollanders, not daring to do anything in war or peace without their leave and licence.

'There happened a commotion whilst I was there; the general sent two of the chief of the Hollanders to the Emperor to demand 500,000 pieces of eight which the Hollanders said he was indebted to them upon an account of war which the Hollanders made in their defence. But during the war the Emperor's crown was in the hands of the Hollanders, and one of those ambassadors had taken out a rich stone of a very great value, which the natives had not forgotten. They cut them off with their company, the manner was as followeth:

'The Emperor of Java at his Court at Japara [Djakarta], finding those two ambassadors appear from the general at Batavia, the Emperor desired them to go into Council, and when they were sat down the Emperor commanded all the passages and avenues to the said council to be manned and securely guarded, then he commanded the house to be set on fire where the Hollanders were, and those that came out to save their lives the Javans killed, and the rest were burnt.

'This news being brought to the general at Batavia, the

general is now sending away four or five ships of war with soldiers to have satisfaction for the wrong done to them. Which if this accident had not fallen out, as far as I could understand, those ships would have been sent to the west coast of Sumatra, to Cillebar [Bencoolen], where our English settled after the Dutch by their villainy circumvented them of Bantam. There being now of us in Batavia twenty English-men who would willingly have adventured to Cillebar, but they would by no means permit us to go thither although we had bought a sloop to carry us away. They took our sloop from us and would not pay us the first cost, putting the men in prison which sold the sloop to us. We demanded the reason wherefore they were so very unkind to us; they replied that there was an Act of fifty years standing that no person belonging to any foreign factory of the Dutch should presume to sell any ship or vessel to any strangers; but we found that the main reason was that we should not go to Cillebar to strengthen our people. For had not this commotion fallen out at Japara, those ships and soldiers were designed for Cillebar under pretence that the King of Cillebar owed the Dutch a great deal of money and that they would be paid in pepper, which was only to do the English a further diskindness, for if they had done that, the English would have had no occasion for a factory there. For the Hollanders' intent was to get the pepper trade into their own hands by this subtle wile, and seemingly not in the least to disturb the English fort but the country all about it.'

As we know now, the lucrative trade in pepper was to be concentrated in Dutch hands for another century, and was the cause of much savagery and suffering to the natives of the East Indies. Some of the trade, no doubt, was gained by 'subtle wiles', but much of it came by bloodshed and murder.

On 1 March Cowley and his two companions successfully signed on in a Dutch ship, bound for the Cape of Good Hope and Holland, Cowley as navigator, the two others as seamen.

As they sailed out of Batavia they saw the *Nicholas* coming in, the last sight we know of Eaton and his men. What was their ultimate fate is not known, though Eaton succeeded in reaching England after committing 'many barbarous insolencies'. As for the remainder, like so many other buccaneers in this region, they probably succumbed to the lotus-eating delights of the islands, and spent the rest of their lives there.

For three months Cowley's journal is filled with nothing but daily calculations of distances made good, courses steered, differences of latitude, and departures. If, to our present-day eyes, his was a haphazard system of navigation, at least it worked well enough, and on 1 June Cowley could write: 'This day we saw the land, it being high and flat, distant 10 leagues, being a round hill flat at the top . . . I reckoned it to be the Cape of Buena Esperancia.' It was indeed, and on the next day the ship anchored in the bay.

On the 4th Cowley went ashore, to discover for himself the truth or otherwise of a strange native phenomenon of which he had been told.

'We also walked without the town to the village of the Hodmandods [Hottentots], so called by the Hollanders, to view their nasty bodies and the nature of their dwellings, which we found as followeth. When we came there we were scarce able to endure the stench of them and their dwellings; they build their houses round, making their fires in the middle of them almost like our Irish huts, the people lying in the ashes having nothing under them but a sheep's skin. The men have but one stone (which is strange), and the women are more to be admired, for they have a flap or piece of skin which groweth from the upper part of their commodities and so falleth down naturally over the slit and covereth their shame, which by hearsay I could not believe before I saw and felt it.

'At our coming into this village the small imps came running about us, dancing and begging of money. One of them being about fifteen years of age and a woman standing by him, which properly might have been termed a beast although she had human shape, I asked the boy if she was his mother. He told me, yes. I told him I would give him no money, but if his mother would show what she had to us, then she should have two pence. The lad replied, "give me two pence and I will make her show you", but we would not give it to the youth but gave it to his mother for to see the strange sight, and she let us see and feel it, it being a thing with them very common, so to do if they see a stranger to ask him to give them two pence to see their shame.[1]

'Their apparel is a sheep's skin over their shoulders with a leathern cap on their heads made as full of grease as it can hold. Their legs are wound about with guts of beasts, from the ankle to the knee, well greased. Those people called the Hodmandods are born white, but make themselves black with soot and smear themselves with grease. Their children be of a good shape when they be young, but by continual use of grease and blacking themselves makes them in time look like negroes, but not perfect black, but of a copper colour. Their noses are like a negro's. When they marry the woman cutteth off one joint of a finger, and if her husband dieth and she marry again, another joint; so many men as they marry, so many joints they lose.

'They are a people which will eat anything that is foul. If the Hollanders here kill a beast, they will get the guts and squeeze the excrement out, and then without washing or scraping, lay them upon the coals and eat them as soon as they are hot through. If one of the company's slaves should have a mind to lie with one of their Hodmandod women, let

1. This account in Cowley's *Journal* has been used on many occasions to discredit his veracity and to pour scorn on him as a serious navigator. The phenomenon, however, is not unknown even today and occurs frequently in the women of the pigmy race, and occasionally, though less frequently, in the women of other African races.

him give her husband a bit of roll tobacco three inches long, and he will immediately fetch his wife to lie with this slave. They are men not prone to the least jealousy of a stranger, but they will beat their wives if they lie with the Hodmandods, but they matter it not if they lie with any man of another nation.

'They are worshippers of the moon. When they expect to see the new moon there shall be thousands of them gathered together by the sea side, dancing and singing, but if it be dark weather that the moon appears not, they will say that their god is angry with them, but when they see the moon, then he is not angry.

'There happened at this time one of the Hodmandods to drink himself dead in the fort. The other Hodmandods came with oil and milk and put it into his mouth, and finding that they could get no life in him, they began to make preparation for his burial, which was as followeth. They came with knives and slashed his body, arms, and legs through the thick skin. Then they dug a hole and set him in upon his breech, clapping stones about him to keep him upright. Then came a company of women howling about him and making a damnable noise, after which they cover the hole and leave him sitting.'

Cowley set sail in the Dutch ship on 15 June, bound for Ascension Island and Holland, taking the northabout route round Scotland. Once more his journal is given up to navigational details, finding nothing of more moment to record than than the odd behaviour of a goat. 'This Wednesday, we have a she-goat on board which we brought from Batavia, who had then two young kids sucking of her (I think they were about three weeks old when she was brought on board, or a month at most), but the said she-goat grew big again, and our men said it was with the water, but in conclusion she brought forth four young ones, which is very remarkable.'

They sighted Ascension on 12 July, and ten days later,

on the 22nd, Cowley was able to celebrate. 'This day I cut the same line which I did when I departed from the westward, and continuing my course to the westward until I am come to the very same place whence I sailed, having this voyage encompassed the terrestial globe of the world. I have been farther to the southward than any man I ever read or heard of; in this voyage I have been in the latitude of 60 degrees 30 minutes south latitude.'

The weather was thick as they sailed to the north of Scotland, giving them no sight of land. They had, in fact, seen none since sighting Ascension Island two months earlier. Cowley's navigation, however, was as sure as ever, and his remarkable voyage came to an end on 28 September 1686, with another exact landfall. 'When it was day we saw the Brill Church and graves, and we came to an anchor in ten fathoms of water till the pilot came on board; then we weighed for the Maas.' There he found a yacht bound for England, 'and on 14 October I arrived at London in my native county of England, blessed be Almighty God for our safe arrival, amen. *Laus deo*'

CHAPTER EIGHT

Dampier's First Voyage Round the World

IN SPITE OF THE DEPARTURE of Eaton and Cowley in the *Nicholas* in the autumn of 1684, a great opportunity arose that winter as parties of English and French buccaneers began, like vultures, to converge on the Gulf of Panama. Had this unequalled concentration of force, amounting to nearly a thousand men, been led by another Morgan, the conquest of part at least of the Spanish empire might have been achieved. The voyage up the coast of the *Batchelor's Delight* that summer may thus be seen as the first reconnaissance venture of the much larger invasion of the South Seas which now followed.

The first to join her at the island of Plate was Captain Charles Swan in his *Cygnet*, which Cook had saluted in the Straits of Magellan before he went off in company with Captain Eaton. Swan had continued to Valdivia, the largest port in southern Peru, where his object was trade, not loot. A previous attempt to open trade with that port had been made by Sir John Narborough in 1670 when he took H.M.S. *Sweepstakes* there without success. Swan's rebuff, as he told Davis when he caught up with the *Batchelor's Delight* on 2 October, was even sharper; as we have seen, his appearance on the coast, however legitimate his intentions, had so alarmed the Spaniards that he ruined her former captain's chances of taking easy prizes. Ringrose, who was on board as supercargo, had been sent on shore under a flag of truce, only to be fired at and several of the boat's crew wounded and taken prisoner. According to Dampier, Swan blamed Ringrose for the affair, since he considered that the young man had misled him under false pretences. A third such failure to do what the South Sea Company was founded for and never achieved was the visit of Captain John Strong in 1690. As with previous visitors, he says in his unpublished journal, the inhabitants of Valdivia 'were so kind as to return us thanks with shot'.

All these voyages were entirely legal, Swan being so proud of his commission from the Lord High Admiral that he refused a bogus French commission when he was offered one. Strong's Letter of Marque is worth summarising because it is typical of the commissions issued during the War of the English Succession: 'And whereas the said John Strong hath given security with sureties by bond to us in our said Court of Admiralty according to the effect and forms set down in certain articles and instructions made by us on 27 June 1689, KNOW YE therefore that we by these presents grant commission to and do licence and authorise the said John Strong to set forth to sea in a warlike manner in the said ship *Welfare* under his own command and therewith by force of arms to apprehend, seize, and take vessels and goods belonging to the French king and his subjects . . . and to bring the same to such port of this our realm as shall be most convenient in order to have them legally adjudged in our High Court of Admiralty . . . provided always that the said John Strong keep an exact journal of his proceedings.'

Failing to dispose of any of his cargo at Valdivia, Swan sailed on up the coast hoping for better luck farther north. Instead, on 3 August he accidentally met Peter Harris (the nephew of the man who had died with Morgan at Panama) with a party of ninety-seven outright buccaneers, each one of whom had twenty-seven ounces of gold in his pocket. This they had won as a result of sacking Santa Maria, on the Isthmus, as they came across by the overland route. Swan began to trade muskets with them at forty dollars apiece, but when his men 'saw the privateers so full of gold, they thought it a better trade than what they followed, and therefore went aboard of Captain Harris, who entertained all that came'.

Having now no one to sail his ship, Swan was forced to join the buccaneers too. 'Assure my employers,' he writes in a pathetic letter home, 'that I do all I can to preserve their interests, and that what I do now I could in no wise prevent. So desire them to do all they can with the King for me, for as soon as I can I shall deliver myself to the King's justice, and I had rather die than live skulking like a vagabond for fear of death. The King might make this whole kingdom of Peru tributary to him in two years' time.' He concludes by expressing his hopes that he will make his wife a lady, if the cruise prospers, 'but now I cannot tell but it may bring me to a halter. Pray present my faithful love to my dear wife, and assure her she is never out of my mind.'

Perhaps Swan was fortunate that his ship was not taken from him. Having sold his cargo to the buccaneers for the surprising sum of £5,000, they permitted him to retain her as an independent command in their organisation. And it must be admitted that he entered into the game with gusto. As the captain of a well-found, well-armed vessel, he and Harris and Davis were soon laying plans to intercept the Lima treasure fleet when it left for Panama.

The prospect of success was enhanced when, in February 1685, they accidentally encountered a party of 280 Frenchmen under Captain Grogniet. Grogniet told them of another party of 180 Englishmen, who had crossed the Isthmus before them under Captain Townley. These they met on 2 March. A further 264 French buccaneers under Rose, Le Picard, and Desmarais joined on 11 April. Among the latter was a certain Raveneau de Lussan, a boy of good birth who had been sent

out to the West Indies by his parents because of his 'rambling
sort of humour'. Like Dampier, he had drifted into the company of buccaneers who now followed the route across the
Isthmus pioneered by Morgan and Sharp. His journal, which
was published in Paris in 1689 and translated in London in
1699, is our only source of knowledge about subsequent
operations from the French point of view, although the forms
which he gives to English names occasionally makes it difficult to follow. Those whom he calls 'David, Suams, Sameley,
Henry, and Brandy', may be identified as Davis, Swan,
Townley, Harris, and an obscure captain whom Dampier
also calls Brandy – a fit name for any buccaneer. Unlike the
English journalists, de Lussan is an unpleasant young man
with a streak of callous cruelty in him, far more interested in
women and pieces of eight than in the countries through
which his band passed like a consuming flame.

Most of the ten vessels belonging to the buccaneers as they
lay in wait for the Lima fleet in the Gulf of Panama were
coasting vessels and canoes: only the *Batchelor's Delight* and
the *Cygnet* were well armed. Davis, as the captain of the
largest ship, was nominally in command, but unfortunately
every privateering captain thought himself as good a man as
the admiral. The consequence was that when the Spanish
fleet came into sight off Pacheque on 28 May, a fine opportunity was lost. Whether this third battle for Panama (if
Morgan's was the first, and Sharp's the second) was lost because of bad seamanship on Grogniet's part, or simply because
the Spanish pilots were more conversant with local conditions, it is hard to say. The buccaneers began the action well
enough with the weather gauge in their favour, but night fell
before many shots had been exchanged, and in the morning
Davis found to his consternation that the Spaniards were now
to windward of him and that there was no sign of Grogniet's
ship. Of course the English imputed the worst motives to the
man whom Dampier calls 'our cowardly companion'. The

enemy's fourteen ships attacked and mauled the buccaneers all day, Harris's little vessel (in which was de Lussan) receiving no less than 180 hits. But they never dared to lay their redoubtable opponents by the board, fearing the buccaneers' reputation for savage close-quarter fighting, and on the second night they withdrew their ships under the guns of the city.

Naturally there were recriminations which resulted in the temporary withdrawal of Grogniet's force. According to de Lussan, what brought matters to a head was an attempt on the part of Townley to seize Grogniet's ship, 'but as he found he had to do with men who, though inferior in number, would not tamely be thus put upon, he was forced to give over his pretensions'. He was indeed the roughest character of them all, quarrelling with most of his colleagues and staining his later career with cruelties worthy of L'Ollonois. For the time being he combined with Davis in an attack on Leon, a large town lying twenty miles inland from Realejo (Rio Lexo to the buccaneers) in Nicaragua. Thomas Gage, an earlier visitor, called it 'the paradise of the Indies, with fine gardens, a variety of singing birds and parrots, plenty of fish, which is cheap, with gay houses where they lead a delicious, lazy, and idle life'. Dampier, however, found it 'not so pleasant as Gage makes it'. Townley led the van composed of eighty of the 'friskiest men', Davis and Swan commanded the centre divisions, and the newly-joined Captain Knight brought up the rear. The vanguard marched boldly into the central square of the town, Townley putting twice the number of the enemy to flight without difficulty, so that by the time the rest arrived the town was in his hands. All the defenders were able to do was to cut down some of the laggards in the open country, one of whom was a stout-hearted old man of eighty-four who had once fought under Cromwell. This veteran – his name was also Swan – refused an offer of quarter, standing alone with his pistol in his hand until he was shot down.

But it soon appeared that the garrison had evacuated the town only to re-group outside, and so the buccaneer captains decided to remit the ransom in order to march back to the coast before a greater force of the enemy had collected to menace their withdrawal.

There was a difference of opinion about what to do next. Davis, Harris, and Knight thought the prospect looked brighter to the southwest. Swan and Townley were for continuing along the Mexican coast. Wafer continued with Davis, but at this point Dampier decided to change his ship to Swan's *Cygnet*. Not, he says, from any dislike of Davis, 'but to get some knowledge of the northern part of this continent', and because he knew that Swan was already toying with the idea of following Eaton across the Pacific.

They had little luck on their cruise, and so the time soon came for Swan and Townley to part. The former, anxious about the problem of provisioning 350 men, favoured a policy of raids in search of victuals. Townley still hankered after the gold and silver. He knew that at Acapulco the famous Manila galleon (which he recalled had been captured by Cavendish in Elizabethan times) landed her cargo of Chinese silks, spices, and muslins, and that there she met a ship from Lima loaded with the gold and silver, which was used to pay for these goods in Asia. Townley proposed to attack the latter vessel in Acapulco harbour, and to do so on his own account if Swan was still reluctant. The temptation was too much for Swan.

The result was a fiasco. Having paddled their canoes silently into the harbour with muffled oars, they found the vessel riding securely under the guns of the fort. Even Townley dared not attack both ship and fort without guns, so they paddled out to sea again, 'tired, hungry, and sorry for their disappointment'. Nor were they any more fortunate in January 1686, when the Manila galleon was due. While both crews were hunting cattle on the coast, she sailed past them without their catching sight of her.

It was here that they decided to part, Townley to try his fortune in the south, while Swan continued north towards Lower California where, like another Pizarro, he hoped to find gold-mines in unoccupied country. Dampier, who was by now on intimate terms with his captain, tried to dissuade him by pointing out that as long as the Cape Horn route was used it was impossible to break the Spanish monopoly of the South Seas. In his view such a grandiose prospect should be postponed until the Northern Pacific had been more thoroughly explored and a search made for the supposed western exit of the North-West Passage. This in fact was the task which Cook set himself on his third voyage a hundred years later, to be completed by Vancouver and the subsequent settlement of British Columbia, though that was much farther north than Dampier ever intended.

A disastrous action at Santa Pecaque on 19 February 1686, settled the matter. This was the worst defeat ever suffered by the buccaneers in those seas. As usual, it was caused by a lack of discipline, for Swan was no true buccaneer leader. The town of Santa Pecaque was unimportant except for the fact that the provisions for the slaves working in the neighbouring silver-mines were stored there. Swan took the town without difficulty; but when he decided to retire, half his men refused to evacuate the place until the other half had carried the provisions down to the shore. Seeing that the convoy to the ship was marching in a slovenly way, the Spaniards ambushed it a few miles out of the town. When two riderless horses galloped into the market place, it was obvious what had happened. Swan promptly led his men out to the attack, but the enemy had vanished, leaving behind them the corpses of fifty buccaneers so cut and mangled that they were scarcely recognisable. Here, says Dampier, died 'my ingenious friend Mr Ringrose. He had no mind for the voyage, but was necessitated to engage in it or starve'.

At this point of his story Dampier's manuscript differs materially from his book. He tells us, for example, that Swan had been warned of impending disaster by his astrologer (whoever he was), and that ghastly groans had been heard in the church the night before the action. More important is the way he evidently persuaded Swan to make up his mind to strike across the Pacific. The project had already been much debated. Swan and his mate, Teat by name, were very earnest for it. Dampier himself, though sick of the dropsy, 'had still a mind for further discoveries, and my advice and counsel was ever accepted by the company as much as any man's; and indeed it was ever a design between Captain Swan and myself to promote it and use our utmost endeavours to persuade the unthinking rabble to it'. What deterred the 'rabble' was that no one knew how broad the ocean was, because before the days of chronometers it was impossible to determine the longitude. If, as Spanish maps suggested, it was 2,400 leagues, they certainly lacked sufficient provisions for the voyage. Even if, as the English held, it was only 2,000, the distance was still enough to dismay the stoutest hearts. Swan and Dampier, of course, favoured the lower figure, though it was actually a gross under-estimate. They pointed out that if Drake and Cavendish could make the crossing, so could they in a stout ship like the *Cygnet*, so much had the science of shipbuilding advanced since their day. It was no good arguing from the precedent set by Eaton, because no one knew what had become of him. We may be sure that it was Dampier who pointed out that at this time of year they might expect a steady favourable wind. But what really turned the scale was Swan's promise that they would look for the Manila galleon on the other side of the ocean, a dishonest argument because what he really wanted to do was to set up as an interloper in the East India Company's trade in those parts. He had had enough of privateering; perhaps he was too fat for such an active form of life. With the proceeds of the sale of his cargo to Harris he had sufficient cash to begin negotiations. In any case, the Mexican coast obviously offered them nothing but further fatigues, hardships and losses.

In addition to the *Cygnet*, they took with them a smaller vessel under the command of Teat to accommodate some of the 150 men who composed the party. Reckoning on sixty days as the maximum amount of time they would be at sea, Swan rationed the maize at half-a-pint a day per man, and even that pittance would not last if the rats on board continued to devour as much as they were doing. No wonder 'most of our men were daunted at the thought of the voyage, thinking that if they did not starve on such a voyage, it would probably carry them out of the world'. Luck, or rather skilful navigation on Dampier's part, was with them. They left Cape Corrientes on 31 March 1686, and sighted Guam in the Marianas group fifty-one days later after a voyage which Dampier logged at 7,302 miles. Cowley's estimate was 7,646, but then he started farther south. For the first 5,000 miles they saw neither fish nor fowl, but the wind was steady the whole time, and they made great runs every day. Since they could not afford to heave to at night, it is something of a miracle that they made their landfall so accurately. Nor would their victuals have lasted much longer. Some of the crew were already plotting to kill the officers and eat them. ' "Ah, Dampier," Swan said with relief on their arrival, "you would have made them but a poor meal"; for I was as lean as the captain was lusty and fleshy.'

It was nightfall when they anchored under the lee of the island, so the Spaniards could not tell what ships they were. When a boat came alongside with a priest in it, the Governor's emissary was promptly secured and entertained by Swan with great civility in his cabin. The captain explained that he only wanted provisions and would pay for what he was given. Until he received such a promise he regretted that he must hold the priest as hostage. In the morning the priest wrote the

required letter, which Swan accompanied with four yards of
scarlet cloth and a lot of gold lace. Whether it was the Spanish
love of a fine uniform, or their fear of these legendary
buccaneers whose reputation had certainly crossed the ocean
(Eaton and Cowley's visit was only a few months previously),
we cannot say, but the provisions were forthcoming and Swan
was as good as his word. They learned afterwards that the
Manila galleon herself had appeared when they were at the
island, but that fishermen had warned her not to approach.
This story 'put our men in a great heat to go out after her,
but Captain Swan persuaded them out of that humour, for
he was now wholly averse to any hostile action'.

And so he continued when they reached Mindanao in the
Philippines, the land of bananas, 'the king of fruits', of which
Dampier gives a luscious description since they were still unknown in England. Swan immediately opened trade negotiations with the Sultan while his men drank themselves silly
and fell an easy prey to the women. In a few weeks the
hospitable natives had divested them of all their hard-earned
silver.

When they found themselves thus beggared, trouble
started. Swan did not intend to move, even though his
crew begged him to go out in search of the Manila galleon.
Their captain still maintained his authority over them: indeed, says Dampier, 'it was very strange to see the awe that
these men were in of him, for he punished the most stubborn
and daring of his men'. But when he had Teat flogged in
public, and when the last of their money was altogether gone,
the ship's company gave him an ultimatum to set sail. For a
few more days he put them off, living on shore while his
mutinous crew waited for him in the ship. Then the gunner,
rummaging in the captain's cabin, accidentally came across
his journal. A certain John Reed, 'a pretty ingenious young
man, and of very civil carriage', who also kept a journal,
wished to compare it with his own. He found that the mis-

deeds of various members of the crew had been carefully noted down for further punishment. When he showed the offending entries to his namesake, who was the ringleader of the mutineers, they decided to enforce the ultimatum. On the morning of 13 January 1687, a gun was fired to attract the captain's attention. He sent his chief mate on board to find out what was the matter. Reed showed him the journal and told him that the captain must come on board immediately. When nothing further had happened by the next afternoon, they weighed anchor with Reed in command. 'If Captain Swan had yet come on board, he might have dash'd all their designs, but he neither came himself, as a captain of prudence and courage would have done, nor sent till the time expired. So we left Captain Swan and about thirty-six men in the city, and about sixteen men we had buried there, the most of which died by poison'– probably administered by jealous husbands.

Later Dampier found out what happened to his fat friend. It appeared that he quarrelled with the Sultan's general, and when about to take a passage home in a Dutch vessel, his canoe overset and he was drowned, an accident evidently arranged by the general, who wanted to lay his hands on the white man's money. Swan had already sent his journal home by an East Indiaman, but no trace of it has ever been found.

It is not clear why Dampier, if he was so friendly with Swan and disliked Reed, did not stay behind with the others. He was certainly determined to desert Reed as soon as opportunity offered, but that opportunity did not present itself for a long time. In the meanwhile the crew of the *Cygnet* cruised aimlessly about the Spice Islands, hoping to hear news of the galleon. When they gave up the hunt they sailed casually south as far as lat. 16°15', where they found themselves on the coast of New Holland. Only a few spots on that desolate coast had been visited at that date, so that Dampier was uncertain if it was part of Terra Australis Incognita, or not.

We cannot tell the exact spot where they landed, but it must have been in the neighbourhood of the present Dampier Land and the Buccaneer Archipelago.

The coast afforded them nothing save an opportunity for Dampier to note the curious behaviour of the aborigines and to write a description of them which may well have served Swift for his Yahoos: the Captain Pocock whom Lemuel Gulliver meets on his last voyage to the land of the Houyhnhnms is obviously Dampier himself – 'an honest man, and a good sailor, but a little too positive in his own opinions'. But he had seen the Australian aborigines and Swift had not. His description of them is such an admirable example of his style and so similar to Cowley's description of the real 'Hodmandods' that one cannot forbear from quoting it: 'The Inhabitants of this Country are the miserablest People in the World. The Hodmandods of Monomatapa, though a nasty people, yet for Wealth are Gentlemen to these; who have no Houses, and skin Garments, Sheep, Poultry, and Fruits of the Earth, Ostrich Eggs, etc., as the Hodmandods have: and setting aside their Humane Shape, they differ but little from Brutes. They are tall, strait-bodied, and thin, with small long Limbs. They have great Heads, round Foreheads, and great Brows. Their Eyelids are always half closed, to keep the Flies out of their Eyes; they being so troublesome here that no fanning will keep them from coming to one's Face; and without the Assistance of both Hands to keep them off, they will creep into one's Nostrils and Mouth too, if the Lips are not shut very close. . . . They have great Bottle-Noses, pretty full Lips and wide Mouths. The two fore-teeth of their upper jaws are wanting in all of them, Men and Women, old and young; whether they draw them out, I know not; neither have they any Beards. They are long-visaged, and of a very unpleasant Aspect, having no one graceful Feature in their Faces.'

The stay in Australia was but short. Between January 1688

Title-page of *The South Sea Wagoner* by Bartholomew
Sharp, 1682

An early buccaneer, wearing clothing made from the skins of animals and carrying a home-made musket

A Spanish gentleman with his slave

Rock Braziliano. From Esquemeling's *The
Bucaniers of America*, 1684

FRANCISCO LOLONOIS.

François L'Ollonois. From Esquemeling's *The Bucaniers of America*, 1684

Sir Henry Morgan. From an anonymous portrait

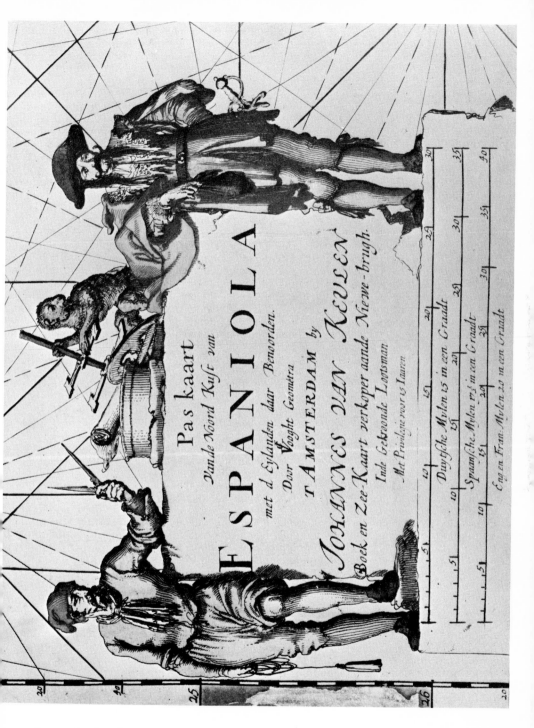

Cartouche showing buccaneers. From the chart of Hispaniola in Van Keulen's *Sea Atlas of the Waterworld*, 1682

The buccaneers' fort at Tortuga. From Dutertre's *Histoire Générale des Antilles*, 1667

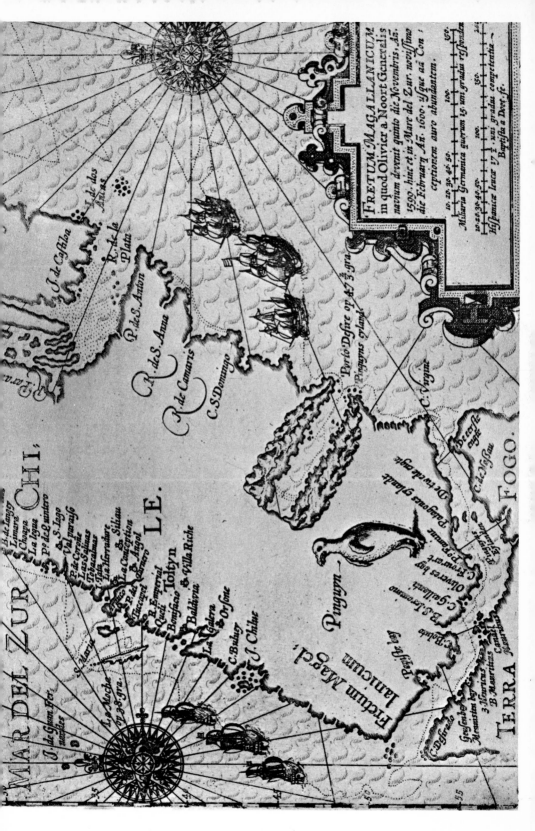

An early chart of South America. From *Voyage of Van Noort*, 1601

William Dampier. From a portrait by T. Murray

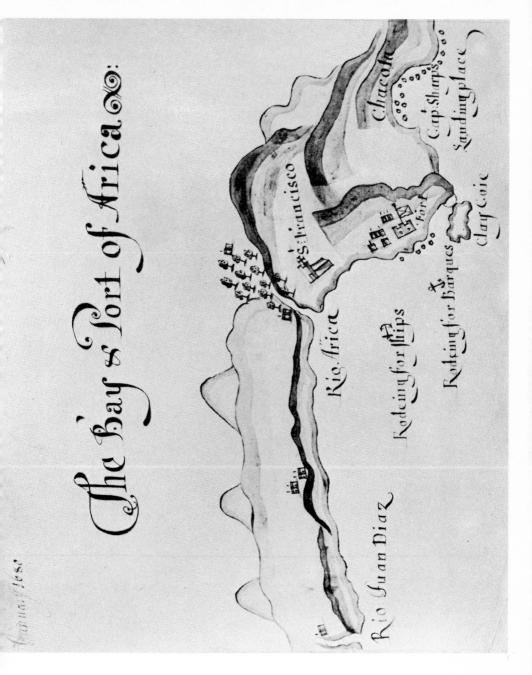

Bay and Port of Arica. From *Bartholomew Sharp's Journal*

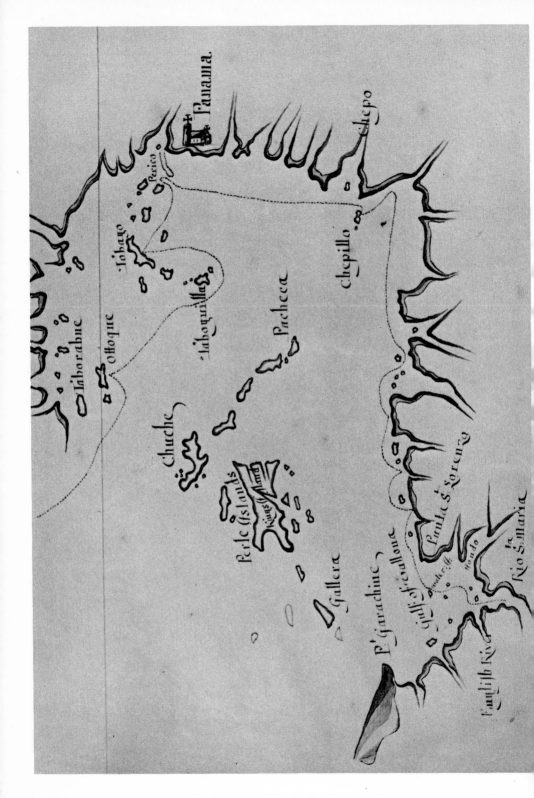

Chart of the Bay of Panama. From *Bartholomew Sharp's Journal*

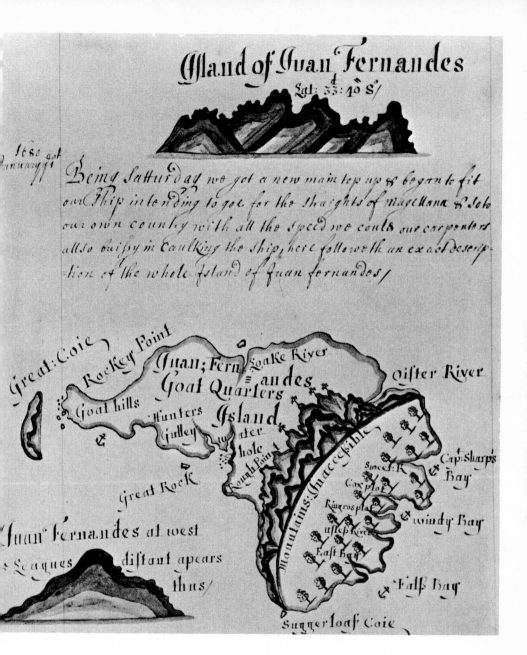

The Island of Juan Fernandez. From *Bartholomew Sharp's Journal*

Bows of a Dutch East Indiaman, *Der Ary*. From a model at Amsterdam

Woodes Rogers and his family, at Nassau. From a painting by William Hogarth

Robinson Crusoe sees the footprint of Man Friday. From an old engraving

and his return to England in 1691, so many adventures befell Dampier that we must pass over them rapidly: it needed another full volume in his Works to describe them. It was in the Nicobar Islands that he finally succeeded in making his escape from the buccaneers, of whose company he was by now heartily sick. He often begged Reed to put him on shore to find his own way home, but Reed was the sort of bully who liked to play cat-and-mouse with anyone in his power. However, at the beginning of May, Reed agreed to let him get up his chest and bedding. Three others – Coppinger the surgeon (the man who had been tricked with false ambergris), Mr Robert Hall, and 'one named Ambrose, I have forgot his surname'– wished to follow his example. After a long argument they were allowed to go, provided they took nothing but their personal belongings and an axe (though someone smuggled a gun on board the canoe that took them ashore). It was a fine, clear, moonlit night. At any moment Reed might change his mind, but they were determined to resist, if need be with their lives. All Dampier possessed was his pocket compass, his precious journal still in its bamboo case, and his sea chest, which was upset in the water as they struggled on shore. But at last he was his own man again. So they walked 'on the sandy beach to watch when the ship would weigh and be gone, not thinking ourselves secure in our new-found liberty till then. About twelve o'clock we saw her under sail and then we returned to our chamber, and so to sleep. This was the sixth of May'.

Much later he found out what happened to the *Cygnet*. Reed continued to act the buccaneer in the Indian Ocean, taking a Portuguese prize off Ceylon; after that he deserted his crew and made his way to New York on board a slaver. Teat got back to England. The rest of the ship's company hoped to sail the ship home, but the worm-eaten vessel sank at her moorings off Madagascar, where the remnant of her crew probably joined the pirates of the next generation.

Dampier himself wandered about South-East Asia for the next three years on board a variety of trading vessels. In the course of his many voyages he ran across Edward Barlow, whose beautifully illustrated journal was only discovered a few years ago. To him he entrusted a packet of letters to the owners of the *Cygnet*, but Barlow never mentions this encounter with an obscure adventurer, as Dampier must have seemed to him, and since we know that he lost his sea chest on the way home, the packet must have gone down with it.

But Dampier still had his own journal. It was all that was left to him, except the ownership of a Malay boy called Jeoly, who was so elaborately tattooed that Dampier called him his 'painted prince'. Besides having an affection for the boy, he regarded him as a sound investment should he ever reach England. In the end the two of them managed to scramble on board through the scuttle of a homeward-bound India-man which, after a terrible voyage, reached the Downs on 16 September 1691.

At this point his journal ends. What happened until it was printed in 1697, when he achieved celebrity and dined with Evelyn and Pepys and was offered the command of H.M.S. *Roebuck* by the Admiralty, no one can say. He had hoped to make some money by putting his Prince Jeoly on exhibi-tion, but had to sell him before he could do so. The new owner was certainly a keen business-man, for the advertise-ment of the exhibition has survived. 'This admirable person,' we read, 'is exposed to publick view every day (during his stay in town) from the 16th day of this instant June at his Lodgings at the Blew Boar's Head in Fleet Street, near Water Lane: where he will continue for some time, if his health will permit. But if any Persons of Quality, Gentlemen or Ladies, do desire to see this noble Person at their own Houses, or any other convenient place in or about this City of London, they are desired to send timely notice, and he will be ready to wait upon them in a Coach or Chair any time they please to

appoint, if in the day time. *VIVANT REX ET REGINA.'*
But poor Prince Jeoly turned out to be but an indifferent
bargain, for he died of smallpox at Oxford a few months later.

Dampier himself seems to have tried to settle down as a
farmer, but he was not the sort of man who could remain long
on shore. As soon as the success of his book made it possible
for him to go to sea again he was off, even though the warship provided for him was worse found than any of the
buccaneering craft he had sailed in and her crew mutinous
at having to serve under a commander with such a past. The
disastrous *Roebuck* voyage, on which he nearly anticipated
Cook in the discovery of the eastern part of Australia, lies
outside the scope of this book. When we next meet him he is
in command of the *St George* privateer, and his character does
not seem to have improved in the interval.

Soon after the publication of his book, Sir Hans Sloane,
whose interest in the journals of the buccaneers has been
noted, got hold of Dampier's manuscript to add to his collection and persuaded its author to sit for his portrait to Thomas
Murray. This admirable picture is now in the National
Portrait Gallery. It shows a long, keen face, with a firm jaw
and a slightly embarrassed expression: after all, he is the only
buccaneer to be represented in that distinguished collection
of national figures. In his hand he proudly displays a copy of
his *New Voyage*. Underneath is written 'William Dampier,
pirate and hydrographer.' Perhaps, on occasion, he was a
pirate. He was certainly proud of his work as a hydrographer.
But it is as a travel writer of the first order that we know him
so well today.

CHAPTER NINE

The Retreat from the South Seas

THERE WERE STILL some five hundred buccaneers left
on the coasts of Mexico and Peru after the departure of Eaton
and Cowley in the *Nicholas*, in September 1684, and of Swan
and Dampier in the *Cygnet*, in March 1686. The highly fissile
tendencies which characterised such bands of adventurers became more marked as the months went by, so that their story
becomes increasingly complicated. The captains who remained on the coast – Grogniet, Townley, Harris, and Davis –
were always quarrelling among themselves and going their
own ways, only to meet up again, usually accidentally, a few
months later. It would be tedious to record their innumerable
landings in search of food or loot. In order to keep the general
picture in focus it will be enough to follow the careers of the
most notable leaders until the end of 1687, when the buccaneers evacuated the South Seas and returned to the Caribbean of their own accord. They were never driven out of the
Pacific by the Spaniards.

Of these leaders Edward Davis in the *Batchelor's Delight*
was the most outstanding. Since he was illiterate, our only
record of his movements are the notes left by his surgeon,
Lionel Wafer, though Wafer never kept a detailed journal
like those of his companions, Dampier and de Lussan. Occasionally these notes may be supplemented by other evidence.
A certain Robert Arnold, for example, deserted Davis in
order to recross the Isthmus and give himself up at Jamaica.
From there his deposition, dated 4 August 1686, was sent
home by the Deputy-Governor with a covering letter deplor-
ing the depredations which he felt would cause 'a great noise'

and would injure not only Spain but 'all Europe'. Arnold was originally a member of the party led by Peter Harris in June 1684, which later met Swan and Cook. Swan, he said, always regarded himself as a legitimate privateer and insisted on fighting under English colours, with the King's Jack at the foretopmast head. When Swan and Dampier sailed west in 1686, Arnold joined Davis until he deserted with thirty-eight others. The last he knew of Davis's plans was that he intended to return via the Straits in a few months' time.

However, Davis continued to cruise off Peru in company with Harris and Knight for over a year. The Galapagos Islands to the north and Juan Fernandez to the south were their usual bases because, lying so far out to sea, both were uninhabited. When at the end of 1686 Knight expressed a desire to return home, they shared out their loot at the old base at Juan Fernandez to the amount of 5,000 pieces of eight per man. What happened to Knight is difficult to say. It would appear that he is almost certainly the same Knight who gave evidence against his former French companions when they were brought up for trial at Jamaica in June 1688 for serving under 'the pirate Townley'. He was told to prepare an account of his own association with the privateers, but then wisely faded out of the picture. He can hardly be the Knight who was a member of the Assembly of Jamaica that year, though it is true that the latter was summoned for using disrespectful language. It is just possible that he is the Knight mentioned by Dampier as joining the *Cygnet* in the East Indies until 'he grew weary of her company and giving her the slip in the night, went away for Achin; having heard that there was plenty of gold there, he went thither with a design to cruise'.

Davis returned north to the Mexican coast, where he met 300 of his old companions on 14 May 1687. By that date Le Picard had become their nominal leader, because both Grogniet and Townley were dead: how they died we shall see shortly. But the majority of Davis's crew were by now anxious to return. 'We continued rambling about to little purpose, sometimes at sea, sometimes on land,' says Wafer, 'till having spent much time and visited many places, we were got again to the Galapagos under the line, and were there resolved to make the best of our way out of these seas.'

Course was therefore set once more for Juan Fernandez. On their way thither they may or may not have discovered Easter Island, so named by the Dutch circumnavigator Roggeveen, who found it in 1722. One cannot be certain about 'Davis Land', as the buccaneers called it, because the position given is very vague. Wafer says that in lat. 27° 20′ S. they saw 'a small, low, sandy island and heard a great noise like that of the sea beating upon the shore right ahead of the ship.' Next morning they descried a long way off 'a range of high land, which we took to be islands', but Davis forbade them to land. The latter may possibly be Easter Island, which does indeed lie in lat. 27° 10′ S., but where could the low, sandy island be in those lonely seas? Later explorers searched in vain for it, though Captain Beechey of H.M.S. *Blossom* agreed in 1825 that Davis Land and Easter Island might be the same thing on the assumption that the small island had subsequently disappeared. If such is the case, 'Davis Land' is not quite as mythical as Cowley's 'Pepys Island', which he claimed to have seen in the South Atlantic.

Before quitting the South Seas they left another group of Crusoes on Juan Fernandez. 'Three or four of our men, having lost what money they had at play, and being unwilling to return out of those seas as poor as they came, would needs stay behind at John Fernando's, in expectation of some other privateers coming thither. We gave them a small canoe, a porridge-pot, axes, macheats, maize, and other necessaries. I heard since they planted some of the maize and tamed some of the goats and lived on fish and fowls. I have heard also that these men were taken off by a privateer vessel which came thither a year or two after, and that one of them is since come to England.' The privateer he mentions was Captain Strong, who records without comment that on 12 October 1690, he took off two Englishmen who had lived three years on the island.

The voyage round the Horn, since they missed the entrance to the Straits in thick weather, was an appalling experience. On Christmas Day 1687 they reckoned their position as lat. 62° 45′ S., seven degrees south of Cape Horn, having failed even to sight Tierra del Fuego on account of a gale which blew uninterruptedly for three weeks. As they turned north they encountered icebergs, 'hills of ice, whence came very cold blasts of wind, insomuch that our men, newly come out of a hot country, could scarcely endure the deck'.

Since they were ignorant of their longitude and even of their latitude because they could take no observations, and since they were exhausted by the gales, and short of food, the crew begged Davis to sail west towards what they thought should be the entrance to the River Plate. They imagined they were only a hundred leagues from land, but having run down five hundred without sighting South America, Davis put the ship's head north again. 'This bred a fresh commotion and we had like to have been all together by the ears upon it.' Some were convinced that they were still in the Pacific. 'But Captain Davis and Mr Knott, the master, begged them for God's sake to keep the same course two days longer, which they did, though we had but a small wind.' The appearance of a swarm of locusts proved that the coast was near, so they landed somewhat north of the entrance to the River Plate. Here they refreshed themselves with ostrich eggs and were surprised to find that the birds would eat any old iron they threw on the ground.

When they reached the Caribbean they encountered a Captain Carter, who informed them that a pardon had been issued to all buccaneers who gave themselves up. Most unwisely they did not take the opportunity to do so, continuing north as far as Philadelphia, where the *Batchelor's Delight* anchored in May 1688 after four years at sea. Thence Davis, Wafer, and Hincent (who had been Wafer's companion on the Isthmus) tried to cross to Jamestown, where they 'thought to settle. But meeting with some troubles, after three years' residence there, I came home for England in the year 1690'.

From this abrupt conclusion to Wafer's narrative it would hardly be imagined that his three years' residence were spent in Jamestown gaol on a charge of piracy. What they had not realised was that Admiral Sir Robert Holmes had just been sent out with an efficient squadron to clear the seas of buccaneers. He was a tough customer with a distinguished fighting record, a fire-eater, 'a rash, proud coxcomb' according to Pepys. Certainly his extraordinary tomb at Yarmouth, Isle of Wight, bears out Pepys's opinion: having captured a marble torso of Louis XIV which was being conveyed up-Channel, Holmes decided to have his own head put upon the shoulders of the *Grand Monarque*.

One of his ships had captured the remainder of Grogniet's party, and brought them in to stand their trial at Jamaica. Another, H.M.S. *Quaker* (surely the most inept name ever invented for a warship), encountered our three heroes in an open boat rowed by a negro slave in the middle of the Chesapeake. They were handed over to Captain Simon Rowe, who took them in H.M.S. *Dumbarton* to the gaol at Jamestown.

Reading between the lines of the lengthy correspondence which followed, it looks as if the bags full of pieces of eight which each of them carried were what first aroused suspicion. Otherwise, why should three men in a boat have been summarily arrested, their belongings seized, and their persons carefully guarded? On 19 August 1688, the Governor of Virginia, Lord Howard of Effingham, informed the President of the Board of Trade and Plantations of their arrest, adding that various counter-charges had been made (probably on the advice of a clever lawyer) against the seizure of their goods. 'But I told them, after I had made them own themselves to be pirates, and set their hands to it, as appears in the enclosed copy, that they were not within the benefit of the declaration [of pardon] because they did not surrender themselves, but were taken. To which they replied that they came with intent to do it, but hearing the proclamation was not published they dare not venture. To which I answered that they knew there was such a proclamation [in fact they had heard of it from Captain Carter], and though I had not then received it, yet had they claimed the benefit of it.'

The fact that the word 'pirate' was now used where 'privateer' had been used formerly must have daunted our heroes and made them all the more anxious to lie their way out of their predicament. Their replies to their examiners show that all three had agreed on the same story and meant to stick to it. Each claimed to be a West Indian trader; they had never set eyes on each other before; they had never been on board a privateer, far less visited the South Seas. When they were asked how, in that case, they were in possession of so much silver and plate, Davis refused to answer and Wafer said he had got it by trading with a privateer. Hincent said the same thing. What blew their case sky high was the evidence of Peter Cloise, the negro. He admitted that he had known Davis for nine years as a privateer in command of the *Emmanuel* (another name for the *Batchelor's Delight*, or the name of a previous vessel?) 'in which he has taken several ships and plundered many towns in Spain', and that the spoil had been divided at Barbados.

Our heroes thereupon decided that attack was the best form of defence. They accused the naval captains of unjustly detaining their goods, of which detailed inventories were given. Davis had three bags of money, some dirty linen, and 'two paper books very material to the matter' – probably a log, though he himself was illiterate. Wafer had thirty-seven silver plates, seven dishes, and some cups (broken), three bags of money amounting to 1,100 dollars, and 84 lb. of broken plate. Hincent had 800 pieces of eight, 106 lb. of plate, and a quantity of ribbons. Needless to say, their own estimates were higher, Wafer claiming 1,158 pieces of eight, 162 lb. of plate, and silks to the value of £40. The only one of the three to put his name to the petition for the return of the goods was 'Lionell Delawafer'. Davis's mark is an inverted E, and Hincent's the figure 2. By prolonging this correspondence they delayed the instructions to prosecute them, because Holmes was at the moment conducting a private war against the magistrates at Jamaica. The petitions emanating from Jamestown gaol soon became blander in tone. They now admitted that they had been in the South Seas, where they procured 'a small quantity of plate and other goods, designing to spend the remainder of their days honestly and quietly'. Charges and petitions alternated until the summer of 1690, when they were given money to buy a passage back to England, the new Governor evidently being heartily glad to be rid of the knaves.

Then Holmes intervened. He demanded a trial as well as his share of the prize money. He said he was sorry to see a man like Davis 'countenanced in England, where the gallows is too good a reward for him'. But Davis and Wafer won in the end. In March 1692 their goods were restored by royal order, with the deduction of £300 'to be applied to the building of a college in Virginia' – now the College of William and Mary at Williamsburg.

Nothing definite is known about Davis after this date. Dampier seems to have met him in London, and he has been identified with a Nathaniel Davis who led another raid on the Isthmus in 1702. But 'Nat' is not 'Ned', far less 'Ed', and it is unlikely that the French Captain Tristian, who volunteered to join them, would have been willing to serve on board a ship commanded by the man who had robbed him of the

Revenge so many years before.

More probably he is the 'Edward Davis, of London, mariner', who joined the notorious Captain Kidd, the only difficulty being that this Davis signed his deposition in a most legible way, unless of course the document is a copy. According to this document in the Kidd dossier, Davis shipped from England in the *Fidelio*, Tempest Rogers, commander, on a voyage to India in 1697. At Madagascar he deserted in order to join Kidd, who had sailed from Deptford in the *Adventure Galley* at the end of 1695 to 'cruise for pirates' in the Indian Ocean. How and why the perfectly respectable, 'trusty and well-beloved' William Kidd had been sent on this duty lies outside the scope of this book. All that we need note is that as soon as he reached his objective he, like Sharp in the West Indies, turned pirate and captured a number of vessels, among them the 'moorish' ship *Quiddah Merchant*, commanded by an Englishman named Captain Wright and carrying an extremely valuable cargo. Kidd's defence is that he was forced (like Swan) by mutineers to seize the vessel: if so, Davis was certainly among the number. At all events he sailed the *Quiddah* (or *Quedagh*) back to Hispaniola where she was left with the less valuable part of her cargo to be disposed of by a merchant from Antigua while Kidd, Davis and others continued to Boston in the sloop *S. Antonio* with the more precious part of the loot on board. According to Davis and others, Kidd took precautions to leave some chests of gold with a friend at Gardiner's Island near Nassau on the way north. Then, for reasons which are still difficult to understand and which belong to the Kidd *cause célèbre* rather than to this book, he entered Boston harbour with the expectation of receiving a pardon from the Earl of Bellomont, the Governor who had been instrumental in appointing him in the first place. Bellomont says he allowed Kidd to anchor and agreed to a pardon only if he could prove his innocence. Kidd was convinced of this and so thought he was safe. But as soon as he landed he was arrested and clapped into Boston jail. Davis was one of the first to testify against him, but then fades out of the picture as the Kidd case loomed larger and larger in the public eye until he was hanged in chains at Wapping Old Stairs.

What has always captured the popular imagination is the story of his treasure. Certainly the inventory is impressive. Setting aside commonplace things like bags of sugar and bales of muslins and 'bengals', he certainly had on board boxes containing 1,111 oz. of gold, 2,353 oz. of silver, 67 rubies, 2 emeralds, 1 large loadstone, 4 diamonds set in gold lockets, a bag of precious stones weighing 5 oz. and another of unpolished stones weighing 12½ oz. What happened to this part of the famous treasure after his execution on charges of murder and piracy has never been noted before and is of such interest that this digression must be pardoned by the reader. In 1704 the Commissioners of the recently founded Greenwich Hospital petitioned the crown for the sum of £6,472-1-0, 'being condemned as the effects of the pirate Kid by the Court of Admiralty'. This granted, they used £4,000 of the sum to purchase the Queen's House at Greenwich from Colonel Sidney (a nephew of the Earl of Romney who, curiously enough, had been one of Kidd's original backers) as the Governor's residence. This building – Inigo Jones's masterpiece – is now the heart of the National Maritime Museum. Whether Kidd was guilty or innocent, such is his legacy to the nation.

To return to our story of Davis and his companions in 1692. Wafer, we know, was later involved in the famous Darien Scheme, which he helped to promote as expert adviser to the Scottish Company which was set up to rival the great English East India Company. He told the Scottish financiers who invited him up to Edinburgh under a veil of secrecy (in Scotland he called himself plain Mr Brown) that five hundred men could settle with good prospects in a part of the world which he knew by personal experience to be a white man's grave. The company offered to employ him as a surgeon, but he wisely remained behind in London to see his *Description of the Isthmus of America* through the press at the time when the first colonists sailed to their death in 1698. One is glad to know that he only received £100 out of the £700 which he asked for his services. A little town called New Edinburgh did indeed arise on the spot where Sharp and Wafer had once landed. The colonists were taken thither by Captain Alliston, one of Sharp's companions, who volunteered his services when he met these simpletons at Jamaica. The inevitable Captain Tristian was there on the coast to welcome them, and even an Indian named Andreas, who asked after his old friends Davis and Swan and then got so drunk that he had to spend the night on board; he cannot be the same Andreas as Sharp's Emperor of Darien, who would now be 128 years old, according to their computation. We need not enter into the international problems raised by the Darien Scheme, or into the debts and deaths which this brief experiment in Scottish imperialism involved. It is curious to think of Wafer and Dampier (whose advice was also asked) as being connected with the Act of Union between England and Scotland, under which part of the losses of the shareholders were made good by an *ex gratia* payment, and it is significant to recall that both the financial enterprises which were floated in consequence of the activities of the buccaneers – the Darien Scheme and the South Sea Company – were financial disasters of the first magnitude.

The last buccaneers to leave the Pacific were the Anglo-French parties originally under the leadership of Grogniet and Townley. They quarrelled and separated in 1685, only to meet again under very different circumstances. It may be recalled that the cause of the quarrel was Townley's overbearing attitude to Grogniet after the battle of Pacheque. A deeper cause for resentment was the way the Catholics were shocked by the iconoclastic behaviour of the Protestants whenever a town was taken. The French, indeed, were given to singing the *Te Deum* as soon as they captured a church; but that did not prevent them from sacking the place as thoroughly as their heretical comrades immediately afterwards. In March, 1686, however, Grogniet's twelve canoes found five others cruising in the offing one fine morning. They gave chase and to their surprise overtook Townley, who gave them the news that Davis and Swan had gone. Now was the opportunity to turn the tables on the bully Townley. 'We finding ourselves to be the stronger party,' writes de Lussan, 'called to mind their former imperious dealings with us, and to show our resentment of it, we made him and his men prisoners. But our design being only to frighten them, we left them for some time under the apprehension of the danger they were in. Then we let the captain know that we were honester men than he, and that though we had the upper hand, yet would we not take the advantage of revenging the injuries they had done us.'

What they really wanted was to patch up an alliance in order to attack the Nicaraguan town of Granada. When they found it void of anything which interested them, they separated once more, Townley's English party being joined by 148 Frenchmen going towards Panama, while Grogniet continued up the coast. The former party met with considerable success, taking 15,000 dollars' worth of merchandise at one place. But what was easily got was easily lost. The loot was put into two canoes while a party of buccaneers marched along the river-bank to guard it. At the same time a Spanish force followed along the opposite bank keeping out of sight under the trees until they saw that the English were compelled to turn inland on account of some thick undergrowth. Whereupon they emerged, shot the men in the canoes, and recaptured the booty. When Townley's men rejoined the river they found the canoes wrecked and the heads of their companions stuck on poles, which so enraged them that they cut off the heads of five of their prisoners.

The story of Townley's buccaneers thereafter becomes a sickening catalogue of executions and depredations marked by an increasing barbarity. It became their practice to compel the mayors of the towns which they captured to pay ransom by threatening to send the heads of the most important prisoners they had taken if this was refused. At one place two such heads produced 10,000 pieces of eight and 120 carcasses of salt beef from recalcitrant authorities. When five of their number were captured in an engagement with two Spanish ships off Panama, their threats were dismissed by the President and by the Bishop, who informed them that England had turned Roman Catholic since the accession of James II. Townley replied by sending five heads accompanied by the following letter: 'Had you used us in this manner when we sent to you for the releasement of our five men, you would have saved the lives of those wretches whose heads we have sent you, and whose deaths you have been the occasion of. We give you a dozen men by way of exchange and require 20,000 pieces of eight for the ransoming of those that are still behind; but in default of which we shall put them out of condition to send us poisoned bullets again.' Another twenty heads produced a ransom of 10,000 pieces of eight, but fortunately for the Spaniards, Townley died of the wounds he had suffered in the late action on the day that the ransom money was received. A letter from the President of Panama confirms this horrible story. 'These new Turks,' he tells the Governor of Costa Rica, 'sent me twenty heads, and I bethought myself that for the prevention of the slaughter of so many Christians I ought to send them their men with 10,000 pieces of eight for the ransom of ninety of our people which they sent us out of the 330 they had taken with them. Thus you see how God is pleased to afflict us on all sides.'

A letter of a slightly earlier date, which Dampier transcribes in his manuscript, gives another example of the style and spelling of these 'new Turks':

'TO THE GOVERNOR OF PANAMA

'If you refuse this last demand and thinke that the imprisonment of three or foure Englishmen is more advantageous to you than the lives of soe many of your Countrymen as are already and what else shall fall into our hands, then you may keep them and we will send you the heads of these for a beginning, and then doe our Countrymen the least hurt in their lives or bodyes and by the helpe of God wee will color your Land Rivers and Sea with Spanish blood of men women and children the whole time wee remaine in these Seas, turning our former Mercy into Cruelty, shewing Mercy nor giving quarter to any.

'Wee will bring our ships near to your walls that you may have the pleasure of seeing them [the Spanish prisoners] hanged at our yard armes.

'Wee will make you know that wee are the Commanders of the whole South Seas, so consider what to choose, for wee waite your sentence of life or death with impatience; if death you shall have the heads by Monday morning.

From the Commanders of the whole South Seas. Feb. 22. 1685.'

Grogniet, too, died of wounds in the spring of 1687, and his men rejoined Townley's party. They continued to fare so well that they were able to retire for a while to the island of Puna. Here 'we lived mighty well, for besides the victuals which the Spaniards brought us daily [under the terms of the ransom], we had brought thither ourselves a great many refreshments; neither did we want charms for our ears in this place, for we had all the musick of the town among our prisoners, which consisted of lutes, theorbos, harps, guitars, and other instruments I never saw anywhere else, wherewith they made a very fine consort'. They had by now captured so much booty that they were no longer interested in silver and plate, only in gold and precious stones. But how could they get it home? Their craft were too small to follow Davis round the Horn, nor had they by now any leader of his calibre. Another crossing of the Isthmus was the only alternative. 'We were persuaded,' says de Lussan, 'that it would be better for us to die with our swords in our hands, than to pine away with hunger.'

So all things were made ready for a crossing well north of the dangerous Panama route. The hulls of their vessels were stove in to dissuade the timorous from any thought of retreat, and on 1 January 1688 this leaderless mob of 280 men began to march across Costa Rica. Many had lost all they had won. The wiser (de Lussan among them) realised the dangers of theft and even assassination at the hands of such desperate gamblers. His precautions were to divide his share of the spoil among half a dozen such penniless men, promising each a share if they ever reached the farther shore. The Spaniards never openly attacked them along their route, but they harassed them continually and burned everything which might serve to satisfy their wants. Ultimately they reached the river which they hoped would take them down to the coast at Cape Gracias a Dios. It was so shallow that they built themselves rafts to pass the rapids, but many of these were overset. The party no longer travelled together, and one small splinter party of five Englishmen were murdered for their gold on the last stage of the journey, just as de Lussan had feared. 'I must freely confess,' he remarks complacently, 'that such a spectacle would have struck no small terror into me if I had still been the bearer of my winnings; I bless God with all my heart that inspired me with a design to quit my treasures being exposed in going down the river, as I was the last after the English, to the treachery of those villains, where I must have infallibly run the same risk as they had done.'

On reaching the coast the English who remained alive were cheered by the sight of a Jamaican vessel, whose captain they asked to return thither in order to obtain pardons for them.

The captain replied that he would do so only on condition that they paid him £6,000 in cash. Fifty Frenchmen coming up while this argument was going on put an end to the matter by overpowering the crew, seizing the ship, and sailing her off to Petit Goave, where they arrived in May after four years' absence.

Young de Lussan's joy at being home again was so great that he could not believe his luck for a fortnight. Even though he was as arrant a buccaneer as any of them, his family was of some standing in France, so he was able to persuade the Governor of Tortuga to arrange a passage back to France with a safe conduct in case he got into difficulties with the authorities. At the same time Governor de Cussy gave him a letter to his father in which he complimented the young man on having made 'the greatest and finest voyage of our age', advising Raveneau senior to send his son's journal to the Minister of Marine. This was in fact done. The narrative was printed in Paris the next year, to be translated into English in 1699, the same year as Wafer's book was published.

With this retreat of the buccaneers, the South Seas could once more be called Pacific for the few years which were to elapse before the war broke out once more. The most dangerous threat to the Spanish monopoly of that ocean was over for the time, but more on account of the faults of the buccaneers themselves than by any resolution of Spanish arms. The cruises of the privateers and traders which are the subject of the later chapters of this book were of a different and more respectable character. They were public acts of war or trade, not the barbarities of private men. But it was the memory of the latter which was responsible for the failure of the many later attempts on the part of French and English seamen to open a channel of legitimate trade in those parts. The age of the buccaneers was over, in the Pacific as well as in the Caribbean, because a European conflict converted those who remained into legal men-of-war.

CHAPTER TEN

Dampier Turns Privateer

O N 4 M A Y 1 7 0 2, the War of the Spanish Succession broke out. Since the vessels of Spain and of her ally, France, were now fair prize, buccaneers of dubious legal standing seized the opportunity of transforming themselves into perfectly respectable privateers. There was a rush of applications on the part of shipowners in England for Letters of Marque to cruise against the enemy, and once more Dampier's thoughts turned towards the South Seas. Though three years previously he had been found, at the *Roebuck* court martial, 'not a fit person to be employed as commander of any of Her Majesty's ships', he was, after all, a skilled navigator with considerably more knowledge and experience of the Pacific than any other man alive. Hence it was with little difficulty that he persuaded a group of shipowners, headed by Sir William Southwell, Thomas Estcourt, William Price, and Michael Mitford, to adventure their ships *St George* and *Fame,* each of twenty-six guns and 120 men, at a cost of £4,000, on a privateering voyage 'in such parts of America where no attempts have yet been made'.

Dampier was perhaps less than honest in the tenor of his persuasions to the owners. He held out hopes of a quick seizure at Buenos Aires of 'two or three Spanish galleons which Captain Dampier gives an account are usually there; and if by that expedition we got to the vaue of £600,000, then to return again without proceeding further. But if we missed of success there, then to cruise upon the coast of Peru for the

Valdivia ships, which commonly are said to bring down store of gold to Lima. But if that design should also fail, then to attempt some rich towns according as Captain Dampier should think fit. And after that we were, at the usual time of the year, to go down upon the coast of Mexico to seek for a great galleon which trades from Manila, one of the Philippine Islands, to Acapulco on the coast of Mexico, and which is commonly reported to be worth thirteen or fourteen millions of pieces of eight.' Dampier, for his part, induced the owners to appoint as their agent on board the *St George* an old crony of his, Edward Morgan, who had been with him in the *Cygnet* under Captain Swan. He refused to sail until Morgan was on board, and the whole expedition was in fact held up until Morgan, who was at that time in prison, was released. The terms for the expedition were 'no purchase, no pay'; in other words two-thirds of the booty to the owners, one-third for division among the crew.

Knowing something of his quarrelsome nature from the evidence of the *Roebuck* court martial, it is not difficult to understand the almost immediate trouble into which the expedition ran. The only contemporary sources of this voyage of the *St George* are an account written by William Funnell, who calls himself mate to Captain Dampier; a vindication written by Dampier after the publication of Funnell's book, in which he describes Funnell as his steward; and a reply to the vindication by Midshipman Welbe, who confirms Funnell's account. Between the three of them, it is not always easy to assess the truth.

We know that the *Fame*, which was to have sailed with the *St George* upon the expedition, gave Dampier the slip before the start to try her luck alone among the Canary Islands. Knowing Dampier, we can perhaps believe Funnell when he says that 'some difference arose between the two captains'. It is all of a piece with what was to happen later.

The *St George*, now alone, weighed anchor on 30 April

1703, and sixteen days later reached Kinsale, in Ireland. Here she was joined by another small ship, the ninety-ton galley *Cinque Ports*, sixteen guns, sixty-three men, under the command of Captain Pickering. They spent four months at Kinsale, refitting and victualling, and were not away until 11 September, bound for the Canaries and the Cape Verde Islands.

It was here that the first real hint of trouble arose. Funnell noted in his journal: 'Here being some disagreement between our Captain and First Lieutenant, our Captain turned him ashore with his chest and clothes and servant, much against both their wills, about twelve at night'. The unfortunate Lieutenant Huxford, thus 'turned ashore amongst a parcel of Banditties and negroes', later 'miserably ended his days, partly with hunger'.

It was while lying here that, according to Funnell, Dampier learned that the Spanish galleons, from which he had held out hopes of a prize of £600,000, had already sailed and were well on their way to Spain. The whole suggestion sounds suspicious, for Buenos Aires was not at that time a recognised gold port; indeed, Dampier says as much and denies the whole story in his vindication. Nevertheless, it was set down, on Dampier's proposal, as one of the first objectives of the cruise.

The two small ships reached Brazil in November, and again there was trouble. Huxford, turned ashore in the Canaries, had been succeeded as First Lieutenant by James Barnaby. Once more there was a quarrel in the *St George*, and Barnaby and eight men quit with their goods. Dampier, accusing them of mutiny, wrote a letter of denunciation to the Governor of Rio de Janeiro, thus making certain that they would be thrown into a Portuguese prison. Again we cannot be sure of the truth, having to choose between Dampier's story of mutiny, Funnell's account of the captain and lieutenant 'falling out', and Welbe's assertion of a drunken quarrel in the 'great cabbin' between Dampier and Barnaby. Here, too,

Captain Pickering of the *Cinque Ports* died and was buried ashore. He was succeeded in command by Thomas Stradling, the senior lieutenant, and one Alexander Selkirk was promoted to be his quartermaster.

From Rio de Janeiro they took the usual course to the South Seas around Cape Horn, crossing the longitude of the Horn on 20 January 1704, and sailing up into the Pacific. The two ships lost each other in the thick weather south of the Horn, but on 7 February, the *St George* sighted Juan Fernandez Island and, on anchoring in the great bay, discovered the *Cinque Ports* which had raced her there by three days.

It was now Stradling's turn to run into trouble, and two-thirds of his crew mutinied and deserted ashore. Dampier seems to have made them see sense, and finally the trouble was patched up, but it was hardly a good augury for success in the venture.

Three weeks were spent at Juan Fernandez, wooding, watering, and laying in a store of goats' meat and oil rendered down from sea lions, with which the beaches were thronged. They were an easy enough quarry. 'They are very much afraid of a man, and so soon as they see him anything near, they will make to the water, for they never go far from it. If they are hard pursued they will turn about and raise their body up with their fore-fins and face you, standing with their mouth wide open upon their guard. So that when we wanted to kill one, to make oil, we used commonly to clap a pistol just to his mouth, as it stood open, and fire it down his throat. But if we had a mind to have some sport with him, which we called lion-baiting, usually six, seven, or eight, or more of us would go with each a half pike in his hand, and so prick him to death, which commonly would be a sport for two or three hours before we could conquer him.' It is not a pretty picture which Funnell thus conjures up under the name of sport. They killed one sea lion which was twenty-three feet long, fourteen and a half feet in girth, and seventeen inches deep in fat, which provided them with a whole barrel of oil for their lamps.

Their stay at Juan Fernandez was cut short by the sight of a ship on 29 February. Leaving their boats and stores ashore, as well as five men, they slipped their anchors and set sail in chase, eager to capture their first prize of the cruise. They came up with her next morning, discovering her to be a French ship, the *St Joseph*, of 400 tons, armed with thirty guns. 'We fought her very close, broadside and broadside, for seven hours; and then a small gale springing up, she sheared off.'

The buccaneers, or privateers as they must now be called, were anxious to try their hand at her again on the morrow, fearful that the ship, if allowed to escape, would give information to the Spaniards about their presence in the Pacific. 'But our captain was against it, saying that at the worst, if the Spaniards should know of our being in those seas and so should hinder their merchant ships from coming out, yet he knew where to go and could not fail of taking to the value of £500,000 any day in the year.' So the *St Joseph* was allowed to escape and duly reached Lima where she spread the news of this new invasion into the Pacific.

The *St George* and *Cinque Ports* returned to Juan Fernandez to collect their hurriedly abandoned stores, together with the five men whom Stradling had left behind. There was, however, a rude disappointment in store. As they neared the island they sighted two ships at anchor there, both French and both carrying thirty-six guns. This was Captain Perrée in the *St Esprit*, and her consort. The *Cinque Ports* was greeted by a broadside as she tried to make her way into the bay and prevented from recovering her slipped anchor. Dampier and Stradling decided to run for it, and they were forced to leave behind them their 'anchors, cables, boats, several tuns of water casked, a tun of sea lions' oil, Captain Stradling's five men, with other necessaries we could ill spare.'

They crossed over to the Peruvian shore and looked into the port of Arica, but were unable to land because of the lack of boats, all of them left behind at Juan Fernandez. Sailing north they reached the latitude of Lima and gave chase to two sail which were trying to make the port. As they came up with the sternmost of the two, they recognised her as the *St Joseph*, which they had fought a few days earlier off Juan Fernandez. The second was the *St Esprit*. It was a further chance to take them before they could give information to the Spanish, 'but our captain thought it not advisable to venture upon her, and whilst the matter was disputing, the two ships got into Lima'.

Dampier's irresolution is difficult to understand and it laid him open to later charges of cowardice. It certainly exasperated his men, and they were even more furious the next day when they captured a Spanish ship, called *La Ritta*, without difficulty and Dampier let her go almost without penalty, 'alleging that if we kept her it would be a hindrance to his greater designs'. She was laden, according to Funnell, with 'snuff, lace, woollens, silk, pitch, tar, tobacco, turtle-shell, beeswax, soap, cinnamon, pepper, balsam, and a pretty good sum of money'. The men were not permitted to 'rummage' her, as was both their right and indeed their duty to the owners, and there can be little doubt that this was the first major mistake along the road which was to lead to the final break-up of the expedition. In fact, Dampier took out of her goods to the value of £4,000 and only two out of forty negroes on board, though negroes were at that time very profitable merchandise. The fact that Dampier allowed her to go without attempting to hold her to ransom was widely believed to be due to 'a private consideration paid by the Spanish captain to Dampier and Morgan'.

Exactly the same thing happened a few days later when they captured a second prize, the *Santa Maria*. Again she was allowed to go free, even though laden 'with several very good commodities'. The excuse was the same, that Dampier 'would not cumber up his ship for that he intended to make a voyage at one stroke upon some rich town on which he had a speedy design'. Morgan, however, had little to complain of in this capture, secretly taking for himself the captain's dinner service of silver plate, valued at 1,000 Spanish dollars, and wrapping it up in his private linen.

The expectation of quick wealth through the ransom of a rich town kept his two crews together for the time, for though he had brought nothing but disappointment and dissatisfaction so far, Dampier's undoubted knowledge of the South American coast at least gave a promise that his 'greater design' might be as phenomenally successful as he prophesied. Sharp had done it during his cruise; Swan could have done it had he been less impatient; and certainly those exploits were well known to this present contingent of the Brethren. So, still in reasonably good heart, they stood up to the Galapagos group of islands, which was to be their base for the exploit, capturing one more prize on the way and another which stood in towards them while they lay at anchor in the Galapagos.

The town Dampier had chosen for his 'greater design' was Santa Maria, 'where we did not question but to get gold enough, because it is the first place that they send all the gold to which they dig out of mines not far from Santa Maria'. On 27 April, with Dampier and Stradling in joint command, a party of 102 men left the ships in boats, bound up the river on the banks of which Santa Maria lies. They spent an uncomfortable night among the islands in the river mouth, lying out in torrential rain in their open boats.

Next morning, while still at anchor, five Indians in a canoe approached. Dampier invited them on board, but they were suspicious of the good intentions of the Englishmen and refused. Presumably in a fit of temper, Dampier ordered them to be fired at. It was a fatal thing to do, for unless all five Indians were killed, there was nothing to stop the canoe

escaping and warning the town of the impending attack. And
Dampier's men were not good enough marksmen for that. In
fact, they missed them all.

The only possibility now was immediate action. Stradling,
with a boat-load of forty-four men, set out to capture the
small Indian town below Santa Maria, Dampier promising to
follow with the remainder in the larger boat as soon as the
tide served, in order to make a combined attack on the
Spanish town later in the day. In spite of being directed by
Dampier to the wrong bank, Stradling and his men had no
difficulty in taking the Indian town, where they waited with
what patience they could for Dampier and the main body.
As they failed to arrive that day, Stradling manned a canoe
and sent it down river to discover the cause of the delay.
They found that Dampier had mistaken the mouth of the
river, run past it, and could find no way up. Led back by
Stradling's canoe, they at last joined him in the Indian town.

All this had now occupied two full days, and any hopes of
taking Santa Maria unawares had evaporated. Nevertheless
Dampier and Stradling, taking thirty-seven men, decided to
make the attempt. 'About twelve this night our men returned
on board, frustrated of their design. They gave us an account
that they were up within a quarter of a mile of the town, that
they were assaulted by their ambuscades, in which one of our
men was killed and several wounded, that our men beat them
from their ambuscades, and would willingly have put ashore,
but Captain Dampier advised that since the Spaniards knew
of our coming and had had so much time as to provide ambuscades for us, it could not be doubted but they had made
the best use of their time and had taken care to convey their
wives and children, and all that was valuable, out of the
town, which is always the first thing they do when they hear
of an enemy. So it was resolved to return. And on 1 May,
betimes in the morning, we went down the river to return on
board our ships.'

So ended Dampier's 'greater design' by which he had promised to enrich the privateers to the tune of £500,000. It was a sorry exhibition of inept leadership, and the picture of Dampier, the skilled navigator, being unable to find the mouth of the river, is not a happy one. There is some evidence that there was a good deal of drunkenness on this expedition, and indeed that Dampier's quarrelsome behaviour largely stemmed from this cause. Such may perhaps be the happiest explanation of his inordinate bungling throughout. This is all the more strange because his chief characteristic as a young man was his singular sobriety compared with his buccaneering companions. According to Welbe, Stradling had asked Dampier before the attack to give each man a dram of brandy to encourage them, to which Dampier had replied that if they took the town they would get brandy enough, but that if they didn't he would want it all himself!

The privateers were now near their lowest ebb. They had failed in their golden dream, and moreover their provisions on board the *St George* were almost exhausted. 'We were so scant of provisions that there were but five green plantains ordered to be boiled for every six men.'

Within a few hours, however, they were once again cock-a-whoop. As they lay at anchor that night, disconsolate and mutinous, a ship blundered alongside and, all unsuspecting, came to an anchor. The privateers were into her in a flash and she was taken without a gun being fired. She was the Spanish ship *Asunciòn*, a large vessel of 550 tons, and deeply laden with flour, sugar, brandy, wine, linen and woollen cloth, and thirty barrels of marmalade of quinces, 'so that now we might supply ourselves with provisions for four or five years'. Funnell and Alexander Selkirk were put on board as prize masters to act on behalf of Dampier and Stradling respectively, and the *St George* and *Cinque Ports*, with the Spanish prize in company, stood across the Bay of Panama to the Pearl Islands, where she was to be 'rummaged'.

Four days were spent in getting out her provisions; during this time another small prize was taken which produced an unspecified sum of money in plunder. This, however, was but small beer compared with the big prize, in which according to Funnell there were 80,000 dollars concealed in the bottoms of the holds. Dampier, still in his non-co-operative mood, refused to waste time in searching for the treasure 'because he thought loss of time would spoil his greater designs'. The great ship was 'dismissed' with the balance of her provisions on board, and Dampier was made the target for a good deal of criticism from these new Brethren that no attempt was made to hold her to ransom. Funnell was particularly outspoken on the subject. According to Welbe, the captain of the Spanish ship himself offered to procure a ransom of 50,000 dollars, requiring three days to do so and proposing to leave his two brothers in Dampier's hands as hostages against his return with the money. Morgan, however, added to his private store of silver plate, taking a second dinner service valued at 800 Spanish dollars, Dampier, in his *Vindication*, pours scorn upon Funnell's suggestion; 'a parcel of fellows who were perpetually drunk, and very fit, you'll say, for guarding a ship in the night or being kept in any decorum' during negotiations for ransom.

It was while the 'great ship' was being plundered that the expedition began to disintegrate. Stradling and Dampier obviously quarrelled, though again Dampier denies it in his *Vindication*. His story of parting in friendship, and of his assisting Stradling with provisions, stores, and the person of the doctor, hardly bears investigation, and both Funnell and Welbe deny it. Whatever the reason, Stradling sailed away in the *Cinque Ports*, 'intending to beat up the coasts of Peru again', and as a first step made for Juan Fernandez, where it will be remembered that he had involuntarily left his stores and five of his crew at the start of the expedition.

They were, of course, not there when he reached the island,

having been taken by the French ships which had greeted him with a broadside at the anchorage on his return after the abortive battle. But while the *Cinque Ports* was replenishing there with goat's flesh and water, another quarrel flared up, this time between Stradling and his mate, Alexander Selkirk, who refused to serve in the same ship with Stradling. He elected to be left on the island, no doubt in anticipation that his stay would not be a long one and that the *St George* would call there before many weeks were out. The *St George*, however, never put in to Juan Fernandez, and Alexander Selkirk's self-imposed stay upon the island was to be so long as later to intrigue Daniel Defoe with its novelty and to be immortalised by him in his story of Robinson Crusoe.

One of Selkirk's reasons for refusing to continue the expedition with Stradling was that the *Cinque Ports* was so unseaworthy as to be in danger of foundering at any moment. He was undoubtedly right, as events turned out, and if one may judge from the events which later befell Stradling, it was certainly Selkirk who came off the better in his voluntary loneliness on Juan Fernandez.

Stradling himself met an unhappy fate. He managed to get the *Cinque Ports* back to the buccaneer base, the deserted Mapello Islands, but of course by then the *St George* had gone. By now his own ship was so leaky and unseaworthy, as foretold by Selkirk, that he had to run her ashore there, losing most of his crew in the act. For some months he and the six survivors spent a precarious existence on the islands, until at last they were discovered by a Spanish missionary. He took Stradling to Lima, where he was promptly chained hand and foot and thrown into *les basses fosses* as a pirate. Five years later he was handed over to the French Captain Porée, who brought him back to Europe, where he was incarcerated in the prisoner-of-war castle at Dinan, in Normandy.

While in prison at Dinan, Stradling began to spread stories of a vast treasure he had amassed from buccaneering in the

Pacific and which he had buried before his capture by the Spaniards. The story was taken up by the French Minister of Marine and the rigours of prison slightly relaxed in the hope that he could be persuaded to talk. It was the moment for which he had been waiting. One night he knotted together his bedclothes and escaped down this improvised rope into a ravine outside the prison walls, eventually reaching St Malo, and from there the Channel Islands. The Governor of St Malo was so angry at thus missing a chance of easy money that he wrote to the Minister, 'If you had agreed, Monseigneur, to have permitted me to send the prisoner back to Peru on board one of our vessels, as he wished, you would now be master of the treasure and, despite your enemies, would have been able to bring it back to this country.' Stradling returned to London in time to be joined with Dampier and Morgan as a defendant in a lawsuit brought on behalf of the owners of the *St George*.

Meanwhile, however, things were going from bad to worse with Dampier. A short cruise along the Peruvian coast produced a few prizes of little worth, which Dampier 'dismissed' after taking a few items from each. They fell foul of a Spanish frigate of thirty-two guns and fought a long-range action with her, which did little but lead to further charges of cowardice against Dampier by the crew.

Just before joining action, the *St George* hoisted the 'bloody flag', a significant action which most of Dampier's later biographers seem to have missed. At this period the 'bloody flag' was the ensign used by pirates, and Dampier himself had sailed under it with Coxon in the first invasion by the Brethren. As a licensed man-of-war, the *St George* should have flown the English ensign, and it was probably at this stage of the voyage that Dampier decided to 'double-cross' his owners and sail on his own account in their ship. After a completely inconclusive, long-range action, the *St George* sailed north and reached the Bay of Tacames where, on landing, they discovered a small ship lying alongside and loaded with plantains. They took her and renamed her *Dragon*, then returned to Nicoya Gulf, no richer than they had left it two months earlier.

But for part of the crew, impatient for a more active policy, the breaking-point had arrived. A local cruise by the *Dragon* having resulted in the capture of a small Spanish vessel of forty tons, the chief mate and carpenter of the *St George*, John Clipperton, together with twenty-one men, mutinied and put to sea in this small Spanish prize, taking with them most of the provisions, all the powder, and Dampier's Letter of Marque, which Clipperton had stolen. Clipperton relented a day or two later, sending a message to the effect that he had landed most of the powder at a place farther along the coast, where the *St George* later picked it up, but of the mutineers themselves there was no further trace.

Clipperton and his men, in fact, stood over to the Mexican coast and, entering the small harbour of Rio Leon, captured two Spanish ships. One was so old and leaky that they sank her without more ado; the other they held to ransom and succeeded in obtaining 4,000 Spanish dollars [about £1,000 sterling] for her. With this money in their hands, they crossed the Pacific to the Philippine Islands and then proceeded to China, where a little successful piracy soon filled their pockets. There they decided to disperse after sharing out the booty, some remaining in China in the service of the 'Great Mogul', others taking passage to India, either to Goa where they entered Portuguese service, or to Bengal to join the East India Company. A few took passage home in Dutch ships, and among them was Clipperton himself. We shall be hearing of him again before this South Seas story is done.

This voyage of Clipperton's of more than 7,000 miles across the Pacific in a small vessel of no more than forty tons was indeed a remarkable feat of seamanship, worthy to be compared with Bligh's later boat voyage of 1,700 miles to Timor after the *Bounty* mutiny. Possibly Clipperton was familiar with Cowley's or Dampier's log of the similar crossing of the Pacific, but this cannot in any way detract from his own personal skill as a navigator on this occasion. Indeed, all through this buccaneering story, one keeps meeting these exceptional instances of remarkable skill in navigation, all the more noteworthy when one takes into consideration the total lack of certainty about longitude at this period.

The *St George* herself was now in bad shape, and during August she was beached in the Middle Islands for repairs. 'The bottom of our ship was in many places eaten like a honeycomb, insomuch that the firm plank was no thicker than an old sixpence. Nay, in some places in the hold we could thrust our thumbs through with ease. Our ship being in this condition, and we in want of planks to new bottom her, our carpenter was forced to make a hard shift and stop the leaks as well as he could with nails and oakum.' One wonders a little at Dampier's improvidence, for only four weeks earlier, when they took the *Dragon*, they found enough cut plank lying there to build a bark of fifty tons.

Nevertheless, the *St George* was made seaworthy again and returned to the fray. It was the season when they could expect the great Manila galleon, bringing the treasure of the Philippines to Acapulco in Mexico for further shipment to Spain. The *St George* took up her station off the Mexican coast. She had a stroke of fortune in taking a small Spanish ship, not from any riches found in her but because she was commanded by an erstwhile buccaneer, Christian Martin, who had been Eaton's gunner in the *Nicholas* in 1684, and who might, had his advice been taken, have led the buccaneers to riches.

For the next month they cruised to and fro, sacking an occasional Indian village and taking an occasional small prize, out of one of which they had the good fortune to take 'some parcels of pearls'. A week or two later they chased a ship, but 'they heaved their things overboard, after which they took to their boat and got ashore. We took possession of the vessel, which was a new vessel of about sixty tons, and in her we found a great deal of powder and shot scattered up and down in all parts of the vessel. We supposed, therefore, that this ship lay here with ammunition to supply the Manila ship.'

Excitement on board was mounting daily in expectation of meeting this fabulous prize at last. Every sail that was sighted was chased, the crew 'immediately getting everything in readiness for an engagement, not knowing but it might be the Manila ship, which we now began to expect shortly to see. We were at this time sixty-four of us, men and boys, all well in health, and did daily wish to have a sight of the Manila ship'.

Probably these few days, with everyone on board a-tingle with the hope of an overwhelming success, were the only days throughout the whole cruise when an utter and complete contentment reigned in the *St George*. Dampier's previous shortcomings were forgotten, and for the time there were no murmurs of mutiny.

On the morning of 6 December 1704, a sail was sighted. She was in no hurry, and the *St George* was soon up with her. 'She proved to be the Manila ship. So we, being all provided, gave her several broadsides before she could get any of her guns clear, for they did not suspect us to be an enemy and were not at all prepared for us. Captain Martin, whom I formerly mentioned, was then a prisoner on board us. He advised to lay her aboard immediately, while they were all in a hurry, and that this would be the only way to take her, but if we gave her so much time as to get out their great guns they would certainly beat us in pieces and we should lose an opportunity of making ourselves masters of the whole of sixteen million pieces of eight.

'And accordingly it happened. For time being delayed in quarrelling between those of us that would lay her aboard and those that would not, the enemy got out a tier of guns and then were too hard for us, so that we could not lie along her sides to do her any considerable damage. For our five-pound shot, which was the biggest we had, signified little against such a ship as she was; but any of her shot, which were 18 and 24 pounders, if any of them happened to strike us, our ship being very much decayed, it would drive in a piece of plank of three or four foot. So being much damaged, and receiving particularly a shot from the enemy between wind and water in our powder-room, by which we had two foot of plank driven in on each side the stem, the signal was made to stand off from the enemy.'

Thus Funnell. Dampier has a different story.

'I ordered my officers to keep enough to windward to be sure of her; instead of this, spite of my heart, they edged away and were so far from having power to command and board her, as I intended, that we lost the opportunity and were forced to leeward. After that I tacked, came about, and had her under my lee bow, and then I hoped to batter her with my chase guns, she having no stern chase to gall us. This I took to be the best way of disabling her, and this way I could have made her yield. Instead of this, to show the world how ready my officers were to board her or perform their duty, the master and the mate left the braces and betook them to the great guns, so in this confusion neither they nor the private men (let 'em talk what they will) ever intended boarding her. . . . For the very man at the helm contradicted my orders and edged her away to leeward once more, at which I offered to shoot him through the head. While things were at this pass, the boatswain being at the braces, I asked him what they did intend to do. He told me to board her. "Clap her on a wind, then," said I. But for want of wind by this time, they being drunk and bewitched, the ship had neither way nor could she keep to.'

Welbe has yet another version.

'She no sooner perceived that we were an enemy but

immediately sprung her luff and hauled close upon a wind, and so got to windward of us, and got time to heave all her boats overboard and her goods from betwixt decks and made a clear ship, and got a tier of guns out. . . . After which we tacked and run along her side, the men being resolved to clap her on board, but the Capt. was so much against it that when the boatswain ordered the men at the helm to edge near her to clap her on board, the Capt. swore he would shoot the man at the helm through the head if he offered to edge near her. After which, we having received several shot under water, one of the men told the captain that our ship was a-sinking and that now was the time to clap her on board. But instead of clapping her on board, the Capt. cried out: "Where is the canoe, where is the canoe?" And was for getting into the boat to save his life, which showed what man of courage and conduct he was. . . . We stood about two leagues off from her, and then the captain said: "Well, gentlemen, I will not say, as Johnny Armstrong said, 'I'le lay me down and bleed awhile,' but I will lay me down and sleep awhile," but he forgot to wake again till 7 or 8 o'clock the next morning. He never so much as left any orders with the officers what they should do, but set a sentry at his cabin door that nobody should disturb him. . . . Now, if so be that Captain Dampier would have done as the officers advised him, which was, when we first came up with her, to have hoisted Spanish Colours and fired a gun to the leeward as a friend, we might have run along her side, she not suspecting us to be an enemy, and then hoisted our English Colours and gave her a broadside and a volley of small shot, which would have been a great surprise to them, and so clapped her on board. In the confusion we might very easily have taken her.'

Whatever the truth of the matter, the great prize was irretrievably lost and the threat of mutiny hung ever more broodingly over the dispirited men. Dampier, with some difficulty, persuaded them to remain a further six weeks on the coast to try their luck, but no single prize came their way.

On arrival at the Gulf of Amapalla, Dampier persuaded twenty-seven of the crew to remain with him for a further spell, and from a remark of Funnell's the terms on which they were to continue the cruise were to the detriment of the syndicate which had sponsored the voyage. This may be so, for certainly the owners received no dividend from this part of the cruise and no full record of it exists. Dampier is stated to have declared that he was going to cruise on the Queen's account, though again no record can be found of any payment by him to the Lord High Admiral on his return. One is forced to the conclusion, in fact, that Dampier and that part of the crew which remained with him had come to a private resolution to cruise on their own account, thus descending once more to the level of piracy. There is some corroborative evidence for this assumption in the affidavit filed for the civil action in which Dampier was joined as defendant. This reads: 'About 6 January said Dampier ordered all persons within the said ship *St George* to come on deck and, having given them a dram of rum or brandy or some other strong liquor, desired all who were willing to go along with him upon their own account, exclusive of the owners, to go on the quarterdeck, and prevailed upon twenty-six or twenty-seven persons whose names he caused to be entered, at the same time offering the bark [*Dragon*] to such as should think not fit to go with him, and said Morgan, who went in said bark, took along with him as much as said Dampier, by combination together, agreed to belong to said owners.'

The remaining thirty-three, who included Funnell, Welbe, and Morgan, made their final break with Dampier here. Dampier claims that this break was none of his making, and further complains that of the twenty-seven men left him, only one was a seaman, the remainder being land-men and boys. The provisions were divided under the supervision of one man from each faction, and four of the twenty-six guns of the *St George* were transferred into the *Dragon* for the use of the breakaway party. Having with great difficulty watered their ship, 'very muddy and on the top of it grew duckweed as it does usually in our ditches', the little *Dragon*, with not even one boat on board in case of wreck or disaster, set sail on 1 February 1705 for the Dutch East Indies.

Meanwhile the *St George* was patched up for her continued cruising in the South Seas. 'The Carpenter stopped the shot-holes with tallow and charcoal, not daring as he said to drive in a nail for fear of making it worse.' In this crazy ship they reached across to the mainland and finally put in at the small port of Puna, which they captured without much difficulty. For two days they ransacked the town, though it is not known what they received in way of plunder, and then put to sea again. A few days later, meeting a Spanish ship at sea, they captured her and joyfully transferred themselves into her, leaving the *St George* to drift and founder as soon as her bottom dropped out.

This was as far as they went in their new venture. Having obtained at least something from the sack of Puna, and having possession, too, of a reasonably seaworthy ship in place of the *St George*, Dampier decided to tempt providence no further. He set his course to the westward in the track of the *Dragon*, bound for India and home on his second voyage round the world.

Only one thing is known of this part of his voyage. When he arrived in the Dutch East Indies he discovered that the loss of his Letter of Marque (to which he had paid little attention when Clipperton stole it) was to cost him dear.

It was the only 'passport' he possessed as immunity from a general charge of piracy. He and his twenty-seven men were thrown into prison. It is not known what was the fate at the hands of the Dutch of the Spanish prisoners he brought over with him in his captured ship. Nor is it known how he procured his release, nor indeed any of his further adventures before reaching home. All that is certain is that he landed in England at the end of 1707, apparently no richer than when he set out four and a half years earlier. One says 'apparently', for the later charge against him and the others is at least circumstantial evidence that something was saved out of the wreck of the expedition. There were even some hints that Dampier and the others met after their return at the Young Devil Tavern, near Temple Bar, to share out the spoil, though the rumours were never proved.

Funnell's party, on their way home, had a similar experience, being thrown into prison at Amboyna for three and a half months after their ship and their goods had been forcibly sold by 'public outcry'. Funnell does not say whether they received the proceeds of this sale, but from the treatment he received in gaol it seems improbable. Ironically enough, it was Dampier's fame as a navigator which saved them from a possibly worse fate, for they expected to be put to death, the memory of the massacre of the English at Amboyna by the Dutch being still vivid enough to make them anticipate a similar result. Funnell attributes their immunity to the fact that a Dutch ship, bound to Batavia, had taken with her the journal kept on board the *Dragon*, 'for they [the Dutch at Amboyna] were sensible that upon that ship's arrival at Batavia it would be presently known that a part of Captain Dampier's company was arrived at Amboyna, and from thence it would spread all through India, and so they knew, if we fared otherwise than well, we should be inquired after.'

Funnell was put on board a Dutch ship, and after a leisurely voyage by way of Batavia, the Cape, St Helena, and Holland, reached England on 20 August 1706, glad to be safely home.

Of Edward Morgan more is known. He claimed to have sold the owner's share of the proceeds at Batavia for £600, for which he accepted a bill payable in Holland. This, in fact, represented the whole dividend which the owners received from the venture. There is no mention of Morgan's private acquisition of the two silver dinner services; perhaps they made their first public appearance at the Young Devil Tavern, near Temple Bar, the silver beakers brimming with the burnt brandy which was for generations the favourite tipple of the true buccaneers. As for the owners, there is a tradition at Malmesbury that one of the daughters of Thomas Estcourt (by then dead) murdered her sister for her share in the proceeds and buried her body under the stairs.

CHAPTER ELEVEN

The Voyage of Woodes Rogers

DAMPIER, AS WAS SEEN IN THE LAST CHAPTER, reached England at the end of 1707 after the disastrous voyage of the *St George*. During his absence Funnell (who had reached home a year before him) had published his journal under the title *A Voyage Round the World*, and though it left much unsaid, it was not complimentary to Dampier's conduct as a commander of an expedition. The full story of the disasters had not yet reached the public – it was to filter out later in accusation and counter-accusation – and because of this lack of full knowledge, Dampier's reputation as a navigator still remained reasonably high.

While he was still out of England, plans were afoot in Bristol to fit out another privateering voyage to the South Seas. A syndicate of merchants, among them Sir John Hawkins, Francis Rogers, and Thomas Goldney, a Quaker merchant, and Alderman Batchelor, a linen draper, fitted out two ships, the *Duke*, frigate, 320 tons, 30 guns, 117 men, and the *Duchess*, 260 tons, 26 guns, 108 men at a cost of over £13,000. In command of the expedition was Woodes Rogers, a relative of Francis Rogers, and between them the two ships carried double the usual number of officers 'to prevent mutinies, which often happen in long voyages, and that we might have a large provision for a succession of officers in each ship in case of mortality'. Among the officers was Dampier, who was signed on as pilot, and thus to make the last of his three voyages round the world. Though little is said about him in Rogers's narrative, his knowledge of the navigation of these seas undoubtedly proved of the greatest value.

One of the sponsors of the voyage who chose to sail as an officer (he called himself 'Captain of Marines') was a very successful Bristol doctor named Thomas Dover. He had made several voyages in Bristol ships as a surgeon, but he does not seem to have practised as such on this expedition, being paid £423 to represent the interests of the owners. His 'kinsman and apothecary', Samuel Hopkins, acted as surgeon's mate until the latter's death during the course of the voyage; he is described as 'a very good-tempered, sober man, and very well beloved by the whole ship's company'. Dover, on the other hand, lived to a prosperous old age, when he published *The Ancient Physician's Legacy to His Country*. His book may have been forgotten, but his true legacy is Dover's Powder, a sedative containing ipecacuanha and opium, which has been used by countless generations. However it was not this, but his prescription of large doses of mercury for all ailments which earned him notoriety in his own day as Dr Quicksilver. One would like to think, though the evidence is not sufficeint to prove it, that the comparative absence of scurvy on board Rogers's ships was due to his advice. Dover may not have been a satisfactory subordinate, but compared with the catastrophic losses suffered by Commodore Anson on a voyage thirty years later, inspired by Rogers's success, the latter was remarkably fortunate.

The *Duke*, commanded by Woodes Rogers, and the *Duchess* (invariably spelled *Dutchess* by contemporaries), commanded by Edward Cooke, who also left an account of the voyage, left Bristol on 2 August 1708, bound for Cork, where one of the syndicate of owners had preceded them to beat up for likely recruits for the voyage. The two crews were made up to a total of 333 men, 'of which above one-third were foreigners from most nations, several of Her Majesty's subjects on board were tinkers, tailors, haymakers, pedlars, fiddlers, etc, one negro, and about ten boys. With this mixed gang we hoped to be well manned as soon as they had learnt the use of arms and got their sea legs, which we doubted not soon to teach 'em, and bring them to discipline. . . . Our crew were continually marrying whilst we stayed at Cork, though they expected to sail immediately. Amongst others there was a Dane coupled by a Romish priest to an Irish-woman, without understanding a word of each other's language, so that they were forced to use an interpreter, yet I perceived this pair seemed more afflicted at separation than any of the rest; the fellow continued melancholy for several days after we were at sea. The rest, understanding each other, drank their cans of flip till the last minute, concluded with a health to our good voyage and their happy meeting, and then parted unconcerned'.

The two ships left Cork on 1 September, joining a small convoy bound for Gibraltar and parting company five days later, making for Madeira as their first port of call. Within a few days Woodes Rogers was faced by his first mutiny on board. He dealt with it swiftly and efficiently, putting the ringleaders in irons and having the chief of them well whipped by his comrades in crime. 'This method I thought best for breaking any unlawful friendships amongst themselves, which, with different correction to other offenders, allayed the tumult.'

Woodes Rogers, unlike his immediate predecessor in the South Seas, was a man determined to stand no nonsense; the contrast between the success of his voyage and Dampier's failure is equally strong. He believed in 'Navy' discipline and had no compunction in using the cat o' nine tails to instil a proper respect in his unruly band. He had a low opinion of buccaneers, considering that they wrote their accounts merely 'to set off their own knight-errantry and to make themselves pass for prodigies of courage and conduct . . . and for anything I could learn they scarce showed one instance of true courage or conduct, though they were accounted such fighting fellows at home'. And he was probably right at that. His voyage was to be no buccaneering expedition – his were legalised men-of-war and he carried a Commission and a Letter of Marque – and he was determined that his whole cruise should conform to the strict rules of privateering action. He was obviously an honest man, but the presence on board of Dr Dover as the personal representative of the owners must have made him doubly careful.

Shortly after the first mutiny was quelled, the *Duke* and *Duchess* crossed the Tropic of Cancer. 'According to custom we ducked those that had never passed the tropic before. The manner of doing it was by a rope through a block from the main-yard, to hoise 'em above half-way up to the yard and let 'em fall at once into the water, having a stock crossed through their legs, and well fastened to the rope that they might not be surprised and let go their hold. This proved of great use to our fresh-water sailors, to recover the colour of their skins which were grown very black and nasty.'

Rogers's next act was to settle the vexed question of 'plunder'. A fairly general rule was that everything found on board a prize above the level of the main deck might be considered as plunder, which was looked upon as the perquisites of the ships' companies and not accountable to the syndicate which had financed and sent out the expedition. It was a system open to much abuse, for choice articles from the holds could so easily be dropped upon the main deck and then picked up again and claimed as legitimate plunder. A further refinement was the division of plunder into two types, known as ship's plunder and cabin plunder, that of the ship belonging to the crew and that of the cabin belonging to the captain. Most captains of privateers made a very good thing out of this sub-division, for the cabin of any captured ship was usually the place where the real valuables were kept.

Rogers, in agreement with his officers and the crews of the two ships, drew up a regular tariff for the division of plunder.

He laid down, first of all, that the senior officers alone should decide what was plunder and what was not. It was then to be divided on a scale which ranged from £10 for every capture for seamen to £100 for the two captains. Both he and Captain Cooke, of the *Duchess*, relinquished their claim to cabin plunder in consideration of each receiving five per cent of the gross before division. Any person who concealed plunder above the value of one piece of eight and did not declare it within twenty-four hours was to be severely punished and deprived of the whole of his share in the plunder. Finally, a reward of twenty pieces of eight was to be paid to the first who sighted any prize of above fifty tons burthen.

According to the custom of the day, it was a fair enough agreement. Rogers, who kept very strict books of account, was patently anxious throughout to justify the faith placed by the owners in his integrity, and this is reflected throughout his journal in his care to have every major decision he took endorsed by a council of officers, each one signing his agreement on each occasion. It left no room for argument and was, moreover, a useful instrument of confirmation of his more drastic disciplinary actions.

The *Duke* and *Duchess*, in their passage south towards the Horn, put in at the Brazilian island of Grande to careen and refit, and Rogers paid a ceremonial visit to the local governor, who entertained him and his officers to an excellent meal. It happened to be the feast day of the Conception of the Virgin Mary, and the English officers were invited to take part in the celebrations. They collected the 'ship's band' of the *Duke*, two trumpets and a hautboy, which the governor 'desired might play us to Church, where our music did the office of an organ, but separate from the singing, which was by the Fathers well performed. Our music played *Hey boys, up we go*, and all manner of noisy paltry tunes, and after the Service our musicians, who were by that time more than half drunk, marched at the head of the company'. Rogers, Cooke, and the rest of the officers joined the procession, 'with each of us a long wax candle lighted', and after two hours of marching around the small town, 'we were splendidly entertained by the Fathers of the Convent, and then by the Governor at the Guardhouse'.

On the following day the *Duke* and *Duchess* repaid this hospitality by a party on board, 'where we treated 'em the best we could. They were very merry, and in their cups proposed the Pope's health to us, but we were quits with 'em by toasting that of the Archbishop of Canterbury; and to keep up the humour we also proposed William Penn's to them, and they liked the liquor so well that they refused neither'.

On the way to the Horn, Rogers mused in his journal on the habits and customs of the countries he passed. Of the Amazon district he remarked that there was 'abundance of petty kings who live upon their particular rivers, on which they decide their quarrels with canoes, and the conqueror eats up the conquered, so that one king's belly proves another's sepulchre'. He wondered too, 'whether the women's hair or breasts be longest'. Farther south, in what is now the Argentine, he had few good words for the Spanish missionaries, whom he thought unduly avaricious. 'Land, corn, cattle, everything is theirs, and they call all the people their sons and daughters, and perhaps there's just cause enough to give many of 'em that title.'

They rounded the Horn early in January 1709, and made for the traditional anchorage of Juan Fernandez with some anxiety, for there was considerable sickness on board both ships, mainly scurvy, and particularly in the *Duchess*, 'their want of clothes, and being often wet in the cold weather, has been the greatest cause of their being more sick than our ship's company'. This was also to be Anson's diagnosis, though he reached the island in far worse shape.

They sighted Juan Fernandez on the afternoon of 1 February, and being unable to fetch it partly because

of head winds and partly because of the contradictory posi-
tions in which it was laid down in the charts, Rogers ordered
one of the boats in to bring off fresh water, of which they had
great need. As the boat was going in they saw a light ashore,
and Rogers hoisted its recall, assuming that French ships were
using the anchorage. The *Duke* and *Duchess* both began to
clear for action on the morrow, for 'we must either fight 'em
or want water, etc'.

On the next day the two ships stood in to the island, again
sending a boat in advance, well armed in case of trouble. As
the boat did not return, Rogers ordered the pinnace ashore to
find out the cause of the delay.

'Immediately our pinnace returned from the shore and
brought abundance of crawfish, with a man clothed in goat-
skins, who looked wilder than the first owners of them. He
had been on the island four years and four months, being left
there by Capt. Stradling in the *Cinque Ports*; his name was
Alexander Selkirk, Scotch man. . . . The reason of his being
left here was a difference betwixt him and his captain which,
together with the ship's being leaky, made him willing rather
to stay here than go along with him at first; and when he was
at last willing, the captain would not receive him.

'He had with him his clothes and bedding, with a fire-
lock, some powder, bullets, and tobacco, a hatchet, a knife,
a kettle, a Bible, some practical pieces, and his mathematical
instruments and books. . . . He built two huts with pimento
trees, covered them with long grass, and lined them with the
skins of goats. . . . In the lesser hut at some distance from
the other, he dressed his victuals, and in the larger he slept,
and employed himself in reading, singing psalms, and pray-
ing, so that he said he was a better Christian while in this
solitude than ever he was before or than, he was afraid, he
should ever be again. . . .

'He might have had fish enough, but could not eat 'em for
want of salt because they occasioned a looseness; except craw-

fish, which are there as large as our lobsters, and very good. These he sometimes boiled, and at other times broiled, as he did his goat's flesh, of which he made very good broth, for they are not so rank as ours. He kept an account of 500 that he killed while there, and caught so many more which he marked on the ear and let go. When his powder failed he took them by speed of foot, for his way of living and continual exercise of walking and running cleared him of all gross humours, so that he ran with wonderful swiftness through the woods and up the hills and rocks, as we perceived when we employed him to catch goats for us.

'He came at last to relish his meat well enough without salt or bread, and in the season had plenty of good turnips, which had been sown there by Capt. Dampier's men and have now overspread some acres of ground. He had enough of good cabbage from the cabbage trees, and seasoned his meat with the fruit of the pimento trees, which is the same as the Jamaica pepper and smells deliciously. He found there also a black pepper called Malagita, which was very good to expel wind and against griping of the guts.

He was at first much pestered with cats and rats, that had bred in great numbers from some of each species which had got ashore from ships that put in there to wood and water. The rats gnawed his feet and clothes while asleep, which obliged him to cherish the cats with his goats' flesh, by which many of them became so tame that they would lie about him in hundreds, and soon delivered him from the rats. He likewise tamed some kids, and to divert himself would now and then sing and dance with them and his cats; so that by the care of Providence and vigour of his youth, being now about thirty years old, he came at last to conquer all the inconveniences of his solitude, and to be very easy.'

Selkirk, though he must have been glad of the sight of men again, had a long memory. When he saw Dampier among the officers of the *Duke*, he refused to be rescued and demanded to be put ashore on Juan Fernandez again. It was only when he was convinced that Dampier was not in command of the expedition that he consented to remain on board. Dampier, on the other hand, spoke up for Selkirk's skill as a seaman to such purpose that Rogers rated him mate on board the *Duke*.

Much refreshed, and with only two deaths among the sick men of the *Duchess*, the ships left Juan Fernandez on 14 February, bound for the traditional buccaneering base in the Bay of Panama, the Lobos Islands. On the way they captured a small prize, which on arrival they fitted out as an additional privateer, naming her the *Beginning*. In the security of the Lobos Islands they careened and tallowed their ships, making plans at the same time for a descent upon the town of Guayaquil, which they proposed to hold to ransom. As each ship in turn was up on the beach for cleaning, the other and the *Beginning* cruised in the neighbouring waters. They brought in a small prize of fifty tons, which was re-rigged and added to the squadron as the *Increase*. Alexander Selkirk was nominated by Rogers to command her.

During the deliberations about the attack on Guayaquil, it became apparent that the crews of the *Duke* and *Duchess* 'began to murmur about the encouragement that they were to expect for landing, which they alleged was a risk more than they were shipped for'. Rogers countered this nascent discontent by revising his list of permissible plunder, which was now to include 'all manner of bedding and clothes without stripping, all manner of necessaries, gold rings, buttons, buckles, liquors, and provisions . . . any sort of wrought silver or gold crucifixes, gold and silver watches, or any other movables found about the prisoners', but excluding 'money and women's ear-rings, with loose diamonds, pearls, and precious stones'. In view of this relaxation of the previously agreed rules of plunder, Rogers inserted a more stringent code of discipline, giving himself powers to punish severely 'any officer or other that shall be so brutish as to be drunk ashore . . . or that shall be so sneakingly barbarous to debauch themselves with any prisoners on shore'.

On the passage southward towards Guayaquil the small squadron took another two prizes, which yielded a quantity of marketable merchandise, a small sum of money, and over a hundred negroes. These were the most valuable merchandise of all, for all the male negroes could be sold for good prices. The females served a double purpose, the younger ones being useful both as cooks, seamstresses, and laundresses, and also as a pleasant means to tap the surplus energies of the crews and thus to give them a diminished urge to mutiny, while the more elderly were reserved as presents for the more important hostages they expected to capture, thus preserving a certain amount of goodwill between the privateers and their victims.

Arrived off the coast, the landing operations were put into effect as planned. The village of Puna, at the mouth of the estuary, was captured without difficulty. The landing party then proceeded up-river in the ships' boats, but fell sadly behind their time-table through under-estimating the strength of the current. As a result they arrived off Guayaquil two or three days later, to discover that their capture of Puna was known in the town.

Rogers was for an immediate attack, but his other officers were dubious, arguing that the town was now alarmed and would put up a stronger defence than the privateers could hope to overcome. Rogers almost carried the day at the council, only giving in finally when it was pointed out to him that, in the event of failure, he alone would have to bear the responsibility with the owners. Instead of the assault, it was proposed to send a trumpeter to the town to announce proposals for a trade in slaves and captured goods, and to demand hostages for the due performance of any bargains struck. Rogers improved slightly on this odd proposal by sending ashore two of his Spanish prisoners, threatening to slaughter all the remainder if they were not back within the hour, with an ultimatum that if the citizens did not purchase his slaves and other goods he would capture the town and burn it.

Rogers knew well what he was doing, and he needed a signal success at the start of his voyage to keep his crews in good heart. There was always a keen local market for goods along this coast, for the Spanish authorities kept a tight economic control of all trade and, having the monopoly, sold at artificially inflated prices. That they were, in fact, buying back their own goods did not concern the local Spaniards in Guayaquil, for they were getting them much more cheaply than they could buy from their own Government.

The Corregidor of Guayaquil was quickly on board and reached a firm agreement to buy 'the goods by the lump, at 140 pieces of eight per bale, one sort with another'. There was some haggling over a fair price for the slaves, of which Rogers now had nearly 150, and considerable difficulty over a demand from Rogers for 50,000 pieces of eight as an additional contribution from the town, for which sum he would forbear to destroy the place and the shipping lying in the harbour.

The Corregidor resisted this demand, on the grounds that the privateers had as yet taken neither town nor shipping and that he had sufficient troops ashore to defend both. 'We all concluded by their dilatory treaty that they only designed to trick us and gain time, upon which we gave 'em this answer, that the ships we could have in a minute, or set them on fire, that we did not fear taking the town at pleasure and that we looked upon it as much our own as if it was in our possession.' These words seemed to take effect, for the Corregidor immediately settled for 40,000 pieces of eight, though he refused to sign any paper to that effect.

On the following day the Corregidor announced that Guayaquil could raise only 30,000 pieces of eight. Rogers immediately threatened to haul down his flag of truce and attack the town, and the Corregidor raised his price to 32,000, which he said was his top limit. 'We ordered our linguist to tell 'em we had done treating, and bid the Spaniards ashore retire forthwith and keep out of shot-guns if they designed to save their lives.' The landing-parties went in almost at once and captured the town without difficulty against no more than a token resistance.

But there was little booty to be found in the town. Rogers received information from an Indian slave that many of the richer inhabitants had fled with their valuables up-river, where most of them had country houses, and he despatched a small party under Selkirk and Lieutenant Connelly to do the best they could. 'The houses up the river were full of women, and particularly at one place there were above a dozen handsome genteel young women, where our men got several gold chains and ear-rings, but otherwise were so civil to them that the ladies offered to dress 'em victuals and brought 'em a cask of good liquor. Some of their largest gold chains were concealed and wound about their middles, legs, and thighs, etc, but the gentlewomen in these hot countries being very thin clad with silk and fine linen, and their hair dressed with ribbons very neatly, our men by pressing felt the chains, etc, with their hands on the outside of the lady's apparel, and by their linguist modestly desired the gentlewomen to take 'em off and surrender 'em. This I mention as a proof of our sailors' modesty, and in respect to Mr Connelly and Mr Selkirk who commanded this party; for being young men I was willing to do 'em justice, hoping the fair sex will make 'em a grateful return when we arrive in Great Britain, on account of their civil behaviour to these charming prisoners.'

The chains and ear-rings were valued by Rogers at £1,200, but it was about all of value that the town yielded. And as it was in the middle of the hot season, and proving difficult to keep the landing-party occupied in the empty town, Rogers was glad to agree to a new Spanish offer to ransom the town for 30,000 pieces of eight, to be paid at the mouth of the estuary, at Puna, in six days' time. He accepted additional hostages for the prompt payment of this sum and, with his men, gratefully dropped down-river to the security of the *Duke* and *Duchess*, still at anchor beyond the mouth.

Rogers, returning to Puna, finally received 25,500 pieces of eight as the ransom money for Guayaquil, but was unwilling to remain at Puna longer for the balance. He could legimately have kept the hostages for non-payment of the whole sum, but sent them ashore probably because they would prove more of a nuisance than they were worth if he took them with him. To the chief hostage he gave 'four old sick negroes and a damaged bale of goods' as a token of his regard, and presented the other three with five negro women between them. The *Duke* and *Duchess*, together with a captured French ship, the *Havre de Grâce*, and the *Beginning* and the *Increase*, then steered to the northward intending to refit in the Galapagos Islands.

They were, however, not finished with Guayaquil yet. Some prisoners which Rogers took there told him that there had been an outbreak of disease shortly before its capture and that the inhabitants had died at such a rate that the floor of the main church had been taken up and a great pit dug beneath it. Bodies had been piled into it until it was full, and it had then been covered over again with the original church floor.

This church had been Rogers's headquarters, and after a couple of days at sea the disease, thus contracted at Guayaquil, swept through the ships. It was somewhat aggravated by their inability to find any fresh water in the Galapagos Islands, and a number of men died before they finally reached Gorgona, where their needs for water were at last satisfied. Here they completely refitted the *Havre de Grâce* and renamed her the *Marquis*. Here, too, they made a rough valuation of their takings so far; gold, plate, and jewels amounted to about £20,000 and captured merchandise to about £60,000. This, of course, was exclusive of slaves.

Here, too, they got rid of their prisoners, of whom they now had some one hundred and eighty, mainly the crews of a number of captured prizes. Some were forced to buy their freedom, others were sent across to the mainland, their return guaranteed by a system of hostages, to raise money to redeem their ships and their cargoes. This raised some 15,000 pieces of eight, only a fraction of the total value, but welcome to the privateers, who found themselves so full of prisoners and captured goods that there was hardly room to move aboard the ships. They sorted out the best of the bales and stowed them in the *Duke*, *Duchess* and *Marquis*, threw overboard 500 bales of papal bulls, sixteen reams to a bale, 'except what we used to burn the pitch of our ships' bottoms when we careened them', and 'a great quantity of bones in small boxes, ticketed with the names of Romish saints, some of which had been dead 700 or 800 years', and let the remainder of the captured goods go with the prizes for the ransom money. They kept the negroes and a few of the prisoners who might later be worth some further ransom, and set sail to cruise in the Bay of Panama.

A few more prizes came their way, producing their quota of prisoners, slaves, and goods, and in one of them they had the good fortune to capture a Spanish family of some wealth, and from around the daughter's waist extracted a gold chain worth £150. They also took a young priest, who proved of great use to them when they put in at an Indian settlement in search of water and fresh provisions. Not only did he act as an interpreter, but also readily gave the Indians an absolution for trading with the ships, an act strictly forbidden by their Spanish overlords. For his helpfulness on this occasion, Rogers set him free without ransom 'and gave him, as he desired, the prettiest young female negro he had in the prize, with some baize, linen, and other things. The young Padre parted from us extremely pleased, and leering under his hood upon his black female angel; we doubt he will crack a commandment with her and wipe off the sin with the Church's indulgence'. Less happy was an experience with another 'black angel' on board: '29 August, we buried one John Edwards, a youth who died of a complication of scurvy and the pox, which he got from a loathsome negro, whom we afterwards gave to the prisoners that she might do no further mischief on board.'

The time, however, was drawing near when they might expect to meet the annual galleon from Manila to Acapulco, for which so many of their predecessors had lain in wait. In preparation for this crowning object of the cruise, the little fleet of three ships returned to the Galapagos Islands, there to stock up with sea and land turtle to eke out the rapidly dwindling store of salt meat. And currently with this provisioning, Rogers, Courtney, now captain of the *Duchess, Cooke,* now of the *Marquis,* and Thomas Dover, captain of marines and owners' agent, drew up their plan for a standing patrol off Cape St Lucas, in California, which Dampier had indicated as the most likely place in which to intercept the prize. They drew up, too, a code of visual signals through which they could effect a rapid concentration should one of them sight the ship. Rogers, as ever a stickler for the recording of all decisions to save later argument, ended his notes on the meeting with an exhortation to the crews of the three ships: 'We resolve with the utmost care and diligence to wait here the coming of the Manila ship belonging to the Spaniards and bound for Acapulco; whose wealth on board her we hope will prompt every man to use his utmost conduct and bravery to conquer.'

By the end of October the three ships were on their station, having had an uneventful passage beyond the fact of a 'she-

Negro' being brought to bed 'of a girl of a tawny colour'. The ships were spread at maximum visibility, covering a line forty-five miles in length, plying to windward by day and driving before the wind under bare poles at night so that they could remain more or less on station.

For the next three weeks they plied up and down, with nothing but an empty ocean to greet them each day. On 19 December, Rogers ordered a survey to be taken of all food-stuffs on board, and by stretching the allowances 'and a rummage of both ships *Duke* and *Duchess* and strictly computing everything that will help prolong our bread', reckoned that his squadron could remain at sea for a further seventy days. But out of this had to be allowed the estimated margin for unforeseen eventualities. Rogers, perusing these figures, came to the reluctant conclusion that they could no longer lie in wait for the galleon. The other captains agreed, the fact was duly recorded in Rogers's journal, and signed by all the officers. 'We all look very melancholy and dispirited, because so low in provisions, that if we should not reach Guam in the limited time, or accidentally miss it, we shall not have enough till we arrive at any other place.'

They decided to put in to the shore to fill their water-casks, and on the 21st made their way towards Port Segura. A gale took them down to leeward of the anchorage and as they were beating back, 'to our great and joyful surprise, about nine o'clock, the man at the masthead cried out he saw a sail beside the *Duchess*, distant about seven leagues. We immediately hoisted our ensign and bore away after her, the *Duchess* soon did the same'.

As the wind fell light, Rogers sent away his pinnace to discover what ship she was. It was a tantalising morning on board. 'The boat, not returning, kept us in a languishing condition and occasioned several wagers whether 'twas the *Marquis* or the Acapulco ship. We kept sight of our boat, and could not perceive her to go aboard the ship, but made

towards the *Duchess*'s pinnace, who was rowing to them; they
lay together some time, then the *Duchess*'s boat went back to
their ship again and ours kept dogging the stranger, though
at a good distance, which gave us great hopes that 'twas the
Manila ship.'

She was indeed from Manila, and a great wave of joy surged
through the ship when the question was finally settled. There
was too little wind to hope to get up with her that day, so
Rogers ordered the two boats to 'tend her all night, and keep
showing false fires that we might know whereabout they and
the chase were'. To save time in the morning he ordered the
Duke to be cleared for action.

At daybreak on the 22nd they saw the prize on their
weather bow, about three miles off, with the *Duchess* about
two miles ahead of her. 'I ordered a large kettle of chocolate
to be made for our ship's company (having no spiritous liquor
to give them), then we went to prayers, and before we had
concluded were disturbed by the enemy firing at us. They had
barrels hanging at each yardarm, that looked like powder
barrels to deter us from boarding 'em.'

The *Duke* closed her rapidly and, drawing alongside, gave
her several broadsides. Rogers then drew ahead and raked her
from the bows, 'so warmly that she soon struck her colours
two-thirds down'. The *Duchess* then came up and gave her a
broadside which produced no reply. It was obvious that she
had surrendered, and the *Duke*'s pinnace was sent over to
bring back her officers as prisoners. She went by the name of
Nuestra Señora de la Encarnación Desengaño.

Two men only were wounded in the *Duke*, an Irishman
shot through the buttock and Woodes Rogers himself. 'I was
shot through the left cheek, the bullet struck away a great
part of my upper jaw and several of my teeth, part of which
dropped down upon the deck.' It was a serious wound and
two days later Woodes Rogers comments: 'In the night I felt
something clog my throat, which I swallowed with much pain,

and suppose its a part of my jawbone, or the shot which we can't yet give an account of.' The wound effectively prevented him from any sort of talking and he had to issue his orders for a time in writing.

They brought the prize into harbour, discovering that she was only the first, and the smallest, of two galleons which had left Manila with the produce of the East. Nevertheless she was a very rich capture yielding, among other goods, 48,698 lb. of silk, 4,310 pairs of silk stockings, 24,289 pieces of chintz, 7,200 'sattins flower'd with gold and silver', and a number of uncut gem stones.

The *Duke*, somewhat battered after her engagement with the Spaniards, was left in harbour, much to Rogers's disgust, while the *Duchess* and *Marquis* sailed on patrol for the second and larger galleon from Manila. Rogers, in spite of his wound, never willingly missed a fight and, as soon as the two ships sailed, sent two men to the top of the nearest hill to act as 'centries' and to make three 'waffs' with their flag if they should see three sail in the offing instead of the expected two. The day was Christmas Day 1709.

Sure enough, on the following morning, the 'centries' made their three 'waffs'. Rogers's first preoccupation was that the prize, so rich and so recently captured, should not escape during the *Duke*'s absence. He took out all the Spanish prisoners, crammed them into a small bark, and anchored her over a mile away from the galleon. He then removed the bark's rudder, sails, and boats and placed a few well-armed men to make certain that the prisoners did not escape. Two lieutenants and twenty-three men were sent to guard the prize. These precautions taken, the *Duke* shook out her sails and made the best speed she could towards the coming battle.

Throughout the night they could see the lights of the *Duchess* and the *Marquis* as they kept in touch with the enemy. At nine o'clock in the morning 'we saw the *Duchess* and chace near together, and the *Marquis*, standing to them with all the sail she could crowd'. Although the *Duke* was still too distant to hear the sound of gun-shot, all on board could see the smoke of battle, and to Rogers it was an added incentive to arrive in time, for he was enough of a seaman to realise that his two small ships held little chance of success against their huge adversary. Only the three ships acting together might have had a chance.

It was as Rogers had feared. By the time the *Duke* got up, both the *Duchess* and the *Marquis* had been sadly mauled. That they continued in the fight when the *Duke* came up is a testimony to the grip which Woodes Rogers, though still in agony from his wound, retained upon his crews throughout the voyage.

But in spite of his resolution, success evaded him. For most of the following day the *Duke* lay abreast the Spanish ship, plying her with round shot, while the other two kept as close as they could, adding their broadsides to those of the *Duke*. But the Spaniard was a big ship, newly built, of some 900 tons burthen, 450 men, and 60 guns, and the *Duke*'s six-pounders were not large enough to penetrate her thick sides. She was named *Bigonia* and among her crew were 150 European pirates with their private fortunes, all of whom had engaged to help defend the ship against attack in exchange for a passage to America. It was certain that they would all fight hard in defence of their own fortunes, which were inevitably bound up with that of the galleon. In addition to her guns, the *Bigonia* carried 'stink-pots', landing one in the *Duke* which blew up a chest of loaded 'cartouches' on the deck and started a fire, and one in the *Marquis* which burst near Captain Cooke, 'with which I stunk several days intolerably'. The *Duke* in addition had two shot through her mainmast, 'which rent it miserably'.

In these conditions the three British ships drew off to lick their wounds and to consult on further measures. The three captains came to the inevitable conclusion that the enemy was too strong. Any chance of success had been forfeited on the previous day, when the *Duchess* and *Marquis* had failed to wait for the *Duke* before beginning to attack. Another consideration against resumption was the further wounding of Woodes Rogers. He had been close when the *Bigonia*'s 'stinkpot' landed in the chest of cartridges and a splinter had entered his left foot, 'part of my heel bone being struck out and all under my ankle cut above half through'.

Back in harbour a serious disagreement blew up. Dover, who had come out as captain of marines of the *Duke* and was himself one of the syndicate of owners, as well as overseeing their interests, had intrigued with the officers of the *Duchess* and *Marquis* to get himself appointed as captain of the prize, which was now renamed *Batchelor*, in honour of the alderman who backed the voyage. Rogers, who had no personal quarrel with Dover, had at the same time no opinion of him as a seaman, particularly in the long and perilous voyage to England which lay ahead. He let fly in a written broadside. We, the chief officers, on behalf of ourselves and the rest of the ship's company of the *Duke*, having taken a rich Spanish prize . . . do hereby publicly protest against the aforesaid commander [Dover] and everyone of those that have already or shall hereafter combine to place him in. The ship now being in safety, we declare against all damages that may arise or accrue to the said ship or cargo under his command, and that the aforesaid combiners, who have put the care of the said ship under an uncapable command, we expect are accountable and liable to us for all damages that may happen. This is our public protest.'

For all his litigiousness, Rogers was unable to remove Dover. But he did secure the right to appoint two second captains who were not accountable to Dover, with the sole responsibility for the navigation and the defence of the prize. Another nominee of his was Alexander Selkirk as master. He also gained the right to put thirty of his own sailors on board for the voyage as against thirty-eight from the *Duchess* and *Marquis*, and even managed to smuggle another five on board undetected by the other two ships.

They sailed on 10 January 1710, on short allowance of a pound and a half of flour and one small piece of meat daily among five men, with six negroes to count as five white men, bound for Guam. Dampier, who had made the same crossing twice before, knew the route so well that the voyage was un-eventful, though the cat o'nine tails had to be produced on occasions when some of the men were caught stealing meat. St Valentine's Day was enlivened when Rogers 'drew up a list of the fair ladies in Bristol and sent for my officers into the cabin where everyone drew and drank the lady's health in a cup of punch, and a happy sight of 'em all'.

They reached Guam on 11 March, and were well-treated by the Spanish Governor, to whom they made a present of two negro boys dressed up in a livery of scarlet serge (out of one of their Spanish prizes). In return they received a gift of 56 bullocks, 60 hogs, 99 fowls, 24 baskets of Indian corn, 14 bags of rice, 44 baskets of yams, 820 coconuts, and 8 cows with calves, and it is an indication of the scrupulous care with which Rogers conducted every aspect of the voyage that the terms of the bargain were so exactly noted down.

From Guam they sailed through the islands to Batavia, where it was necessary to careen the ships for the long voyage to the Cape, their next port of call. When the *Marquis* was hauled down it was discovered that her bottom was so eaten by worms as to be 'like a perfect honeycomb', and it was decided to sell her on the spot. The Dutch Governor of Batavia, however, jealous of his country's monopoly in these waters and anxious to put as many difficulties in the way of the Englishmen as possible, refused to allow a sale of the ship to any Dutch national. In the end the poor old *Marquis* changed hands at no more than 575 Rix dollars, her new owner being one of the English traders among the islands.

It was a ludicrous sum, even for a ship whose bottom 'was like a perfect honeycomb', but it was the best that Rogers could do in the circumstances.

Apart from a stay of three months at the Cape of Good Hope while awaiting a Dutch convoy for Holland, there is little more to record of this most successful foray against the Spaniards in the Pacific. The convoy passed the Faroe Islands, north of Scotland, on 15 July 1711, and made contact with a squadron of Dutch warships sent out to strengthen the escort through the dangerous areas of the North Sea. On the morning of the 23rd the Texel was in sight, and they anchored later that day in the estuary. There were some vexatious legal delays in answering a charge from the Dutch East Indies Company that the three English ships had indulged in illegal trading in the Dutch possessions in the East, but in the end the charge was dropped and on 14 October, in the security of an English convoy, the *Duke*, *Duchess*, and *Batchelor* came safely up the Thames, to drop a final anchor off Erith.

No sooner was their presence in the river known than representatives of the English East India Company attempted to take possession of them on a charge of infringing the Company's monopoly of trade in the East, in spite of Roger's assertions (which he had already made to the Dutch Company) that he had taken no prizes in those seas. It required a bribe on the part of the owners amounting to over £6,000 – a huge sum in those days – to persuade the Company to relinquish its claims. Ultimately the prize goods were sold for a total of £147,975-12-4. The cost of fitting out the expedition had been £13,188-12. The Lord Chancellor decreed that the owners should receive £98,650 and the crews £49,325, but when all the heavy legal expenses had been paid, together with the bribe already mentioned, the former only received £50,109-8-10. Of the officers and crew, Dr Dover, who was an owner as well as an officer, received £3,302-12, which included payments as chief medical officer, storm, and plunder money. Dampier seems to have received £1,500, most of which was still owing to him at the time of his death in 1715. Selkirk probably got £800. Rogers himself, to whose exertions all the success was due, received only £1,530-6-4 by way of pay, though his shares of the plunder and the proceeds added to this, certainly produced a very handsome sum.

Woodes Rogers's account of the voyage, which appeared in 1712, was widely translated and his success undoubtedly inspired Anson's famous circumnavigation in the *Centurion* thirty years later at the outbreak of the next war with Spain. Rogers himself became one of the wealthiest citizens of Bristol, presenting the cathedral with two magnificent silver candlesticks which tradition says were part of the loot won in the Pacific, but since they have an English hallmark of 1712 this can hardly be the case. His correspondents included such men as Addison, Steele, and Sir Hans Sloane, who acquired his original manuscript for his collection. Nor could the Government dispense with the services of such an able and influential man. When in 1717 an expedition was put in hand to suppress the pirates which had begun to infest the Caribbean now that the war was over, Rogers was the obvious choice to command it. At the same time he was appointed 'Captain-General and Governor-in-chief in and over our Bahama Islands in America, the King reposing especial trust in his Prudence, Courage, and Loyalty'. His work during the fifteen years he held that office belongs rather to the history of piracy than to that of buccaneering. A memorial to this most successful of all privateers is the conversation piece painted of him and his family by Hogarth in 1729, which represents him outside the fort at Nassau.

The voyage may have made the name of Woodes Rogers famous in his own day, but later generations associate it rather with that of Alexander Selkirk. When Rogers and Selkirk returned home the former introduced him to Steele, who wrote up his extraordinary experiences on Juan Fernandez in *The*

Englishman for 2 December 1713. It was either this paper or, more probably, the appearance of the second edition of Rogers's book in 1718 which fired Defoe's imagination. In the interval there had appeared a pamphlet of a dozen pages purporting to be by Selkirk himself, under the title of *Providence Displayed: or a very surprising account of one Mr Alexander Selkirk . . . With some pious ejaculations that he used, composed during his melancholy residence there. Written by his own hand, and attested by most of the eminent merchants upon the Royal Exchange.* In fact, it is nothing but Rogers's account with a few small alterations, Selkirk was alive when *Robinson Crusoe* was published, but it is doubtful if there is anything in the Bristol tradition that Defoe met him there. Defoe had long been an avid reader of voyages; he may even, as we have seen, have had a hand in the English translation of Esquemeling. Voyages were all the rage now and a buccaneer marooned on a desert island gave him just the situation he wanted to write a best seller. *The Life and Surprizing Adventures of Robinson Crusoe of York, Mariner: who lived eight and twenty years all alone in an uninhabited island on the Coast of America, near the Mouth of the Great River Oroonoque; having been cast on shore by Shipwreck, wherein all the Men perished but himself. With an account how he was at last strangely delivered by Pyrates. Written by himself,* appeared in 1719, to be shortly followed by fictional biographies of the pirates Avery and Singleton and even a fictitious *New Voyage Round the World,* exploiting the popularity of Rogers's book. In Defoe's story Crusoe was wrecked in 1659 and left his island in the Atlantic (not the Pacific) in 1686. As far as we know, Selkirk never himself benefited by any of the publications which immortalised him. He remained a mariner to the end of his days, having joined the Navy to be rated master's mate in H.M.S. *Weymouth,* on board which ship he died in 1721.

CHAPTER TWELVE

French Voyages to the South Seas

THE ENGLISH and French buccaneers, who opened the
door into the South Seas in the sixteen-eighties and nineties,
were soon followed by a host of more legitimate privateers
and traders when the War of the Spanish Succession broke
out. Many years before this the English had made half-hearted
attempts to open a legitimate trade with the ports of Chile
and Peru, in spite of Spanish claims to a monopoly in those
parts, but they never met with any success. Sir John Narborough in the *Sweepstakes* in 1670 and Captain Strong in
the *Welfare* in 1690 had been forcibly repulsed at Valdivia.
We have seen how, when the same thing happened to Captain
Swan in 1685, he was forced into turning buccaneer even
though he set out as a legitimate trader. With the outbreak
of the war with France and Spain, the prospects of privateering in those seas became far more attractive than such ill-
rewarded efforts at trade.

For the French it was otherwise. With the crowns of France
and Spain in alliance and the stories of the wealth of those
parts ringing in their ears (de Lussan's narrative, originally
published in 1689, ran through almost as many editions as
Esquemeling's book), the example of the early buccaneers was
followed by shipowners at such ports as La Rochelle and St
Malo, notorious homes of corsairs who, like the Elizabethans
of old, were hired by contractors and speculators to do some
forcible trading in hitherto forbidden areas. In some cases
the ships fitted out for this purpose turned to piracy as soon

as they entered the Pacific; but during the last fifteen years of the reign of Louis XIV most of them tried with varying degrees of success to trade with their Spanish allies. The consequence was diplomatic embarrassment at high levels until, in 1711, the King withdrew his patronage of such efforts.

On the earlier and more piratical ventures one may mention the voyage of Massertie in 1692–4. Following buccaneering precedent, Juan Fernandez and the Galapagos Islands were used as bases for a cruise of uninterrupted piracy which ended with the distribution of 30,000 livres to each of his officers and 15,000 to each member of the crew. On his return to La Rochelle he aimed higher for his next cruise by getting a naval officer named De Gennes sufficiently interested to submit a project for a semi-official privateering venture. The court agreed (Madame de Montespan, for example, contributing 1,000 livres) to provide a royal ship of fifty guns to accompany four privateering vessels the following year. But the expedition was not a success. It began with a quarrel between the commander and the captain of one of the ships, significantly call *Le Séditieux*, and it ended with the prospect of famine in the Straits of Magellan.

Hopes of legitimate trade became brighter with the founding of the Compagnie de la Mer du Sud and the Compagnie de la Chine in 1698 as what may be called subsidiaries of the French East India Company. Unlike its English contemporary, the South Sea Company (which was also, as we have seen, inspired by the advice of such men as Wafer and Dampier), the French company sent a number of vessels to the Pacific before it vanished in the ruins of the fantastic financial schemes of John Law in 1720, the same year as the South Sea Bubble. Having been granted (without official Spanish approval) a monopoly of trade and colonisation in all areas west of the Straits of Magellan, the company sent Captain de Beauchesne Gouin (De Gennes having refused to serve a second time) with a force of 700 soldiers and cadets, together with a large number of potential colonists, in the ship *Comte de Maurepas* to see what the prospects were. The crew included a certain M. Jouan, an ex-buccaneer who claimed to know all about the navigation of those seas. But a mistake was made before they sailed by paying the cadets, with the inevitable consequence that this *assez belle troupe* of young men in their blue uniforms with white feathers in their caps got abominably drunk in the local cabarets, after which many of them deserted. One optimistic character among the passengers (of whom we shall hear again) was a certain Abbé Noël Jouin, who was attracted by the promise of being appointed bishop of the new colony if it was established and evidently saw in the expedition a grand opportunity of combining spiritual with material advancement. Although imprisoned for a short spell on his return on a charge of fraud, the adventurous Abbé soon turns up again on the Pacific coast. De Beauchesne Gouin had a hard passage through the Straits and met with the usual hostile reception at Valdivia, but he succeeded in selling his cargo farther north for 400,000 livres, a sum which, even if insufficient to pay for the cost of fitting out three vessels, at least inspired the company to a second venture.

The port of St Malo, long known for its hardy privateers and corsairs, became the headquarters of the speculators in South Sea voyages. Of these the wealthiest and most persistent was Noël Danykan, whose name was perpetuated by a grateful skipper in an island in the Falkland group. In spite of political difficulties, in spite of jealousy between the old East India Company and the new Compagnie de la Mer du Sud, St Malo merchants were soon fitting out ships for the Pacific with or without official commissions.

One voyage which was quite above board was that commanded by Pierre Perrée, Sieur de Coudray and later Sieur de Villestraux, in 1701–3. He was the first to meet with a civil reception in Peru – salutes, reviews, dinners, and the like –

though the local merchants were too afraid of the attitude
of the Governor to trade on any large scale. Perrée's second
expedition in the *St Esprit* in 1703 was part of the larger
affair. Though he left four months after Perrée, the commander-in-chief, Captain Trublet in the *St Joseph*, reached
Juan Fernandez before his consorts. There, in March 1704,
he found Dampier in the *St George* and after a short
encounter turned and ran. But when shortly afterwards the
two other ships of the expedition arrived, it was Dampier's
turn to flee in such haste that he left a landing party and
considerable stores to be captured by the French (see page
143). When both sides met again off Callao, a few days later,
the French proceeded to take refuge in Lima, much to the
embarrassment of the local authorities. Trublet claimed that
he had come to drive the English privateers off the seas, for
which task he demanded facilities to refit. The Governor of
Lima agreed that he could usefully reinforce the scanty
Spanish naval patrols along the coast, though at a later date
he was reprimanded by the Council of the Indies for per-
mitting even this infringement of the monopoly. Nor were
the attempts to chase Dampier away in the least successful
because of the crazy condition of the French ships. Nevertheless, Trublet returned with seven million livres, and Perrée's
voyage paid 3,576 livres for every 1,000 invested.

Although the French and Spanish authorities remained at
sixes and sevens on the question, French aid to Spain was now
a distinct possibility. In 1706 this was actually requested, so
that the *Aurore* frigate was sent out under Captain de la
Rigaudière Froger; but apart from transporting official
bullion safely home, no use was made of him in a fighting
capacity. A larger force of three ships followed the next year.
One turned back after losing 230 men in a month from
scurvy; but Captain Chabert, commanding the other two,
acted as escort to a convoy of fourteen vessels whose return
caused a sensation at the court of Versailles. At the King's

levée, on Easter Day, 1708, a chamberlain was able to
announce to a bankrupt court that these ships had returned
from the Pacific with thirty million livres in gold and silver
– bullion which would, had it not been for Chabert, have
been sent to Spain by the usual Panama route. Some have
called this a patriotic loan to the nation on the part of the
inhabitants of St Malo, whereby France's war finances were
partially restored, but M. Dahlgren, the erudite historian of
these voyages, has shown that only public money was involved.
Some of it belonged to members of the Spanish aristocracy
who were brought back to Europe in Chabert's ships; but
the privateers, and through them the inhabitants of St Malo,
not only took a generous commission on the deal but also
falsified the value of the cargo and in some cases embezzled a
lot of money by burying it in the sand.

The only person who did not join in the general thanks-
giving was our old friend the Abbé Jouin who, having taken
a passage home, found himself once more arrested as soon as
he stepped ashore on another charge of fraud. The depositions
at his trial suggest that he had been enjoying himself in a far
from clerical manner at Lima. He was accused of living a
scandalous life there, abandoning his clerical clothes, inviting
women to his house, and wining and dining to his heart's
content. The prospect of a bishopric had evidently faded into
the horizon of the Pacific, but a report to the Government at
this time showed that there was so much commercial activity
on the coast that he could be sure of finding some pickings,
and no doubt this was ample consolation for the lack of pre-
ferment in the Church. 'The number of French ships, large
and small, who trade in these seas is so extraordinary that
hardly a day passes without the appearance of a vessel on the
Pacific coast; it is almost impossible to stop them because
often they unite together against some defenceless port, where
they land their cargoes by force and thus achieve by violence
their liberty to trade.'

While Chabert was still abroad, news reached the French Government in April, 1708, that a large expedition was being fitted out in England. The Minister of Marine was informed that 'many English milords were fitting out an armament of seven vessels, from 44 to 64 guns in strength, to cruise in the South Seas; that they were to be commanded by an English *flibustier* named *Dampierre* and by a Frenchman whom he wished to employ and who, by feigning consent, knows the details of the enterprize'. Actually this was Woodes Rogers's expedition in which Dampier served as navigator, and his two ships (not seven) did not sail until October. But since the aim of the expedition was stated to be the capture of French ships and the seizure of Juan Fernandez as a base, the St Malo privateers determined to attack it. Assuming the whole-hearted co-operation of Spain, they drew up an elaborate plan of action with which to put their determination into effect.

The Spanish Government, however, hesitated to give assent to a scheme which involved, among other things, the fortification of Valdivia and instead contented themselves with warning the local authorities that such an attack might take place. With a view to protecting the interests of his fellow citizens as well as doing himself some benefit, Captain Alain Porée, a distinguished citizen of St Malo, sailed for Chile in the *Notre Dame de l'Assomption*. When off the Falklands in January, 1709, he encountered two ships which he thought were French. Actually they were Rogers's *Duke* and *Duchess*. Rogers says that he 'spy'd a sail' and gave chase for twenty-four hours, but that he lost the enemy in thick hazy weather the next day. A few months later he captured Guayaquil in spite of the warning previously given, upon which the Governor turned to Porée for protection, as another Governor had done when Dampier was off that coast in the *St George*. But once more the combined Franco–Spanish force was unsuccessful in finding the invaders, Rogers having retired to take his ease in the Galapagos Islands. He did indeed hear that several 'stout ships' were after him, but that they had now returned to France after a quarrel with their Spanish allies. According to him, French trade in those parts had by now assumed vast proportions, amounting to goods worth £25 million sterling in a good year, but that as a result the market was flooded with French goods. It was certainly the prospect of laying his hands on some such cargoes which first drew him to the South Seas.

Ineffective as was Porée's cruise from a war-like point of view, nevertheless he returned with four million livres as payment for the cargo he took out. The Government tried to tax him six per cent on his gains, much to the anger of his backers, who told the authorities that 'to arrest a man of such consequence in the town of St Malo would set a terrible example, because he alone benefited the State by putting such money into circulation. If he was forced to retire from business, twenty others would do the same, to the detriment of the prosperity of the realm.' Yet in the end Porée had to pay the tax in order to get himself out of prison.

Failing a licence to trade, it was nearly always possible for a St Malo shipowner to get permission to send a ship on a voyage of discovery. No important discoveries were, indeed, made, but the chart of the southern part of the American continent was greatly improved as a result of these voyages. Many skippers, of course, claimed as new discoveries islands which had long since been seen by others. This was especially true of the Falkland Islands. In 1594 Sir Richard Hawkins discovered them and gave them the name of Hawkins Maiden Land. Six years later the Dutch circumnavigator Sebald de Weert called them the Sebaldines. Ambrose Cowley called one of the outlying islands (if such indeed it was) Pepys Land in 1684, claiming it as a new discovery. Captain Strong in 1690, though he made no such claim, called the channel between the two main islands Falkland's Sound, and that name in the end came to be applied to the whole group. However, in Frézier's chart of 1716 they are called Isles Nouvelles, though he admits Hawkins discovered them, and the geographer Delisle in 1720 gave them the name of Malouines because, he said, they were discovered by ships from St Malo.

In spite of the nationalistic nomenclature of the group, we should not underrate the importance of the cartographical work of such voyages. On that led by Jean Doublet in 1707–11 there sailed one of the pupils of Cassini, the great cartographer; his name was Père Louis Feuillée, and he now called himself King's Mathematician and Botanist. His object was to obtain astronomical observations which would elucidate the vexed question of longitude, and he certainly produced, as a result of his experiences, the best map of South America to date. He may, indeed, be regarded as the first of the long line of scientific voyagers in the Pacific which culminates with Bougainville and Cook.

But even the excuse of a voyage of discovery soon became of no avail. Spanish representations against the trading voyages of the Malouins became so strong that though the privateers agreed to abide by any limits laid down, the authorities refused to trust them. After 1711 the Compagnie de la Mer du Sud ceased to fit out any more voyages, though illegal adventures continued to be made. Many of these were made, not only on the coasts of Chile and Peru, but also across to China and back in order to collect more cargo to sell in South America, without the necessity of returning to France. The captain of one of these voyages, that of the *Dauphin* and the *Grande Reine d'Espagne* in 1711, has the honour of being the first French circumnavigator, and had the venture not been strictly illegal, his voyage would undoubtedly have made more stir at home. Nevertheless, few men of substance could disregard the royal ordinance of January, 1712:

'His Majesty being informed that several French merchants have sent ships into the South Seas without permission of either His Majesty or that of the Catholic King to trade there, and deeming it necessary to put a stop to such captains and masters of vessels, and generally all his subjects of whatever rank soever, to make any such voyage, navigation, or commerce in the South Seas, under any pretext whatsoever, without permission of His Catholic Majesty, under pain of confiscation of such vessels and cargoes when reported: His Majesty commands the Count of Toulouse, admiral of France, to execute the present ordinance, together with the intendants, commissaries, and officers of the Admiralty, by publishing it in all places.'

One would have thought that such an official broadside would have shattered all schemes for the development of a Pacific trade. It is true that most St Malo merchants now turned their attentions elsewhere, but the files of the Ministry of Marine provide evidence that corsairs continued to sail into those forbidden seas. When, for example, the Minister heard of the departure of the *Ste Rose,* the Governor of the town was severely reprimanded and the names of her backers demanded. They, of course, feigned ignorance of her destination. To judge by the fines imposed in this and other similar cases where it was shown that the vessel had visited South America, such voyages must still have been worth while, or the contractors would never have set them on foot.

So the quarrel between the merchants of St Malo, Nantes, and La Rochelle with the Government continued until the war was ended by the Treaty of Utrecht, which specifically restored the Spanish claim to a monopoly in those seas. Louis XIV had to be satisfied with the restoration of the *status quo* in this matter, and the English were well content to gain tangible territorial acquisitions elsewhere, and above all the monopoly of the Atlantic slave trade contract, or *asiento,* at the expense of admitting that the South Seas should continue to be the exclusive preserve of Spanish shipping. English merchants, unlike the French, had never been deeply attracted by the prospects of South American trade; their South Sea Company wisely refused to live up to its name and restricted its activities to the Atlantic. Privateering – as the the Woodes Rogers voyage proved – was far more profitable, so that when a new war with Spain broke out a few years later, Shelvocke and Clipperton could renew the activities in which men like Swan and Dampier had been the pioneers.

One French voyage which, as Shelvocke admits, was of particular use to English seamen was that on which a certain Monsieur Frézier, describing himself as Engineer-in-Ordinary to the French King, was sent as a supercargo to examine the coasts of South America and to report on the garrisons, fortifications, peoples, and prospects of trade in those parts. It is typical of the ambivalence of French policy at this date that he was thus sent as a Government spy at the very time the royal ordinance, which has already been quoted, was issued. Whatever his motives and instructions, we are indebted to him for the best description of Chile and Peru at the beginning of the eighteenth century. He was an exceptionally intelligent and civilised person, though he admits he was no sailor. When the ship in which he took his passage out, the *St Joseph* of St Malo, rounded the Horn, he wrote: 'I compared the easy life of the most wretched persons ashore with that of a man of some consideration aboard a ship in a storm; the fine weather we had in Europe when we set out with those dark days which were not above six hours long, and afforded us no more light than a fine moonshine night: the beauty of the fields coloured with flowers with the horror of the waves that swelled up like mountains; the sweet repose a man enjoys on a green turf with the agitation and perpetual shocks of so violent a rolling that unless a man grasped something that was well made fast there was no standing, sitting, or lying; all this, added to the remembrance of the terrible night in the Straits of Le Maire, did so dispirit me that I was overcome with grief.'

By the time the ship reached calmer latitudes he was in the mood to enjoy himself and to carry out punctiliously the errand on which he had been sent. On his return he was allowed to publish his description of the area in a book full of practical details about ports and anchorages winds and currents, fortifications and trading prospects. American Indians and Spanish ladies, and even the notes of the music of the favourite dances at Lima. The book, in fact, is a real Baedeker of South America, ornamented with fine engravings and illustrated by accurate charts which later voyagers found invaluable. It was well worth translating into English, and the edition published in London in 1717 was suitably dedicated to the Prince of Wales as Governor of the South Sea Company. The translator took the opportunity of inviting the astronomer Halley to contribute an appendix in order to answer some of Frézier's criticisms of his chart of the variation of the compass.

As regards prospects for French trade, Frézier is not encouraging. Since the small size of the population on the coast limited purchasing power, he thought it was futile to send out so many ships. There was already a glut in textiles, the chief French export, yet he reckons that there were no less than fifteen St Malo ships on the coast at the time of his return to France in November 1713,

In spite of such expert advice, in spite of royal ordinances and international treaties, the illegal commerce between St Malo and South America was by this time so strongly entrenched that it needed a full scale naval expedition to eradicate it. In 1716 the Spanish Government despatched a squadron of men-of-war commanded by a French officer of doubtful reputation named Martinet. He was to do what the French king was apparently incapable of doing – suppress the corsairs and traders from French ports. Since the Spanish

Navy was unable to fit out its own ships for this purpose, recourse was necessary to the ships of France, and we find no less a person than the Abbé Jouin appearing upon the scene for the last time to negotiate (needless to say on false pretences) the purchase of three St Malo vessels for the purpose. With this typically shady deal, he fades out of history, leaving behind him the reputation of being the only chaplain who could say a Mass in under a quarter of an hour. Perhaps it was for this, and not for his negotiations, that he received the Cross of the Order of St Louis.

Armed with orders from the Spanish Government to seize all French shipping which he found on the coasts of Chile or Peru, Martinet reached Arica in the autumn of 1717. There he seized five St Malo ships, sequestrated their cargoes, and imprisoned their crews. This action, taken in conjunction with the bankruptcy of the Compagnie de la Mer du Sud in the Law catastrophe of 1720, marks the end of French attempts, legal or illegal, to open a trade in the South Seas. None the less, by that date France had benefited to the extent of some five hundred million livres from a traffic which was chiefly conducted by Malouin corsairs and merchants, whose trading habits are indistinguishable from those of the Elizabethan sea dogs of old.

CHAPTER THIRTEEN

Clipperton and Shelvocke: the Last
of the Privateers

SO HUGE A PROFIT HAD BEEN MADE by the cruise of the *Duke* and *Duchess* – the equivalent today of something like £8,000,000 – that it was bound to prove a tremendous magnet for further adventures into these fabulous South Seas. As its vastness gradually became known, and as stories of similar French voyages reached this country, some of the merchants of London began to dream of emulating those of Bristol. Copies of Woodes Rogers's book were scanned eagerly for the clues to his success; and his method of holding a council to approve every action, and his meticulous recording of every decision, were highly praised. It was this that was thought to reveal the secret of his success, and it is probable that too implicit a faith in his methods and an insufficient appreciation of his qualities as a leader were mainly responsible for the catastrophe which was to follow.

The new syndicate's first task, of course, was to search for a suitable man to whom they could entrust the command of the expedition. One of the chief shareholders remembered that he had a relative who had served in the Navy and who, indeed, had held a commission as a lieutenant. Rogers had rigorously applied naval discipline in the *Duke* and *Duchess* venture and he had won through triumphantly. To the syndicate the prospect of discipline as practised by a naval officer, allied to a promise by the man concerned to adopt

Rogers's mode of decision by council, was a passport to success. They jumped at the chance. The chosen leader's name was George Shelvocke, and he proved to be about the most unfortunate choice which the syndicate could have made.

The expedition was to consist of two ships, the *Success*, 36 guns, and the *Speedwell*, 24 guns. Shelvocke, naturally, was appointed to command the *Success*. As he had had no experience of the South Seas, he was given as his second captain in the ship, Simon Hatley, who had served as a petty officer under Courtney in the *Duchess* until he was captured by the Spaniards. Additional experience in the South Seas was represented by John Clipperton, appointed second-in-command of the expedition, whom we have already met with Dampier in the *St George* venture, while a further naval influence was to be found in the appointment of William Betagh, formerly a purser in the Navy, as Captain of Marines aboard the *Speedwell*. The total cost of fitting out the two ships was £14,000, which included the money which Shelvocke subsequently wasted in Flanders in obtaining a commission from the Holy Roman Emperor.

That England was not yet at war with Spain, and as a result unable to issue Letters of Marque, proved no more than a minor irritation. If George of England was still at peace with the Spanish Crown, Charles VI, the Holy Roman Emperor, was not. It was easy enough to slip across the Channel with one of the ships to Ostend, which was in Charles's dominion, change their names, sign on sufficient Flemings to warrant this arbitrary adoption of foreign nationality, and obtain the Emperor's commission to cruise against his enemies. These negotiations were given to Shelvocke as his first task, and he sailed across in the *Speedwell* to put them into effect. The new names for the *Success* and the *Speedwell* were to be the *Prince Eugene* and the *Staremburg*.

Hardly had Shelvocke left the Downs in November 1718, for his passage to Ostend, than England and Spain were at war. That it was bound to come had been virtually certain since the battle of Cape Passaro, fought between the English and Spanish fleets in the Mediterranean in August 1718, during the period of unofficial war, but it was not until 4 December that the official declaration was made. As there were obvious advantages in operating under English Letters of Marque rather than under the Holy Roman Emperor's Commission, a pinnace was hurriedy despatched ordering Shelvocke to stop all negotiations, discharge any Flemish sailors he might have signed on, and to return to England, shipping only enough brandy and wine to suffice the two ships for their voyage into the Pacific. Then, as now, wine and brandy were cheaper to buy on the Continent, and as it would remain on board, no duty would have to be paid for it.

Shelvocke took it upon himself to ignore these orders. He negotiated the Commission with the Emperor, signed on ninety Flemings instead of the sixty which had previously been thought sufficient for the purpose, broached a hogshead of brandy for 'entertainments' in his cabin, and fired away five barrels of powder in unnecessary salutes. He seemed surprised on his return to the Downs to discover that the syndicate was not best pleased with his actions so far. Their displeasure is understandable, for their first action now had to be to discharge the ninety Flemings, paying each of them two months' wages and providing transport for them back to Ostend. And they made their displeasure obvious by depriving Shelvocke of the chief command and giving it to Clipperton. In order not to concentrate all the South Seas experience in one ship, Hatley was transferred from the *Success* to the *Speedwell*, becoming second captain to Shelvocke.

That Shelvocke was deeply hurt by this change in supreme command is certain. 'I shall not speak untruth if I affirm that Capt. Clipperton was neither an officer, nor fit to be one,' he

wrote, and in the same breath he accused Clipperton of con-
spiring with the officers of the *Speedwell* 'to toss me overboard, when they would be rid of a trouble'. Yet to the
Gentlemen Adventurers, the sponsors of the expedition, he
wrote after the switch: 'I am easy, perfectly easy, and very
heartily thankful for all your favours. For God's sake, Sir,
pardon small faults: I starve without your friendship . . . I
shall with the greatest cheerfulness show Captain Clipperton
all the respect in the world.'

It is not easy to hold the balance as between Clipperton
and Shelvocke in the true cause of failure of this new expedition. Clipperton kept no journal, and died in England before
he could answer the charges which Shelvocke later made
against him. The chief mate of the *Success*, however, George
Taylor, did keep a journal, but gave it before publication to
William Betagh, who is a tainted witness. A second journal,
of whose author there is now no trace, was also kept in the
Success, but did not see the light of day until it fell twenty
years later into the hands of the Rev. John Harris, who, combining it with Taylor's, published an account of Clipperton's
actions in his mammoth collection of voyages in 1744. Shelvocke kept a journal in the *Speedwell*, but, like Betagh, he
is a prejudiced witness, more anxious to justify himself by
incriminating Clipperton than to render an honest account
of his transactions. We know, too, that in the end he cheated
the syndicate and had to flee the country to avoid a lawsuit,
which is hardly an argument in his favour. Finally, William
Betagh wrote an account of the voyage; but as his sole object
was to vilify Shelvocke, he must also be considered un-
reliable.

In addition to his published account, Shelvocke submitted
a report to the Lords Commissioners of the Admiralty. This
report, now in the manuscript collection of the Admiralty
Library, has as yet not been published. This does not make
it any the less suspect, though as it contains slightly less

vituperation against Clipperton and Betagh than the account
which he subsequently published, it is possibly rather more
reliable. It is on this report, coupled with the less controversial
passages of Taylor's journal, and the account published in
Harris's *Voyages*, that this present recapitulation is mainly
based, though a few of Betagh's remarks appear to have
enough of truth in them to be considered as valid criticisms
of Shelvocke's conduct.

The two ships proceeded down the Channel in December,
and were held up in Plymouth for two months while the
wind blew obstinately from the west, preventing them from
putting to sea. It relented on 12 February 1719, backing to
the south-east, and on the next day the *Success* and the *Speedwell* began their long voyage to the South Seas. It was hardly
a propitious start, for such a movement of the wind almost
certainly presaged a period of stormy weather.

It is impossible not to believe that Shelvocke, before ever
he left Plymouth, had determined to give Clipperton the
slip at the first opportunity. His chance to do so now came
even earlier than he can have imagined. Two days out from
Plymouth the inevitable heavy weather arrived with a hard
gale from the south-east. While Clipperton in the *Success*
hove-to, and, as admitted by Shelvocke, ordered the *Speedwell* to follow suit, the latter instead drove away to the north-
west, and continued this course for two days after the storm
had abated. So, at the very outset of the voyage, the two ships
became widely separated, with Shelvocke steering a course
that made the separation ever more distant.

The first rendezvous, in case of such a separation, was the
Canary Islands. Clipperton reached them on 5 March. He
spent the agreed period of ten days there waiting for the
Speedwell and then proceeded to the second rendezvous, the
Cape Verde Islands. Still failing to meet with Shelvocke, he
sailed for the third rendezvous, Juan Fernandez Island, reaching the Pacific through the Magellan Straits. He was sailing

with a discontented crew, for he had neglected to take out of the *Speedwell* before departure his ship's share of the wine and brandy, probably expecting to be able to draw supplies *en route*.

Shelvocke reached the Canary Islands two days after Clipperton had left. He, too, waited there for ten days, though he must have known that the *Success* could hardly be astern of him after the course he had steered in the great storm. He then proceeded to the Cape Verdes, but again missed Clipperton, this time by several days.

By now, all was uproar in the *Speedwell*. Most of the officers were not on speaking terms, the crew was in a permanent state of mutiny. Every evening Shelvocke forced the officers to visit him in his cabin, and the night was spent in drinking healths to the Gentlemen Adventurers who had financed the expedition. With his double ration of brandy and wine, there was no lack of the means of conviviality.

Four of the crew deserted at St Jago, in the Cape Verdes, and the gunner and the chief mate, Turner Stevens and Andrew Pedder, were put ashore by Shelvocke to make their own way home. Stevens and Pedder were both, according to Shelvocke, remarkably quarrelsome men, but their discharge did little to quieten the mutinies of the crew. One suspects that it was the sight of Shelvocke, and his son whom he had on board with him, more or less permanently drunk while the men had no share of the liquor which was the greatest cause of dissatisfaction.

It is in the narrative of his stay at the Cape Verde Islands that we get a virtual verification of his intention to avoid a meeting with Clipperton, for here there is a deliberate falsification of dates to make it appear that his arrival there was later than, in effect, it was. It was certain that, at the Cape Verdes, Shelvocke would hear news of the *Success*, as indeed he did, though he kept it a secret between the surgeon, Nicholas Adams, and himself. It would then be his duty to sail as soon as possible in pursuit of the *Success* to effect the junction of the two ships. But by falsifying his date of arrival he safeguarded himself from a charge of deliberate loitering should Adams later divulge the secret.

One other incident here is also revealing. Six silver goblets had been issued for drinking purposes to the officers. Shelvocke ordered them to be hammered down to make four 'circles to adorn the outside of a fine pail, made by the cooper, for the more glorious drinking of Hipsy, a liquor compounded of wine, water, brandy, and sugar, which by the admirers of it is also called meat, drink, and clothing'. Shelvocke suffered from gout and reckoned that this was as good a treatment as any for this disease.

The *Speedwell*, on leaving the Cape Verdes, should have proceeded direct to Juan Fernandez Island, in the Pacific, which was the next agreed rendezvous. Shelvocke explains his inability to do so because of the mutinous conduct of his crew and his need for 'refreshment' *en route*. This, indeed, may be so; it certainly made highly unlikely any meeting with Clipperton when the Pacific was at last reached.

From the Cape Verdes Shelvocke therefore crossed the South Atlantic to Brazil for his 'refreshment', anchoring off St Catherine's Island. Shortly before arrival there, the *Speedwell* fell in with a Portuguese trader. There is a curious discrepancy in the accounts of what transpired. According to Shelvocke, he sent Hatley across to buy tobacco, and was justifiably annoyed when he returned with 'unnecessary trifles; viz., china cups and plates, a little hand nest of drawers, four or five pieces of china silk, sweetmeats, etc'. According to Betagh, this little expedition of Hatley's developed into a piece of pure piracy against a friendly neutral. He describes how the Portuguese captain was made to shiver with fear by the description of 'that piece of discipline used by the merry blades in the West Indies, called blooding and sweating, which is done by making the captain, on the ill report of his men or his declining to discover where his money is hid, to run the gauntlet naked through the pirate crew; each of them furnished with a sail-needle, pricking him in the buttocks, back, and shoulders. Thus bleeding, they put him into a sugar cask swarming with cockroaches, cover him with a blanket, and there leave him to glut the vermin with his blood.'

Having thus, according to Betagh, got the Portuguese captain into a receptive frame of mind, Hatley proceeded to help himself. Into his boat went 'plantins, bananas, lemons, oranges, pomegranates, three or four boxes of marmalade and other sweetmeats, some Dutch cheeses, and a large quantity of sugar. If it had stopped here [remarked Betagh] it was well enough and might pass as a present, but after this came above a dozen pieces of silk, several of which were flowered with gold and silver worth, at least, three pound a yard retail, several dozen of China plates and basins, a small Japan cabinet, not to mention what the men took, who on seeing the Portuguese so brisk at handing their things into the boat, concluded immediately they had as good a right to a present as anyone else. So on board they go, laying hold on what came next to hand. In short, as 'twas all a present, I can't see who could pretend to restrain them. Among other things, Hatley brought the last and handsomest present of all, a purse of 300 gold moidores'.

These were the two accounts, as presented to the world after the return of Shelvocke and his men. It must be remembered that Betagh's whole object when he wrote his account was to present Shelvocke in as evil a light as possible. Yet there is unquestionably some valid foundation for his story, for when finally Shelvocke was brought to book there were included in the complaints against him one from the Portuguese Ambassador on behalf of the captain who had been so terrified by the threat of 'blooding and sweating', alleging piracy against the Portuguese ship. There was also some evidence that this 'prize' never found its way into the account with the owners. Certainly not the embroidered silk, for within a few days of the capture Shelvocke and his son were strutting on board 'in a cinnamon coloured suit of fine silk, all wondrous gallant and gay'. Hatley, for his part, double-crossed Shelvocke by failing to declare the golden *moidores* he had acquired, bribing his boat's crew with ten apiece to hold their tongues while he pocketed the remainder.

The *Speedwell,* while lying off the Brazilian coast, came into company with a returning French ship, the *Ruby*, commanded by M. de la Jonquière. She was one of the squadron under Martinet, hired by the Spanish Government to curtail the activities of the French corsairs on the Pacific coasts. (See page 194.) The *Ruby* was on the way home. She had, in consequence of the seizures on the Pacific coast, a treasure in her holds valued at no less than three million dollars. De la Jonquière was slightly apprehensive of what Shelvocke might do, for his crew was sickly and he could muster less than 100 sound men out of his total complement of 420. He need not have worried, however, for Shelvocke at the time was facing another of the many mutinies in his ship, and the men would not have followed him. And in any case, de la Jonquière took very good care to keep his secret to himself. A few days later another French ship, this time on her way out to the South Seas, came in to anchor. She was the *Wise Solomon* of St Malo, and, like the *Ruby*, had been hired by Spain to assist in driving the French out of the South Seas. She was later to cause Shelvocke some annoyance when next their paths crossed.

The *Speedwell* sailed from St Catharine's Island on 8 August, having loitered there for eight weeks. Gone now was any lingering chance that Clipperton might still be waiting for Shelvocke at Juan Fernandez. One is strengthened in the assumption that this avoidance of a meeting was entirely Shelvocke's doing by reason of a new set of rules drawn up in the *Speedwell* for the division of prize. These now operated far more unfavourably for the owners. Clipperton, who for all his faults was otherwise a reasonably honest man, would never have subscribed to so bare-faced a reversal of the owners' rights. Shelvocke recorded that he was forced to make this new arrangement to pacify his mutinous crew, but if so he certainly made sure that he too was to benefit under the new rates of distribution. The new rules were only made possible by dismissing the owner's agent, Mr Hendry, from his post and reappointing him as purser.

The long stay at St Catharine's had made it certain that the passage around the Horn would not be an easy one. It was late in the season for the southern passage, for they could not now reach the latitude of Cape Horn before October, the normal period for the prolonged and vicious gales from the south and west. The *Speedwell* found it so. 'Gloomy' and 'dismal' are the adjectives which Shelvocke used in his account. For over a month the little *Speedwell* tossed wildly in those inhospitable waters, meeting nothing but 'the continued series of contrary tempestuous winds which oppressed us ever since we had got into this sea'. They oppressed Hatley even more acutely, so that he shot the only other living creature in sight – 'a disconsolate black Albatross who accompanied us for several days as if he had lost himself'. Hatley's name, of course, has long been lost to history, but this particular albatross lives on in Coleridge's immortal poem. It was in fact Wordsworth who, in 1797, drew Coleridge's attention to this passage in Shelvocke's narrative as they walked over the Quantock Hills discussing the genesis of the *Ancient Mariner*.

The poem is not only true about the shooting of the albatross; it is true also about the shortage of drinking water. By mid-November, when the *Speedwell* had at last won her way into the Pacific, she was down to her last seven butts of water, 'and those lying in such a manner that half the hold must have been unstowed to get at them'. In this predicament, Shelvocke made for the island of Chiloe, close to the mainland coast and still some 800 miles short of his destination, for further 'refreshment'. It is perhaps noteworthy that by this stage of the voyage he and his officers had got outside the entire stock of wine and brandy for the two ships.

By pretending to be a Frenchman, and calling himself Capt. le Janis le Breton of the ship *St Rosé*, Shelvocke succeeded in holding at bay the suspicions of the Spanish Governor for long enough to complete with wood, water, and fresh provisions. It is to his credit that he did this in spite of the behaviour of his officers and men, who fired on an Indian canoe, landed and took prisoner two Indian men, ravished the local women, and slaughtered cattle wholesale. Shelvocke himself had at first the design of sacking Chacao, the main town on the island, but thought better of it when he missed it in his first navigation of the island.

The Spanish Governor, rightly suspicious of this 'Capt. Le Janis le Breton and his ship *St Rosé*', produced no more than ten hams as provisions for the *Speedwell*, accompanied by orders to be gone as soon as they were on board. Shelvocke could do nothing more by persuasion, and naturally helped himself from the Indian settlements. He sailed from the island on 17 December with 'our decks full of live cattle, such as European sheep, hogs, guanacoes [a species of llama], poultry in great abundance, and hams, etc.; as also a good quantity of wheat, barley, potatoes, maize'.

Upon the recommendation of a Frenchman in the crew – a man who had deserted from the *Ruby* at St Catharine's in the hope of another fruitful cruise in the South Seas – Shelvocke decided to try his hand at the town of Concepcion, farther up the Chilean coast. He arrived off the port on 23 December and was fortunate in capturing a small ship of 150 tons called the *Solidad d'Anday*. She had little in her of value, but was, of course, good for a demand of ransom money. A smaller craft of twenty-five tons, the property of a Spanish priest who ran a side-line in market gardening, was also brought in. The news of a third ship, laden with wine and brandy, caused Shelvocke to sit up and take notice. He sent away a cutting-out party of twenty-five men under the command of a lieutenant to bring her in, or to secure her cargo should she be found to have beached herself. It proved an unhappy venture, for the party was ambushed and mowed down by a line of riderless horses, linked bridle to bridle by ropes, which the Spaniards drove at them. Five men lost their lives or were captured.

This ill-fortune was counterbalanced the same night when a Spanish ship, the *St Fermin*, came in from sea straight into the arms of the privateers. She was easily captured, and in her holds she carried a mixed cargo of sugar, rice, chocolate, linen, and baize. Also out of her was taken a collection of silver plate, including ten wrought silver candlesticks, destined for the Jesuits' church ashore, and 6,000 dollars in money.

With these two ships in his hands, Shelvocke sent a message ashore under flag of truce demanding a ransom of 16,000 dollars. He received back an offer of 12,000. After two days of bargaining, and discovering that the Spaniards were not prepared to raise their offer, he burnt the *Solidad* and re-iterated his original demand, this time for the *St Fermin* only. It was not in fact an unreasonable sum to demand, for the ship was new and worth from four to five times the amount demanded in ransom.

The Governor again offered 12,000 dollars, and after an acrimonious correspondence Shelvocke accepted it, threatening to burn the *St Fermin* if the ransom was not paid in twenty-four hours. The money, however, was not forthcoming and Shelvocke's ultimatum expired with no sign of movement from the shore. He put the *St Fermin* to the torch, and she blazed furiously as the *Speedwell* put to sea. It was not a wholly unproductive start to the venture, though if Shelvocke had tempered his correspondence with the Governor it is possible that he might have got his ransom. The letters are printed in his journal and are not exactly a model of tact.

As the *Speedwell* put to sea she towed astern the small boat she had captured from the priest on the first day. The *Speedwell's* carpenters had given her a half-deck, and Shelvocke renamed her the *Mercury*, intending to use her as a small auxiliary in his planned depredations along the coast.

Shelvocke at last steered for Juan Fernandez, the rendez-vous where, long since, he should have joined up with Clipperton. As he approached the island he hove to, sending in the *Mercury* for such news of the *Success* as could be discovered. There is another clue to his intentions in an unguarded side-note to his journal: 'Upon accidentally seeing some uncertain tokens of my consort's having been here, suddenly depart.'

Clipperton had, in fact, arrived at Juan Fernandez over four months earlier. He had had a difficult voyage in the *Success*, mainly because Shelvocke had his supply of liquor and he found it hard to pacify his crew at this want of sustenance. His ship, too, had been sickly during the passage, and there had been several deaths from scurvy, including William Pridham, his master-gunner, whom he buried in the inhospitable wastes of Tierra del Fuego.

He had hoped to find the *Speedwell* awaiting him at Juan Fernandez, but as we know, Shelvocke had no intention of keeping the appointment. In the darkest days of the passage, with the crew sick and dispirited, Clipperton had tried to raise their enthusiasm by assuring them that at Juan Fernandez they would at last receive their liquor. But with no sign of Shelvocke, he was forced to the conclusion that the *Speedwell* had been lost on the voyage and he gave this opinion to his crew, 'to pacify them and to hinder them from cursing continually Captain Shelvocke for running away with their liquors, which, however, some of the sick men did with their dying breaths'.

Clipperton's troubles were not yet over, however, for four of his men, tempted by 'the beauty and fertility of this island, compared with the dangers and difficulties they were sure to meet with in the South Seas', deserted and decided to annex the island as their private kingdom. Two were later recaptured with some difficulty, but the remaining two had to be left in the doubtful possession of their island paradise, 'who are to be reputed successors to Governor Selkirk, though for anything I know we have not the slightest memoirs of their administration'.

His invalids having recovered, and having restocked his vessel with fish, goats' meat, and fresh water, one more task remained to Clipperton; to leave a message for the errant Shelvocke should he eventually make his way to the island. On a 'remarkable' tree, facing the landing place and so prominent that it was impossible to miss it, he had an inscription cut. It read:

'Captain John —— W. Magee, 1719.'

The reasoning behind this odd message is obvious. The name of Clipperton was well enough known to the Spaniards from his earlier adventures in these waters and he did not wish it to be known that he had returned on a second privateering venture. But his surgeon, William Magee, had never before been to the South Seas, and his name would mean nothing to any inquisitive Spaniard who might take it in his head to visit Juan Fernandez. It would mean a great deal to Shelvocke, however, who could not fail to connect it with the *Success*. In addition to the inscription on the tree, Clipperton had a large wooden cross set up on the beach, at the foot of which he buried in a bottle a written message, setting out a code of signals by which the two ships could recognise each other should they meet later on the high seas.

This done, the *Success* put to sea in search of Spanish prizes. She was by now weakly manned, having lost thirty of her crew through death and two, the joint rulers of Juan Fernandez, by desertion. Those still on board were, if not actively mutinous, vividly aware of the dangers they ran; one small ship, weakly manned, in waters in which every man's hand would be against them. In spite of their daily curses directed at Shelvocke, they could have wished the *Speedwell* to be with them at this juncture. Clipperton was well aware that a few quick and easy prizes were necessary to revive their waning spirits.

They came up with their first victim a fortnight later, though she proved hardly a good omen for future success. She was a small ship laden with dung, and although she was thoroughly searched, she produced no more than 'two jars of eggs, as much treacle, and a couple of pieces of eight in ready money'. Better fortune was in store, however. In the course of the next week the *Success* captured three good prizes, the *St Vincent* of 150 tons, the *Trinity of* 400, and a smaller ship of 75. All were rich prizes, producing not only useful quantities of high quality goods and reasonably big sums of ready money and plate, but also large numbers of negroes and Indians, who would fetch a good price in any trading on the coast. The smallest of the three ships proved, in fact, the most acceptable to Clipperton, for in addition to several passengers, among whom was a countess who might well be worth a considerable ransom, she carried 400 jars of wine and brandy, 'which were articles very much wanted'.

With these three captures, Clipperton was faced with a decision of considerable difficulty. Quite apart from their cargoes and the cash they carried on board, the ships themselves and their crews had a considerable value if held up to ransom. To enable this to be done entailed sending an officer and about a dozen men on board each one as a prize crew to make sure that the vessel remained in company until the opportunity arose to hold her to ransom. But the *Success* was already undermanned through sickness and death, and each prize crew weakened her still further. One result of this was that the prize crews were smaller than was usually thought prudent in captures of this kind.

The taking of a fourth prize, the *Rosario* of 200 tons, brought the inevitable result. When she struck her colours Clipperton sent across a prize crew of Lieutenant Serjeantson and eight seamen. The *Rosario* carried twelve passengers and her captain, estimating the probable size of the boarding-party from the number of prizes already clustered round the *Success*, told them to hide below decks in the hold and to seize any Englishman who came within their reach.

When Serjeantson and his men boarded the *Rosario*, his first action was to order all the crew on deck to assemble in the captain's cabin, on the door of which he placed one of his eight men as a sentry. He and the other seven then loosed the topsails to take the ship back to the *Success*. With this done, the next obvious task was to discover how rich was the cargo of this newly-captured ship. Leaving one man on deck to steer, Serjeantson and the other six descended into the hold, one by one, to 'rummage'. And one by one, as they went down the ladder, they were neatly knocked on the head by the passengers. This accomplished, the passengers had no difficulty in overpowering the sentry and setting the Spanish crew free. The single helmsman left on deck was, of course, no match for passengers and crew combined.

Clipperton only discovered what had happened when he saw the *Rosario*, which had been sailing towards him, turn about and make for the shore. He set sail in chase, but could not catch the fleeing *Rosario*. She, however, could make no harbour in her haste to escape, and ran ashore, where she dashed to pieces on the rocks. The whole of her crew and passengers, and the English prisoners, scrambled to safety, and Serjeantson and his eight men were sent down to Lima for interrogation and imprisonment.

Under interrogation they not only revealed Clipperton's movements, but also the fact about the buried bottle at Juan Fernandez and the two deserters who had made the place their kingdom. The Spanish viceroy at Lima thereupon ordered a search to be made on the island, and both the bottle and the two 'kings' were soon in his hands.

Clipperton, with his remaining prizes, put in at La Plata Island. He realised that he now had more Spanish prisoners than he could reasonably handle with so small a crew, and wisely decided to put most of them ashore. A further problem was what to do with the considerable cargoes he had already captured. To transfer them all to the *Success* would be to fill the ship to overflowing; to retain one of the prizes as a cargo-carrying consort would be severely to limit his mobility. He therefore filled the smaller prize with the captured goods, which were valued 'at ten thousand pounds and upwards', put on board thirteen English and ten negro sailors, and sent her off to Brazil under command of his second captain, Mitchell. The object was to open a trade in Brazil, convert the goods into money, and return with the proceeds to England for the benefit of the owners.

Sharp and Davis, as has been seen, made no great difficulty of this return journey round Cape Horn, though they had good ships adequately manned. For Mitchell, it was a sterner undertaking with a crew of only twenty-three men, though by no means an impossible one. Not that it ever came to the point of attempting it, for at the Island of Velas a few weeks later, where the *Success* put in for water, Clipperton recognised many articles of clothing in the hands of the Indians there as originally belonging to Mitchell and his men. While it is not certain that Mitchell and his party met their deaths there, it is quite certain that they never reached Brazil, let alone England.

Events were at this stage when Shelvocke in the *Speedwell* at long last reached Juan Fernandez. The bottle at the foot of the cross, buried by Clipperton, was, of course, no longer there, its secret signals now known to the Spanish authorities. The cross itself had also been removed by the Spaniards. And the two 'kings', who might have given useful information, were languishing in a Spanish prison. All that remained was the inscription on the 'remarkable' tree: 'Captain John —— W. Magee.' This was duly read by Lieutenant Brooks whom Shelvocke had sent in advance to the island in the *Mercury*, and it told him that Clipperton had undoubtedly been there. This was the 'uncertain token of my consort's having been there' of Shelvocke's marginal note and the reason which made him 'hurriedly depart'. It was also the occasion of an undignified abuse of Brooks on his return on board, Shelvocke flying into a rage at this unwelcome evidence of Clipperton's presence in these seas.

Accompanied by the *Mercury*, Shelvocke stood away to the northward towards the coast of Peru. He was making for Arica, where he hoped to find some Spanish shipping to capture and hold to ransom. As he approached the coast he sent the *Mercury* ahead to look into the harbour, discovering on his own arrival that she had taken the *Rosario* 'of about 100 tons and laden with cormorant's dung, which the Spaniards call guano'. It is the first mention in any English book of this useful commodity, and Shelvocke adds a note about its remarkable properties as an aid to agricultural fertility. The owner of the *Rosario*, 'a man perfectly honest but straightened in his circumstances', got his ship back the following morning by the prompt payment of a ransom of 1,500 pieces of eight. Another small boat captured produced two jars of brandy and forty pieces of eight in ransom.

Hilo, seventy-five miles to the northward, was to be the next port of call, and the hopes of the men on board rose when the masts of one large and three small ships were seen in the harbour. But Hilo was to produce no dividend for the *Speedwell*. The large ship turned out to be the *Wise Solomon* of St Malo, the French ship which Shelvocke had last encountered on the coast of Brazil. She had been hired by the Spaniards to protect their shipping from the attentions of the foreign corsairs. The *Speedwell*, of course, was just such a ship. Shelvocke, in his journal, voiced his indignation at being thwarted by a Frenchman, especially when the *Wise Solomon* fired three or four warning shots at her. 'This warmed me pretty much,' he wrote, 'and immediately brought to, to consult what was best to be done. I at first thought of showing my resentment in the highest degree, and thought it not impossible to have destroyed him, having converted the *Mercury* to a brander [fireship] who might, without any great difficulty, have roasted this insolent Frenchman.' However, discretion proving the better part of valour, Shelvocke 'clapped the helm a-weather and stood out again'.

Continuing the cruise to the northward, Shelvocke again sent away the *Mercury* to precede the *Speedwell* in the search for prizes. Hatley was placed in command of her, with Betagh as his second.

We have two completely differing accounts of what happened next. According to Shelvocke, the *Mercury* captured two prizes, one of which was worth 150,000 pieces of eight. 'Flushed with this success, Betagh prevailed upon Hatley, and the greatest part of the people with them not to join me again, telling them that there was sufficient for themselves to appear like gentlemen as long as they lived.' He goes on to describe how Betagh and his gang 'kept Hatley warm with liquor', prevailing upon him to sail to India, in which design they were frustrated by a Spanish warship which duly captured them. Betagh is then accused of treason, Shelvocke insisting that he signed on as an officer in the Spanish ships expressly for the purpose of bringing the *Speedwell* to book.

This story is patently false for it is quite certain that the

Spaniards lost no ship at this period worth 150,000 pieces of eight. Betagh's account, however, is little better. He states that Shelvocke was determined to 'lose' the *Mercury* and her crew, and having sent her off up the coast on her own, sailed away and left her to her fate. There might be some truth in this, for Hatley already knew too much for Shelvocke's peace of mind about how the owners were being cheated, while Shelvocke and Betagh had been at loggerheads since the start of the voyage. Also, of course, the fewer survivors at the end of the voyage, the larger the share of each. It is quite true, however, that after their capture Hatley was maltreated by the Spaniards while Betagh was highly favoured. Betagh's reason for this hardly rings true. He says that the Spaniards discovered on Hatley's person ninety-six gold *moidores*, the balance of the money he had taken out of the Portuguese trader off the Brazilian coast, and that this so enraged them that they threw him into prison. His own good fortune he attributes to a discussion with the Spanish captain in which they discovered that each was an admirer of Admiral Sir Charles Wager, at that time one of the Lords Commissioners of the Admiralty. It seems an insufficient reason for his lenient treatment while in the hands of his enemies.

Wherever the truth may lie between these two versions, the *Mercury* was undoubtedly captured by the Spanish and her crew made prisoner. Some months later they were sent overland across the South American continent and shipped to Cadiz, returning to England at the end of the war. They arrived in time for Betagh to add his account to the controversy which was then raging over Shelvocke's conduct of affairs.

Shelvocke, having lost the *Mercury*, took a small ship at anchor at Granchaco and then, hearing of a rich ship lying at Paita, continued his voyage to the northward until he came abreast the town. There was indeed a ship lying there, but she proved to be far from rich, being laden with nothing but timber and jerked beef. Beyond the ship, however, lay the town, and Shelvocke determined to make an attempt at capturing it. He landed with forty-six men at his heels, to find the whole place completely deserted. They spent a couple of days searching for anything of value to bring off to the ship, but there was nothing there beyond a useful store of foodstuffs and 'some pans to cook it in'.

An offer to ransom the town for 10,000 pieces of eight received the same dilatory treatment as usual, and Shelvocke's threat to burn the place if the money was not forthcoming provoked a reply from the Governor to the effect that he could hardly care less, since it was high time the town was rebuilt. The ransom, of course, was not produced at the expiration of the time allowed and Shelvocke put this city to the torch. Consisting mainly of wooden houses, it burned merrily.

The sound of gunfire from the *Speedwell* brought Shelvocke and his men down to the shore, to discover a Spanish 'warship' lying in the entrance of the harbour. Shelvocke's account of his desperate battle with her is certainly exaggerated, for she was not one of the regular ships used for the suppression of buccaneering. She was more in the nature of an auxiliary, manned almost entirely with negroes and Indians, and it was always difficult to make those races face up to gunfire. That the *Speedwell* managed to get out of harbour relatively undamaged, and with no man either killed or wounded, is evidence enough of the quality of the enemy.

Safely out of Paita, the bows of the *Speedwell* were turned towards Juan Fernandez, where it was decided to lay up for a period. Shelvocke's latest adventures along the coast had alarmed the Spanish, and it was certain that no ship of any consequence would be allowed to sail until it was thought that the seas were once more free of buccaneers. To lie low in Juan Fernandez for a few months would not only tempt the Spanish shipping out once more, it would also give an opportunity of a welcome recuperation to the crew of the

Speedwell, who were now beginning to grow sickly.

The island was reached on 6 May and most of the crew put ashore in tents to recover their health. Three weeks later, in a violent storm of wind, the *Speedwell* was driven ashore on to the rocks, where she pounded badly and quickly sank. Only one man was lost in the wreck, but what worried Shelvocke more was that most of the money and prize goods captured so far in the voyage now lay beneath the waves. He did, however, manage to save 1,100 dollars which he kept in his cabin and brought ashore with him, together with some bars of virgin silver and a silver dish weighing seventy-five ounces.

After two weeks of useless self-commiseration, Shelvocke at last came to his senses. He succeeded in persuading the men to begin the building of a boat, partly from the timbers of the wrecked *Speedwell*, partly from trees growing on the island. And in spite of the many difficulties and an almost continuous state of mutiny among the men, a boat of sorts was built and successfully launched in a little under four months.

If the troubles in building the boat were great, those of the mutiny were greater. Again we have only Shelvocke's word for this part of the story, and again it does not entirely ring true. According to his journal 'my officers deserted from my conversation to herd with the meanest of the ship's company', and they allied themselves to 'one Morphew, who both made and mended their shoes before the *Speedwell* was lost, to be their champion and speaker'. We cannot know how much of the truth Shelvocke is telling in this description of the affairs upon the island, but we do know that he signed new articles under which the owners were deprived of all their share in the venture, that he agreed to an immediate division of the rescued booty in which his share was six times that of the others, and that he agreed to a division of the muskets among the men instead of keeping them in his own hands. It is true that he says he was forced to agree to all these measures, but in the light of his subsequent conduct it seems unlikely that he made any considerable attempt to resist the men's demands. His signature of the new articles, under which he was a considerable gainer, is a damning piece of evidence against him.

Twelve of his men either refused, or were prevented from leaving the island with him when at last the little *Recovery*, which was the name he gave his newly-built boat, finally put to sea. Shelvocke admits that he 'found means to manage them, and took all their arms, ammunition, and the rest of their plunder from them, and threatened that if they were found within musket shot of our work or tents, that they should be treated as enemies'. With these twelve were left behind an equivalent number of unfortunate negroes and Indians, for whom there was no room in the boat. What was the fate of these two dozen men, English, negro, and Indian, is not known.

Having no salt on the island for preserving meat, the *Recovery* was victualled with some hundreds of smoked conger eels and 'four live hogs which were fed all the time on putrified carcasses of seals'. They had one cask of water, 'of which not a drop was to be had without sucking it out through the barrel of a musket'. One gun had been salved from the *Speedwell*, and for ammunition they had 'two round shot, a few chain bolts and boltheads, the clapper of the *Speedwell*'s bell, and some bags of beach stones to serve for partridge'.

For six weeks the little *Recovery* roamed the sea, picking up here and there from the coast a small quantity of food as a variation from the diet of conger eels. Finally, at the entrance to Pisco Harbour, they captured a ship of 200 tons, laden with pitch, tar, copper, and plank. She was the *Jesús Maria*, and although her captain offered to ransom her for 16,000 dollars, she was worth more than that to Shelvocke and his men as an exchange for the *Recovery*. 'Now,' he remarks, 'we had room enough to enjoy ourselves in some cleanliness at least, an article we had been perfect strangers to ever since we had departed from the island of Juan Fernandez.'

Steering up to the northward, Shelvocke decided once more to attack the town of Paita. He had only forty men now left out of his original crew, but the *Jesús Maria* was a Spanish ship and by flying a Spanish ensign, Shelvocke reckoned he could get into the harbour without arousing suspicion and capture the town by a *coup de main*. It turned out as he hoped, and his boat carrying the landing party of twenty-four men reached the shore 'without giving the least umbrage to the inhabitants, who were so thoroughly unconcerned that when my people landed they found the children playing on the beach'.

The town, however, produced nothing of value beyond a few bales of coarse cloth, and oddments of a similar nature. 'But though we had so little success in our land enterprise, we took a booty as we lay at anchor in the ship, which might have been made valuable if discretion and prudence had the management of it, for want of which it proved a troublesome incendiary.' This was fifty jars of Peruvian wine and brandy, and to a crew so long starved of liquor it was probably as eagerly appreciated as a substantial haul of pieces of eight.

If Paita had been captured in the morning by an English stratagem, it was recaptured in the evening by a Spanish one. Small groups of Spaniards came down from the hills in the dusk, and by shouting bogus orders to 'march a regiment to the left', to 'send 200 men to the right', and to 'attack in the centre', they so terrified the privateers that they bustled back to the ship without waiting to test the strength of the Spanish assault. Paita was recaptured by no more men than had taken it in the morning.

Shelvocke took the *Jesús Maria* northward to the Bay of Panama, anchoring off Gorgona Island for water. Here, by a majority vote of the crew, it was decided to abandon the cruise

and return by way of Asia. And in anticipation of this home-
ward voyage, Shelvocke changed the name of the ship from
the *Jesús Maria* to the *Happy Return*.

Judged only on the evidence of Shelvocke's journal, this
was an extraordinary decision. If he is to be believed, he had
taken no prize worth the name since leaving Juan Fernandez
and thus there could be nothing of value in the ship. In view
of the evidence which was later produced in the charge against
him, it is certain that in fact there was a very considerable
booty on board, and indeed the decision only makes sense if
this was so.

Two events put a stop to this plan. One was the action of
the minority of the crew who voted against return. They
bored holes in the bottom of the water-butts so that the
precious fresh water on board drained away. The other was
the wind, which blew fixedly from the west, a dead muzzler
for a passage to China. Both these circumstances forced Shelvocke across to the Mexican coast, where at Quibo he was able
to fill up with fresh water again. Here, too, the last of the
Peruvian wine and brandy captured at Paita was reached, a
relief to Shelvocke, one imagines, 'for while they had anything to drink I judged it unsafe to lay my head on my pillow,
which almost wearied me out of my life'. Again belief is
strained, for at the start of the cruise Shelvocke was a
notorious drinker, and leopards do not change their spots as
easily as that.

A few days later, on 25 January 1721, a sail was sighted
from the *Jesús Maria*. Recognising her as 'Europe built, and
fearing she was one of the enemy's men-of-war, I clapped on
a wind, and in half an hour it fell calm. Soon after we saw a
boat rowing towards us, which proved to be the *Success*'s
pinnace, commanded by Mr Davidson, their first lieutenant.
My first interview with him was attended by an astonishment
equal on both sides; he could hardly believe that he saw us
in so mean a condition, and I could scarce believe that the

Success (if in being) had been all this while wandering up and down these seas'.

For Clipperton, meanwhile, the luck had turned. After his early run of successes he had experienced nothing but set-backs. After the loss of Serjeantson and his men in the *Rosario* he had captured but few prizes, and these of no worth, except for a ship called the *Prince Eugene*, which had on board the President of Panama, who was then the Marquis de Villa Roche, and his family. These of course were prisoners of quality and thus probably worth a substantial ransom. Clipperton at the time may possibly have rubbed his hands at the thought of the dollars that the Marquis and his family would bring, but he certainly lived to curse the day on which he captured him. His wits were not equal to those of his prisoner, and he was double-crossed all along the line.

Putting in at the island of Velas, in search of fresh provisions for the crew, Clipperton allowed the Marquis and his wife to go ashore to arrange a ransom, leaving their child in the *Success* as a hostage. They returned with the Spanish Governor of the island and, having agreed on a substantial sum as ransom, the wife and child were released, the Marquis being held. At the same time, on the Marquis's guarantee of prompt payment, the *Prince Eugene* was restored to her captain and allowed to sail to the mainland with the remainder of the Spanish prisoners. Of course the ransom money never arrived. The first part of Villa Roche's plan had succeeded; his wife and child, the Spanish prisoners, and the ship were free. Though he himself was still a prisoner, he had already a design for fooling Clipperton later through which he hoped to obtain his own freedom at no cost to himself.

At the same time he set out to suborn the crew and incite them to mutiny. He succeeded in depressing them considerably by his accounts of the measures being taken by the authorities to hunt them down, and stressed the precariousness of their position alone in this hostile ocean. He told them, too, that if they deposed Clipperton from the command, they would receive more lenient treatment on their inevitable capture. His words took root, and poor Clipperton found himself facing a serious mutiny. Villa Roche found two willing accomplices in James Roch, the ship's corporal of marines, and Joseph Maynard, a boatswain's mate. A plan was formed to maroon Clipperton and the officers on Lobos Island, to shoot all others of the crew who would not join the mutiny, and to run off with the ship. The conspiracy was discovered just in time, and Roch and Maynard found themselves lashed to the grating to receive four dozen each with the cat o' nine tails. For a time it discouraged any more thoughts of mutiny though it did little to raise the morale of the ship's company. And their morale needed raising badly.

It was obviously time for Clipperton to be off, for only with the *Success* at sea could he really keep control of the crew. Abandoning any lingering hope he may have had that the ransom money agreed by the Marquis would be paid, he set a course to the southward in the hope that the luck would change. His plan now was to attack the town of Coquimbo, in the expectation of not only being able to hold it to ransom but also of finding some shipping in the harbour. It was a new success that was most needed to hold his crew together, rather than the flogging of malefactors, and Clipperton had sense enough to realise it.

On the way south he took a small prize with a useful cargo of tobacco, sugar, and cloth. Again Clipperton was faced with a dilemma, whether to send a prize crew on board or to take out of her such of the cargo as he might later sell and then let her go. He chose the former and sent across Lieutenant Milne and twelve men. With his new prize in company, he pressed on for Coquimbo.

As the *Success* opened the harbour, the masts of several ships at anchor were plainly visible. No doubt many English hearts began to beat a little faster at the thought of rich pickings at last. But as the *Success* stood in towards the shore, it was noticed that three of the ships were cutting their cables and loosing their topsails. And they were, moreover, recognised by the cut of their sails as Spanish warships. Clipperton turned and ran, and was only saved when the mizzen-topmast of one of the pursuers carried away under the press of sail she was carrying. Less fortunate, however, was Clipperton's prize. She was retaken, and with her the lieutenant and men whom Clipperton had sent on board as prize crew.

In those days, when the treatment accorded to prisoners, and especially privateering prisoners, captured in those waters was arbitrary and savage, it is pleasant to be able to record that, in the case of Lieutenant Milne and his men, their treatment was extraordinarily handsome. The Spanish captain was Don Blas de Lesso, twenty years later to achieve a more lasting fame as Governor of Cartagena when Admiral Vernon attacked it in 1742. At first annoyed to discover that he had captured only the prize and not the *Success*, he used the flat of his sword on Milne and had him thrown below decks, where he was stripped and robbed by the Spanish sailors. Later, realising what he had done, he sent for Milne and apologised for his behaviour. He ordered a new suit of clothes to be made for him, kept him at his table during the return to Coquimbo, arranged a free passage for him and his men to Panama, gave him a jar of wine and a jar of brandy for his use on the passage, and presented him with 200 pieces of eight for his own use. Milne and all twelve men duly reached England in safety.

This last setback off Coquimbo 'revived the ill humours among Clipperton's men, who did not indeed plot again but became exceedingly dejected'. On Clipperton himself it had an even worse effect. He began to seek for consolation in the bottle, 'and as this vice generally grows upon people under misfortunes, he grew at last to such a pitch that he was hardly ever cool or sober. And though it is true that drunkenness is rather an aggravation than an excuse, yet if we consider that this poor man was a mere sailor and had not had the benefit of a liberal education, that he fell into it purely through despair, and that he still showed upon all occasions great marks of a humane and generous disposition, together with an inflexible honesty in regard to his owners' concerns, we cannot help pitying him because it is impossible to say how far human nature is able to bear, without the help of certain supports, such a heavy load of misfortunes as this poor gentleman met with'. Thus the Reverend John Harris, that worthy divine who spent more time in collecting the journals of sea voyages than ever he did over the souls of his parishioners.

Having achieved nothing to the southward, the *Success* turned her bows north. Food was now running short and Clipperton was forced to make Cocos Island on his way in order to lay in an additional store. Here they found good supplies of fish, fowls, eggs, turtle, and coconuts, and a month later, well victualled and with the crew in good health, they set sail and steered for the coast of Mexico. The time of year was approaching when the great annual galleon from Manila was due, though any hope that the little *Success*, alone and undermanned, could capture her was indeed slight.

The *Success*, in fact, was more undermanned than she need have been, for the Marquis de Villa Roche had been busy again at Cocos Island. He had persuaded eleven men to desert the ship there, promising to send a ship for them as soon as he regained his liberty. Of course he never did; and one must suppose that these wretched men lived out the rest of their lives in this unfrequented island just below the equator. There is no record of them being captured and taken to Lima, and the English among them never reached home.

Closing the Mexican coast, a sail was sighted and Clipperton had the pinnace manned and sent in chase. Those on board the *Success* were encouraged to see that she struck her colours as the pinnace closed her, and there were hopes that she might prove rich enough to compensate for the long period of ill fortune which the *Success* had experienced. It was not to be. The prize which they had captured was the *Jesús Maria*, and in her of course was Shelvocke and what was left of the crew of the *Speedwell*.

So, nearly two years after leaving Plymouth, the two captains met up again. As one might expect, there are two versions of what transpired during the few days they remained in company, one by Clipperton, one by Shelvocke. Clipperton, having been appointed in command of the whole expedition, attempted to take Shelvocke under his command in order to have the benefit of a joint force in the hoped-for meeting with the Manila galleon. The original orders, however, named the *Speedwell* as the second ship, and Shelvocke countered this suggestion by pointing out that the *Speedwell* had disappeared and that since his ship was now the *Jesús Maria* the original orders were no longer binding upon him. Clipperton then tried another tack. He knew the state of affairs on board the *Jesús Maria*, for Hendry, originally appointed as agent for the owners but relieved in that position by Shelvocke and made purser instead, had rowed over to the *Success* and refused to go back. He of course could give first-hand evidence of what had taken place on board the *Speedwell* at St Catharine's right at the start of the voyage, when the owners' agreement had been replaced by the new set of rules. Clipperton, still anxious for a joint attack on the Manila ship, therefore proposed to Shelvocke that 'if he and his crew would refund the money shared among themselves contrary to the Articles with the owners, and agree to put it in a joint stock, then all faults should be forgot, both companies would unite, and proceed to cruise for the Acapulco ship'. Not unexpectedly, perhaps, Shelvocke refused to entertain such a proposal.

Shelvocke, in his account of the meeting, mentions nothing

of these two proposals of Clipperton's. Instead he surrounds the few days in which the two ships remained in company with a long vituperation of Clipperton for deserting him, criticisms of his past exploits in which he accuses him of mishandling his attacks and losing for the owners thereby hundreds of thousands of pieces of eight, and veiled suggestions that his earlier decision to send Mitchell to Brazil with the captured goods was in reality an attempt to divert them to his own pocket. Since, when he wrote this account, Clipperton was already dead and unable to reply, he may have thought he would be safe enough. What he did not know was that Taylor's journal was even then in the hands of Betagh, or that a second journal kept in the *Success* was extant, although this in fact did not appear for another twenty years.

Clipperton, discovering that Shelvocke was too elusive a man to be held to any agreed plan of action, abruptly squared away on 7 March for the East Indies. It was already past the season for the sailing of the treasure galleon, and it was clear to him that he would find nothing but trouble by remaining with Shelvocke. The long-promised ransom money for Villa Roche had, of course, not arrived and so the Marquis remained a prisoner on board the *Success*.

Clipperton drank heavily all the way across the Pacific. The deadly scurvy hit the *Success* hard, six of the small crew dying of it and the remainder being so weak that they could hardly work the ship. In this pitiful condition they reached Guam, Clipperton too drunk in the cabin to bring the ship into harbour. Davidson, the senior lieutenant, brought her in.

It was not an auspicious moment for a British privateer to arrive. The war with Spain was over, and not unnaturally there were hard feelings ashore at the sight of a British ship in a Spanish harbour heavily laden with Spanish treasure and goods captured in what were still thought to be exclusively Spanish waters. But for the moment Clipperton was in a strong position. He still had Villa Roche on board, and the

Spanish Governor ashore was unlikely to take extreme measures with so important a hostage still in enemy hands. He agreed to trade, and the much-needed fresh provisions began to arrive on board in exchange for arms and ammunition, at that time the chief needs of the Spanish garrison.

At the same time, talks were opened about ransoming the Marquis. Eventually a sum was agreed and guaranteed by the Governor. It must have appeared a fool-proof case to Clipperton, but he should have known Villa Roche better by now. He made the mistake of sending the Marquis ashore, accompanied by the owners' agent, Mr Godfrey, and the surgeon, Mr Pritty, who were to return with the cash. He even gave the Marquis a five-gun salute on his leaving the ship.

With Villa Roche in his hands, the Governor's tone changed. He at once cut off all supplies of fresh provisions, demanded the return of the Marquis's jewels and any church plate which had been captured, more powder and shot, and two negroes as slaves. At the same time he informed Clipperton that he was holding Godfrey and Pritty as hostages for the quick acceptance of his demands. More sinister still, he had a battery of guns erected at the rocky point which guarded the entrance to the harbour.

Clipperton's reply was that he would demolish the port, burn all ships in harbour, and carry his war throughout the Spanish possessions in those seas. This, of course, was bluff, and the Spanish Governor knew it was bluff. He called it, and all the *Success* could do was to weigh her anchor and try to fight her way out past the Spanish battery to the open sea, leaving Godfrey and Pritty behind in the hands of the Spaniards.

She was fired on as soon as she began to move. Below, in his cabin, Clipperton had reached the climax of a particularly vicious drinking bout, singing at the top of his voice and incapable of movement. Davidson, the first lieutenant, was killed early on in the engagement, and command of the

Success fell to Cook, the next senior. It says much for the punctilio of the period that, in the midst of the battle, Cook would not accept the post until all the officers on board had signed a paper indemnifying him from personal responsibility for his actions in this tight corner.

There was no wind when the *Success* weighed. They tried to tow her out with one of the ship's boats, but a lucky Spanish shot sank it before they were half-way to the entrance. The *Success*, unable to steer for lack of wind, drifted on to the rocks below the Spanish battery and lay there immobile, a sitting target for the enemy's guns. All attempts to tow her off failed.

One by one the ship's anchors were laid out ahead and the hawser brought to the capstan to try to pull her off. They moved her a little, but not enough to bring her into deep water. When all the anchors and hawsers were gone, they used guns as anchors and the mainmast shrouds as hawsers. Finally, two days later, they got the *Success* afloat and won their way out to the sea. 'Thus they lost both their bow anchors and cables, the stern and kedge anchors, four hawsers, four of their lower-deck guns, nineteen barrels of powder, two men killed and six wounded, having stood no less than fifty hours a fair mark for the enemy to fire at. At ten in the forenoon they brought-to, and began to splice their rigging, not a rope of which escaped a shot; as for the masts and yards they were all severely peppered, and the carpenters worked all night stopping the holes in the ship's bottom.'

After a precarious voyage in her shattered condition, the *Success* reached the Chinese port of Amoy, where Clipperton soon found himself in trouble with the customs. 'The Chinese, in general, are very justly reputed the craftiest people in the world, and it is an invariable maxim of their policy to choose the cunningest man they can find to execute the office of Hoppo [Master-General of the Customs], and after saying this we need not descend to the particular character of the man

Captain Clipperton had to deal with. I shall only add that the people of Amoy, in general, are thought to be the least nice in points of honour, or principles of honesty, in China.' As a sample of their 'principles of honesty' Clipperton found himself presented with a bill for 1,700 dollars, or £400 sterling, for port charges, which he was forced to pay in cash without an appeal being allowed.

At Amoy, Cook revealed himself in his true colours. After being elected to command the ship in the departure from Guam, he began to encourage the crew in opposition to Clipperton, and in China he engineered the first real mutiny which Clipperton had to face. On the grounds that the *Success* was now unseaworthy, he demanded the immediate distribution of the prize money, claiming for himself thirty shares as acting second captain. When Clipperton refused, pointing to the owners' rules which laid down that the money was not to be divided until the return to England, Cook called in the assistance of the Chinese authorities ashore, who were never backward in making trouble whenever foreign ships were concerned. Clipperton found a detachment of Chinese soldiers arriving on board with orders from the port authorities to pay out the prize money at once. Since he could not argue with muskets, he was forced to comply. But even as he did so, and perhaps anticipating new and exaggerated demands once the precedent had been established, he arranged to safeguard the owners' share by shipping it home on a Portuguese East Indiaman. Between £6,000 and £7,000 were transferred to the ship *Queen of Angels* and consigned to London: showing no profit to the owners, it is true, but at any rate enough to cover their expenses in fitting out the *Success*. The *Queen of Angels* unfortunately caught fire at Rio de Janeiro during her passage to Europe, and as a result of the costs of salvage the money which Clipperton had sent home had dwindled to no more than £1,800 by the time the owners received it.

Cook, backed up by the crew, refused to allow Clipperton

to include the names of those killed or taken prisoner in the distribution of the prize money. Excluded, too, were Hendry and Dodd, two officers of Shelvocke's who had elected to come home in the *Success* rather than continue in the *Jesús María* at the meeting of the two ships. The division was therefore made, Clipperton receiving £1,466-10s as his share, Cook getting £733-5s and the remainder lesser amounts down to £97-15s-4d, which was the share of a deck-hand.

Leaving Amoy, Clipperton took the *Success* to Macao, the centre of the Portuguese East India trade, with the intention of proceeding from there up-river to Canton, where the British East India Company had its 'factory'. Cook, in order to justify his actions in forcing the premature division of the prize money, now needed to have the ship condemned as unfit for the voyage home, for only that could provide an adequate reason to the owners for breaking into the prize fund before the expedition returned home. He had no difficulty in persuading the crew to back him up, and when the first survey of the ship pronounced her seaworthy, it was not too difficult to get the Chinese authorities ashore to order a second one. As a result of this second survey, the *Success* was condemned, and in a forced sale to the Chinese authorities themselves, fetched no more than 4,000 dollars, a fraction of her true value. As if to prove his confidence in her, Clipperton contracted with the new owners for a passage in her to Batavia, and from there shipped in a Dutch East Indiaman for Holland. He reached his home in Galway in June, 1722, only to die a week later. As his epitaph, one may best quote the words of John Harris. 'It may indeed be objected that, on his arrival in Holland, he ought to have returned thence to London and given the proprietors the best account in his power of the undertaking and of his management. But when we reflect first on his sending home their moiety of the profits in the Portuguese ship, which by the way very nearly reimbursed the expense they had been at in fitting-out the *Success*, the purchase money of the ship being taken in, and if we next advert to the weak condition he was in when he went to Galway, where he did not live a week, we may very well excuse him. He might very probably have hoped that the comfort of seeing his wife and children might contribute to restore his health and enable him to make a voyage to London when in a condition to settle his accounts; or if he found himself so very low as absolutely to despair of recovering at all, it was very natural for him to desire the satisfaction of seeing his family in his last moments. But above all we ought to remember that it was not in his power to do more for the proprietors than he had done, and therefore he was at the greater liberty to take all the care he could of his private concerns. It is a very easy matter to censure the conduct, blacken the memory, and misrepresent the actions of a poor man in his grave, but from the plain and faithful account of all his transactions I dare say every impartial reader will agree that he was an object of pity rather than resentment, since after so many long voyages in which he suffered so many and so great hardships, he died at last of a broken heart with a broken fortune.'

The rest of the *Success*'s crew found their own way home. Twenty of them paid six dollars for a passage to Canton in a Chinese boat, 'and of this number Mr Taylor, the mate, was one. But before they came to sail he had a foresight of the danger and therefore chose to lose his money and wait for another conveniency. And he had reason to look upon this loss as a piece of frugality, since the next news they heard was that the boat had been taken by a pirate and that most of the people had lost their things'. We can be thankful today for Taylor's 'foresight', for without it we would not have had his journal, and as a result would have known less of Clipperton than we do.

What happened to the nineteen who 'lost their things' is not known; presumably they were able to work their passage

231

home in returning East Indiaman. Those who escaped the
pirate were charged five pounds each for a passage, 'being a
very great favour'. By the end of 1722 they were all home,
and on the whole with very little to show for their four years
of toil and hardship.

But to return to the *Jesús Maria*. With the departure of
the *Success* for China, Shelvocke once more found himself
alone. Whether this was by design or not, we cannot say,
though in his journal he describes, in a considerable state of
self-pity, the intolerable hardships to which he was put by
what he calls his desertion by Clipperton. Yet he is so
obviously a bare-faced rogue that it is difficult to believe his
remarks. So many assertions in his journal can be so easily
disproved.

He put in to the roadstead at Sansonate and had the good
fortune to take a sizeable ship named the *Sacra Familia*. Being
a better ship than the *Jesús Maria*, he and his men moved
into her. But even as he did so, he received a letter from the
Spanish Governor ashore informing him that articles of peace
had been signed between Britain and Spain, and demanding
the restitution of the *Sacra Familia*.

Shelvocke for some reason disputed this statement, giving
as his reason his inability to understand Spanish. He also
refused to deliver up his prize, and was at once declared a
common pirate by the Governor as the result. And then
occurred an extraordinary act on Shelvocke's part. Having
virtually defied the Governor, he ordered Brooks, his lieutenant, and five of his men to row ashore under a flag of truce
to trade for provisions. It may only be a coincidence that
Brooks and Shelvocke had quarrelled earlier in the cruise at
Juan Fernandez, over the discovery of Clipperton's message,
and later again at the same island over so stupid a reason that
the former would not drink the health of the Old Pretender
on the anniversary of his landing in Scotland. Whether this
had anything to do with it or not, it was certain that Shel-

vocke, by ordering him to row ashore, was sending him to certain captivity. He did in fact send him to his death, for Brooks and his men were never seen alive again.

Proceeding northwards, the *Sacra Familia* had the luck to run into a small ship well laden with dried beef and pork and live hogs. This was indeed a welcome capture, for Shelvocke could now provision his ship plentifully for the forthcoming voyage across the Pacific. And three days later an even greater stroke of luck came his way. Still northward bound, and of course oblivious to the ending of the war, he took a fine prize. She was the *Concepcion de Recouva* and had a number of important passengers on board. In his journal Shelvocke gives her lading as 'flour, loaves of sugar, bales of boxes of marmalade, jars of preserved peaches, grapes, limes, etc.' In fact it was the 'etc.' which was the important part. It consisted of 108,636 pieces of eight [dollars] in coin, equivalent to £25,348, and this large sum of money never found its way into the accounts of the owners.

All that Shelvocke needed now was water, and he continued his journey north to the Californian coast to get it. He put in at Porto Seguro and the friendly Indians ashore there soon filled his water-casks for him. And while there he made a discovery of considerable interest. 'The soil,' he wrote, 'is a rich black mould which, as you turn it fresh up to the sun, appears as if intermingled with gold dust, some of which we endeavoured to crush and purify from the dirt. But though we were a little prejudiced against the thoughts that it could be possible that this metal should be so promiscuously and universally mingled with common earth, yet we endeavoured to cleanse and wash the earth from some of it, and the more we did the more it appeared like gold. But in order to be farther satisfied, I brought some of it away which we lost in our confusions in China.' This was a pity, for had Shelvocke succeeded in getting it safely home to England, he might have been able to anticipate the Californian gold rush of 1849 by well

233

over a century. As it happened Shelvocke was so demonstrably a liar by the time his journal was published that no one was prepared to believe in the truth of this particular statement.

With his total crew now reduced to thirty-nine souls, Shelvocke set out on his trans-Pacific passage. As in the *Success* before him, scurvy attacked his company, 'which was undoubtedly in the greatest measure owing to the quantities of sweetmeats they were continually devouring'. Six men died on the passage, and when at last the *Sacra Familia* reached the Canton river, there were no more than seven men strong enough to handle the sails.

As in the case of Cook before him, Shelvocke's need was to get rid of the ship before dividing the prize fund. It was, perhaps, not quite so vital a procedure in his case, since he could still contend that his liability to the owners came to an end with the loss of their ship, the *Speedwell*, though the fact that he still flourished his Admiralty Letter of Marque made this contention untenable in law. There was, however, still some lucrative work to be done before getting rid of the ship. Shelvocke came to a fraudulent arrangement with the Chinese authorities under which a charge of £2,000 for harbour dues was charged on the *Sacra Familia*.[1] Over a half of this found its way back into his own pocket. Next, the ship was sold for a nominal £700. It is difficult to accept this as a true sale, for when one adds together the money Shelvocke received out of the prize distribution and his share of the charge for harbour dues, the sum is still a good deal short of the amount he brought back to England with him.

With the ship sold, the prize money on board was divided up among the thirty-three survivors of the voyage. Shelvocke's share was 11,325 dollars, or £2,642-10s. sterling, while the grommet, or ship's boy, drew 943 dollars, the equivalent of

1. It is interesting to note that the *Cadogan*, an East India Company ship lying at Canton at the same time, was charged £320 for harbour dues. She was twice the tonnage of the *Sacra Familia*.

£202-4s-2d sterling. Shelvocke's son, whose rank in the distribution list is curiously entered as 'nothing', collected no
less than £660.

In this final distribution Shelvocke once more ran true to
form. As well as cheating his owners, he cheated his own ship's
company, for 10,032 dollars were not entered in the prize
fund. This sum was the value of 627 double doubloons in
gold, which Shelvocke took out of the *Concepción* and hid
from the crew.

Shelvocke and his son took passage home in the East Indiaman *Cadogan*, and after an unadventurous voyage reached
Dover in July, 1722. 'Thus ended a long fatiguing voyage of
three years, seven months, and eleven days, after having sailed
considerably more than round the circumference of the globe,
and having undergone a great variety of troubles and hardships, both by sea and land, and made some discoveries which
it is hoped are worthy the notice of the curious.'

Shelvocke reached London with a little over £7,000, which
he succeeded in putting away in a place of safety before being
arrested. The two charges against him was piracy, preferred by
the Portuguese and Spanish ambassadors. They referred to
his plundering of the Portuguese ship off the coast of Brazil
at the start of the voyage and his capture of the *Sacra Familia*
after the cessation of hostilities between Britain and Spain.
The news of his later action against the *Concepción* had not
yet reached the Spanish ambassador. In the trial of the action
it was alleged that the *Sacra Familia*'s cargo was valued at
100,000 pieces of eight, but no doubt this was wildly inflated
for the purpose of the trial. Shelvocke was acquitted on both
counts for lack of evidence, neither of the ambassadors having
taken the precaution of bringing witnesses to England.

No sooner freed on this charge of piracy than Shelvocke
was re-arrested at the instance of the owners and charged
with fraud. He was committed to the King's Bench prison,
but managed to escape before the trial could be begun. He

fled the country to France, presumably with his £7,000, and spent the next three or four years of his life in writing his account of the voyage. As we have seen, he lays the blame for its failure entirely on Clipperton, and had it not been for the journal which George Taylor kept in the *Success*, he might have succeeded in making people believe his story. It was Betagh's account, based largely on Taylor's journal and published two years after Shelvocke's, which finally made clear his own sorry behaviour throughout the whole expedition. History does not record his end, but it is known that he was still in hiding abroad in 1728. Both father and son are buried in the church of St Nicholas, Deptford. On his tombstone the following eulogium of Captain Shelvocke was inscribed before it was destroyed by a bomb: 'He performed a voyage round the globe of the world, which he most wonderfully, and to the great loss of the Spaniards, completed. . . . He was a gentleman of great abilities in his profession, and allowed to have been one of the bravest and most accomplished seamen of his time.' Never was the truth of Dr Johnson's dictum that 'in lapidary inscriptions a man is not upon oath' better illustrated. It is an interesting point that it was his son George, who had accompanied him as a passenger on the expedition, who arranged all the details for the publication of the book in England. The son, in fact, turned out better than the father, ending his career as secretary of the General Post Office.

The most damaging charge against Shelvocke's behaviour on this voyage is one made by Betagh, and repeated by so objective a chronicler as the Rev John Harris, that Shelvocke deliberately abandoned a large proportion of his crew at various stages of the voyage in order that there should be fewer to qualify in the final share-out. It is true enough that out of a total of 106 men on board at the start of the voyage, no more than thirty-three were still there on arrival in China, a prodigious rate of loss. Shelvocke himself accuses most of them of desertion, but the actual circumstances of their departure makes this seem unlikely, for most of them were either ordered ashore by Shelvocke or sent by him cruising in small boats off the enemy coasts in South America. If Shelvocke genuinely thought that these subsidiary cruises could bring substantial results, then we must add foolishness to dishonesty as cardinal points in his character.

This voyage of the *Success* and the *Speedwell* was the last of the privateering voyages into the South Seas. With it, the game was played out, for when, some twenty years later, Britain and Spain were once again at war, it was the Royal Navy which was to take over the part. How well they were to play it is, however, no part of this story.

CHAPTER FOURTEEN

Epilogue

TO SEE THE VOYAGES AND ADVENTURES described in this book in a proper perspective, it is necessary both to look back to the attempts made by English and French seamen in the days of Drake to break down the Spanish monopoly in the Caribbean, and to look forward to the commercial war with Spain known as the War of Jenkins's Ear, in which naval power, rather than the unregulated efforts of private adventurers, was used to the same end. When the West Indies station was established and regular squadrons began to be sent out, to protect and further the interests of colonies settled by planters who owed no allegiance to Spain, the age of the buccaneers and the privateers was over. Only the pirates remained, and they were being rapidly swept off the seas.

As we have seen, a new area for buccaneering enterprise was found when Sir Henry Morgan opened the gate to the South Seas by his capture of Panama. Morgan was followed by men like Sharp, Dampier, Cowley, and hundreds more of the same type. The consequence was the same in the Pacific as in the Caribbean, since Spain claimed sovereignty over both seas. Since legitimate trade in this new sea was discouraged as vigorously as it had been in the West Indies, honest traders like Swan turned buccaneer as easily as had his predecessors in the Caribbean. The voyages of such men, and indeed the expert advice of some of them, resulted in the foundation of the notorious South Sea Company, which, however, was originally formed in good faith in the expectation that trade with South America would become possible. The long period of European wars, in which Spain was ever a principal enemy, effectively prevented any legitimate trade, so that the English company had to content itself with its interests in the Atlantic, rather than the Pacific, until the bubble burst. As we have seen, the similar French company was more active, because France was nominally in alliance with Spain, but that, too, vanished in a financial crash largely due to Spanish intransigence, with the result that the Pacific became once more a closed sea to all shipping save that of Spain.

The historical importance of the buccaneers and privateers lay as much in their narratives as in the exploits they performed. The popularity of the writings of such men as Dampier and Woodes Rogers directed the attention of the public to the last area of the surface of the globe which could be explored by the sailing ship. Collections of voyages, such as that begun by Hack and continued on a massive scale by Harris and Churchill, gave wide publicity to an area which seemed to offer infinite possibilities in the form of the mythical Terra Australis Incognita, which had figured on so many maps from the days of Mercator. In the case of Woodes Rogers, there can be little doubt that it was his experience as a privateer that directly inspired the conception of the voyage of Commodore Anson round the world in 1740-44. That was the last voyage in the long history of the search for the Manila galleon, which goes back to Drake and Cavendish. What is new and significant about Anson's voyage was that it was made by a naval and not by a private squadron. As regards long voyages, the days of the private men-of-war and of the individual adventurer were over. The work of searching for the supposed continent, which resulted in the charting of the Pacific, was to be undertaken by official expeditions set on foot by the Admiralties of Britain and France. Byron, Wallis, and Cook, Bougainville and La Pérouse, cannot be classed with the earlier privateers because their origins and motives were entirely different; but they all had in mind the experience of their buccaneering predecessors in those seas and all used the information which they had collected.

The literary influence of the seamen whose stories we have told in these pages has been even more lasting than the economic or cartographical. Their narratives began that boom in the picaresque sea adventure story which Swift and Defoe (always the best thermometer of popular taste) first exploited. Among the great classics of the nation, they inspired such masterpieces as *Gulliver's Travels, Robinson Crusoe, The Swiss Family Robinson,* and *Treasure Island,* as well as a host of lesser books in all languages. And where the novelist led, the poet followed. It was during a walk over the Quantocks in the summer of 1797 that Wordsworth mentioned to Coleridge that he had been reading Shelvocke's book and had been struck by the account of Hatley shooting the albatross south of Cape Horn. And in *The Rime of the Ancient Mariner* it fell to Coleridge to capture in a stanza whatever there is of magic in the whole swashbuckling story:

'The fair breeze blew, the white foam flew,
The furrow followed free:
We were the first that ever burst
Into that silent sea.'

That, perhaps, was the most remarkable achievement of all those recorded of the Brethren of the Coast.

List of Sources

CHAPTER ONE

THE BRETHREN OF THE COAST

Apart from the editions of Esquemeling mentioned in the text, the chief contemporary accounts of the buccaneers are: Père Labat, *Nouveau voyage aux isle de l'Amérique* (1722); J. B. Dutertre *Histoire Générale des Antilles* (1667); Père de Charlevoix, *Histoire de l'Isle Espagnole* (1730); *Memoirs of a Buccaneer* (Le Golif) ed. t'Serstevens (1952). The most scholarly general account is that by C. H. Haring, *The Buccaneers in the West Indies* (1910), which is based on the Calendars of State Papers, Colonial, and on the Sloane MSS in the British Museum. See also M. Besson, *Les Frères de la Côte* (1928); James Burney, *Chronological History of the Discoveries in the South Seas*, Vol. IV (1816); J. F. Jameson, *Privateering and Piracy in the Colonial Period* (Boston, 1923); M. Vriejman, *L'Identité d'Esquemeling* (Paris, 1934); J. R. Moore, *Defoe in the Pillory* (Indiana, 1939).

CHAPTER TWO

SIR HENRY MORGAN

Of the innumerable biographies of Sir Henry Morgan, only one is reliable – that by Brig.-Gen. E. A. Cruikshank, published in Canada in 1935. Contemporary sources are plentiful: the relevant volumes of the State Papers, Colonial; C. Leslie, *A New History of Jamaica* (1740); the account of Morgan's raid in Esquemeling and in the *Voyages of Capt. Barth. Sharp* (1684); Sir Hans Sloane, *Voyage to the West Indies* (1707). The most important unpublished source is W. Beeston's journal, British Museum, Add. MSS, 12,430. Use has also been made of F. Cundall's *The Governors Of Jamaica*, 1936.

CHAPTER THREE

THE FIRST INVASION OF THE SOUTH SEAS

Detailed references to the various MSS in the Admiralty Library, the British Museum and the National Maritime Museum which describe Sharp's voyage as a whole or in part will be found in an article contributed by C. Lloyd to *The Mariner's Mirror* in 1956 – there are no less than three Sharp MSS, two by Ringrose, two by Cox and two by Coxon. Printed versions of the voyage include the second (1684) edition of Esquemeling, which contains the account signed W. D.; *The Voyages and Adventures of Capt. Barth. Sharp and others in the South Seas*, printed by Philip Ayres or P.A. in 1684; the second volume of Esquemeling, 1685, contains Ringrose's narrative; William Hack's *Collection of Original Voyages*, 1699, contains an edited version of Sharp's MSS.

CHAPTER FOUR

WHAT HAPPENED TO SHARP

As for Chapter III. On Hack's *Waggoner*, see E. Lynam, *The Mapmaker's Art*, and R. A. Skelton in *British Museum Quarterly*, 1955. On St Lo, see R. D. Merriman in *The Mariner's Mirror*, 1945. On the Phips treasure hunt, see C. H. Karraker, *The Hispaniola Treasure* (Pennsylvania Univ. Press, 1834). The trial of Sharp will be found in the Public Records Office, H.C.A. 1/51, and the ship-lists in Adm. 8/1. See also Calendars of State Papers, Col. 1681/5 and 1685/8.

CHAPTER FIVE
THE SUPPRESSION OF THE BUCCANEERS
IN THE CARIBBEAN

Secondary sources are the same as for Chapter I; the relevant volumes of the Calendars of State Papers are the chief primary sources. For Dampier, see his *Voyage to Campeachy* (Argonaut Press, ed. C. Wilkinson, 1931) and his *New Voyage Round the World* (ib. ed. Gray, 1927). For Blackburn, see *Notes and Queries*, 4th Series, IX, p.289. For the attack on Vera Cruz, see narrative in *The Voyages of Capt. Sharp* (1684).

CHAPTER SIX
THE SECOND VOYAGE INTO THE SOUTH SEAS

Dampier's journal is in the British Museum, Sloane MSS 3236. It is printed in the collected edition of his works published by Knapton in 1729. The best modern editions are those edited by John Masefield (1906) and Sir Albert Gray (1927). An edition of Wafer's *Description of the Isthmus of Panama* was published by L. E. Elliott-Joyce for the Hakluyt Society in 1934. The MS of Ambrose Cowley's journal is B.M. Sloane MSS 54; the first half was lost on the island of Gorgona but was reconstructed from memory for publication by Hack in 1699 in his *Collection of Voyages*. The Hack MS version of the second half is in the Admiralty Library, MSS 4. See also State Papers, Colonial, and Burney op. cit.

CHAPTER EIGHT
DAMPIER'S FIRST VOYAGE ROUND THE WORLD

Swan's letter is in the State Papers, Colonial Series, 4 March 1685. Strong's journal is in the British Museum, Harl. MSS 5101; extracts from it are printed by Miss F. H. Dyer in *The Mariner's Mirror* Vol. xiii; there is another account of the voyage in Sloane MSS 672. For Narborough's voyage, see the narrative by Capt. Wood in Hack's *Original Voyages* (1699). The best general account of the buccaneers in the South Seas is in Burney, op. cit. The edition of the journal of Raveneau de Lussan used is that bound up with the 1704 edition of Esquemeling.

CHAPTER NINE
THE RETREAT FROM THE SOUTH SEAS

For Davis, Wafer, and de Lussan, see sources for Chapter VIII. For Knight see C.S.P.Col., 1688, No. 1796. For the documents in the trial of Davis and Wafer see ib., 1/65. Nathaniel Davis's narrative is printed in the Hakluyt Society edition of Wafer, op. cit. The Kidd references are based on Minute of Court of Directors, Adm. 67/3, and Colonial Office papers 5/860 in the Public Record Office.

CHAPTER TEN
DAMPIER TURNS PRIVATEER

The main source for this voyage is William Funnell's *Journal*, published by Knapton in 1707, Dampier's *Vindication*, 1707, and Welbe's *Answer to the Vindication*, 1707. Another remarkable source are the MS papers of F. H. Goldney, summarised by Dr Rogers in *The Mariner's Mirror*, 1924, pp. 366–381. The minutes of Dampier's court martial are in the Public Record Office. Other references can be found in the Calendars of State Papers, Colonial Series. The account of Stradling's ultimate fate is to be found in de la Villestraux's *Deux Corsaires Malouins*, published in Paris, 1929, quoting the Archives Nationales (Marine).

CHAPTER ELEVEN
THE VOYAGE OF WOODES ROGERS

Woodes Rogers, *A Cruising Voyage Round the World*, published by Bell and Lintot in 1712. Edward Cooke, *A Voyage to the South Seas*, published by Lintot and Gosling the same year. A useful modern edition is that by G. E. Manwaring, 1929. Rogers's official letters are in the Public Record Office; his journal is in the British Museum, Sloane MSS 4459, No. 29. An article on the financial aspect of the voyage by B. M. H. Rogers is in *The Mariner's Mirror*, 1933. Selkirk's supposed pamphlet is printed in the *Harleian Miscellany*.

CHAPTER TWELVE
FRENCH VOYAGES TO THE SOUTH SEAS

E. W. Dahlgren, *Les Relations Commerciales et Maritimes entre France et les côtes de l'océan Pacifique* (1909); de la Villestraux, *Deux Corsaires Malouins* (1920); Frézier, *Voyage to the South Sea* (trans. 1717); Burney op. cit.

CHAPTER THIRTEEN
CLIPPERTON AND SHELVOCKE: THE LAST OF THE PRIVATEERS

Shelvocke's Journal is MSS 14 in the Admiralty Library. His book, *A Voyage round the World by way of the Great South Sea* was published in London in 1726; a modern edition by W. G. Perrin appeared in 1928. William Betagh's account, *A Voyage round the World*, appeared in 1728. Taylor's journal, and one other by an unknown author, form the basis of the accounts printed in the great collections of voyages by Harris, Kerr, and Churchill. See also Burney, op. cit., iv, pages 520–553.

Index

244

Coxon, J., 27, 37–41, 61–9, 82
Crooke, W., 15
Crossing the Line, 163
Cygnet, 89; see Swan

Dampier, W. with Sharp, 38, 50; at
  Campeachy, 71; as author, 76;
  first voyage, 109 ff.; in Australia,
  119; and Darien Scheme, 133; in
  St George, 139 ff.; with W. Rogers,
  160 ff., 187, 189
Daniel, Capt., 5
Danykan, N., 186
Dartmouth, 60, 63
Dassigny, P., 59, 93
Dauphin, 191
Davidson, Lt., 220, 226, 227
Davis, Edward, 94 ff., 124 ff.
Davis, John, 13
Davis, Nathaniel, 130
Davis Land, 126
Defoe, D., 11, 183
Dick, W., 51, 57
Dinan, 149
Doublet, J., 191
Dover, Dr T., 161 ff.
Drake, 24
Drake, Sir F., 24
Dragon, 151, 156
Duchess, 161 ff.
Duke, 161 ff.
Dumbarton, 128
Dutch E. I. Co., 181

Easter Island, 126
Eaton, Capt. J., 89 ff.
Endeavour, 27
Esquemeling, J. (or Oexmelin),
  10 ff., 15, 18, 23, 28
Estcourt, T., 139, 159
d'Estrées, Adm., 11, 32, 72
Evelyn, J., 30, 78
Evertsen, J., 32

Falkland Islands, 190

Fame, 139
Fernandez; see Juan Fernandez
Feuillée, Père L., 191
Frézier, M., 193
Froger, Capt. de la R., 187
Funnell, W., 140 ff., 160

Gage, T., 113
Galapagos Islands, 43, 93, 190
Gennes, Capt. de, 185
Gibraltar, 21
Godfrey, Mr, 160
Golif, Louis Le, 8
Gopson, R., 81, 82
Gorgona, 97, 219
Gouin, Capt. de B., 185
Graff, L. de, 6, 72, 73
Grammont, Capt., 6, 72, 73
Granada, 134
Greenwich, Queen's House, 132
Grogniet, Capt., 111 ff., 125, 133
Guam, 97, 117, 175, 180, 226
Guayaquil, 44, 168–73
Gulliver's Travels, 120
Guzman, Don, 26

Hack, W., 40, 49, 58
Harris, Rev. J., 199, 200, 224, 230,
  236
Harris, Capt. P., 32, 36–41
Harris, Nephew of, 110 ff., 125
Hatley, S., 197 ff.; shoots albatross,
  205
Hawkins, Sir J., 160
Hendry, Mr, 225
Hincent, J., 81, 128, 129
Hogarth, W., 182
Holmes, Adm. Sir R., 74, 128, 130
Honduras; see Mosquito Coast
Horn, Cape, Sharp at, 53; Cowley
  at, 88; Davis at, 127; Rogers at,
  165
Horn, Van, 72, 73
Hottentots, 105
Howard, Capt., 57

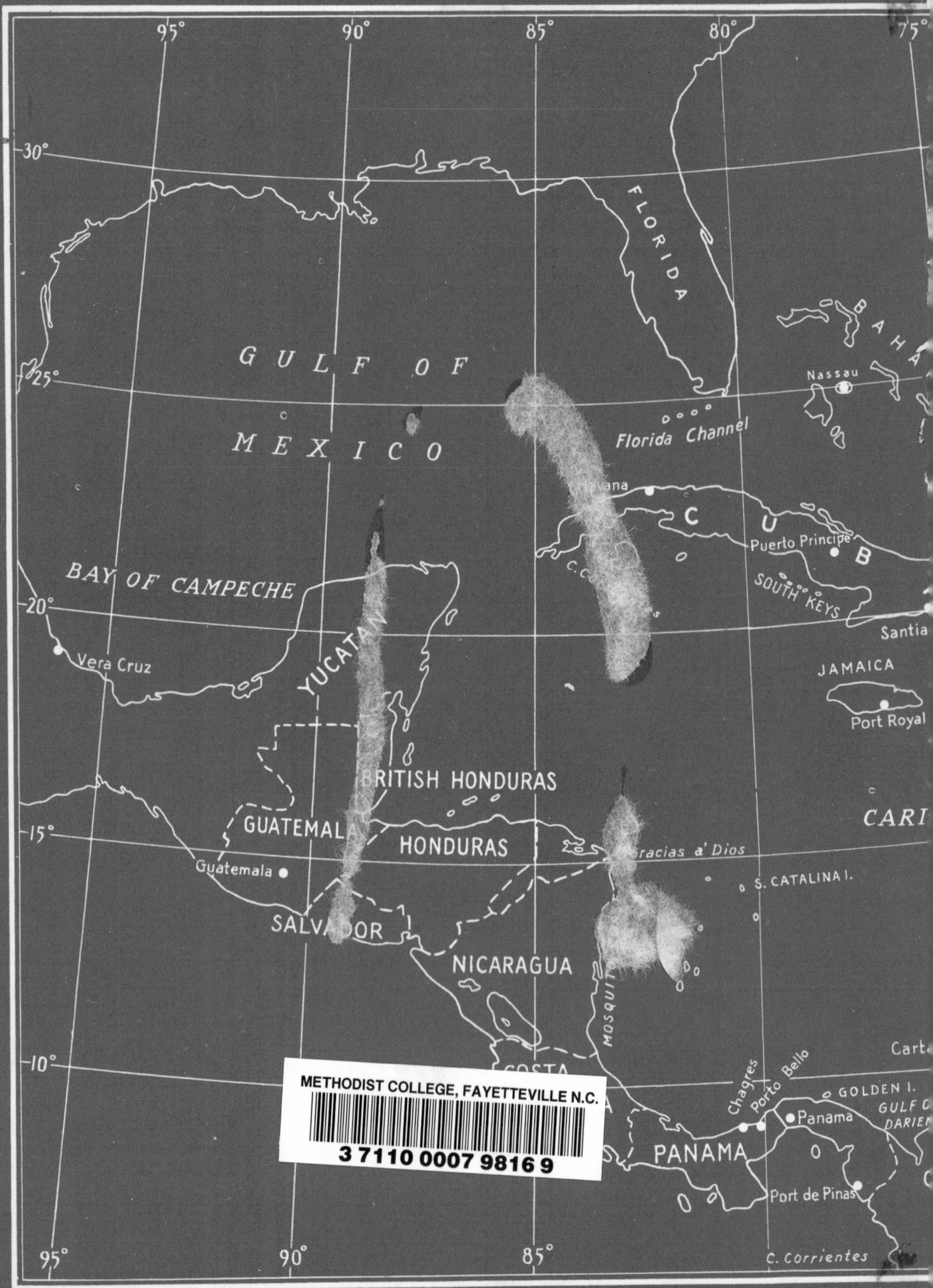
95°
90°
85°
80°
75°
30°
25°
20°
15°
10°
GULF OF
MEXICO
FLORIDA
BAHA
Nassau
Florida Channel
C U B
Puerto Principe
SOUTH KEYS
Santia
JAMAICA
Port Royal
BAY OF CAMPECHE
Vera Cruz
YUCATAN
BRITISH HONDURAS
GUATEMALA
HONDURAS
Guatemala
SALVADOR
NICARAGUA
MOSQUIT
S. CATALINA I.
CARI
Carta
GOLDEN I.
GULF O
DARIEN
Chagres
Porto Bello
Panama
PANAMA
Port de Pinas
C. Corrientes